Environmental Law, Crime, and Justice

Environmental Law, Crime, and Justice

Ronald G. Burns, Michael J. Lynch,
and Paul Stretesky

LFB Scholarly Publishing LLC
New York 2008

Library of Congress Cataloging-in-Publication Data

Burns, Ronald G., 1968-
  Environmental law, crime, and justice / Ronald G. Burns, Michael J.
Lynch, and Paul Stretesky.
      p. cm.
  Includes bibliographical references and index.
  ISBN 978-1-59332-276-2 (alk. paper)
  1. Environmental law--United States--Criminal provisions. 2.
 Offenses against the environment--United States. 3. Environmental
policy--United States. 4. Environmental justice--United States. 5.
 Offenses against the environment. I. Lynch, Michael J. II. Stretesky,
Paul. III. Title.
  KF3775.B875 2008
  344.7304'6--dc22

2008012890

ISBN 978-1-59332-276-2 (paperback)

Printed on acid-free 250-year-life paper.

Manufactured in the United States of America.

Dedication

To the rarely appreciated—the present and future generation of environmental researchers and practitioners and their commitment to improving public health.

Table of Contents

Tables

Figures and Images

Acknowledgments

Several people aided us in the course of writing this book by reviewing sections of the manuscript and providing us with materials used in this book, or through discussion of the book's contents. Special thanks are owed to Dr. Thomas Mieczkowski, University of South Florida; Jennifer Suggs, a chemist for the U.S. EPA, National Enforcement Investigations Center, Denver, Colorado for materials and advice; Stephen V. Lynch for evaluating issues related to portions of the legal discussion; and Pam Carlisle for her technical assistance. Special thanks are also due to LFB Scholarly's editors, including Leo Balk, who invited us to prepare this book, and to the academic editors, Trey Williams and Marilyn McShane.

Criminology and the Neglect of Environmental Harms

The origins of criminology can be traced to three interests. First, was an interest in reforming law and justice in order to make them less arbitrary and capricious and to promote their uniform application. Next emerged an interest in the prevention of crime and how law and justice might be better employed for this purpose. The final step was the emergence of interest in the offender, explaining and identifying the causes of crime in the offender, and using this knowledge to control crime. These three interests or concerns remain the cornerstones of modern criminology.

Building on these interests throughout its history, the primary focus of criminology has been directed toward controlling street or common crimes, dissecting its causes, and utilizing law and criminal justice responses to control this form of crime. This general tendency remains the core of criminology despite periodic calls to pay greater attention to the crimes of the powerful. While the need to address crimes of the power elite has existed for quite some time; it has had little influence on the general focus of criminology.

In the early part of the 20th century, a few scholars began to note that street crimes and criminals (and even the forms of justice and law applied to them) were not the most serious issues in society. In their writings, E.A. Ross, Willem Bonger and Edwin Sutherland, argued that the harm caused by street crime paled in comparison to the crimes of the elite or powerful offender. This view was supported by the work of the "muckrakers," early 20th century journalists who exposed these harms which included the use of monopolies to build empires in ways that damaged the social fabric, employed force against the working class to maintain substandard wage and working conditions that benefited the empire builders, and the production of commodities that were often unsafe for mass consumption. The significant social problems generated by free market practices were addressed by legislation regulating the content of food, drugs and cosmetics, laws defining monopoly and related unethical or market restricting behaviors as illegal, and laws that promoted workers' rights, unions, safe working conditions, and the minimum wage.

As decades past, it became more obvious that societies also needed to address other costs associated with industrialization and unconstrained economic growth. By the middle of the 20th century it had become abundantly clear that unbridled economic growth was the culprit behind much environmental pollution and destruction. In major cities and small industrial towns, air pollution had become so rampant that killer smogs settled on the inhabitants of London, New York and Los Angeles, and even in unknown places such as Donora, Pennsylvania, where intensive industrial labor was performed. Across the U.S., rivers, lakes and streams were becoming so polluted as to be unusable and public health dangers. Even vast water bodies such as the Great Lakes were not immune, and toxic levels of pollution there led scientists to declare Lake Erie dead. Major rivers, some flowing through the downtown areas of leading cities, contained such high levels of human waste and pollution that they caught fire. In the decades that followed these disasters—the late 1960s, 1970s and early 1980s—societies began to assemble a broad range of environmental laws and regulations to address these problems.

For four decades, environmental pollution had been a growing concern for academics in a number of disciplines, as well as to policymakers and social activists. In the last decade, these concerns have been enhanced by increased rates of disease associated with industrial waste, growing evidence of global warming, which is a form of heat pollution, and increased rates in the extinction of species and old growth and rain forests. Taken together, these signs of environmental damage paint a bleak picture of the world's environmental health and its future. Yet, despite this bleak picture and the persistent recognition of the dangers posed to society by this level of pollution and its association with the interests of powerful classes of economic and social actors, criminology has made little effort to reform itself and little headway in the study of environmental law, mechanisms for promoting environmental (and human) health, or the study of environmental justice or environmental crime. Indeed, a generous estimate would be that there are three or four dozen criminologists in the *world* today who devote significant attention to the study of these critical and widespread social harms and problems. The majority of criminologists remain wedded to an old criminological view of crime and justice where the street criminal and street crimes dominate the landscape.

One of the goals of writing this book is to expose criminologists—but perhaps more importantly the next generation of criminologists—to the variety of issues involved in the study of environmental law, crime and justice; to illustrate the serious nature of these problems; and to demonstrate how criminologists can and should become involved in studying environmental crime, law and justice. Environmental harms associated with pollution of the air, land and water kill and injure more people than street crime on an annual and daily basis. Financially, the losses associated with environmental damage are enormous—so enormous that they are difficult to estimate in any accurate manner, so large as to make the losses to street crime seem paltry. To be sure, there is something frightening and foreboding in the thought that a criminal might steal your property or physically attack you. Yet a significantly large portion of the U.S. population is regularly attacked—and more likely to be assaulted, killed or robbed—by exposure to environmental pollution and toxic waste. The difference is that the latter attack, which occurs through the environment and not directly at the hands of a visible offender who confronts a victim, appears ubiquitous, and because it appears so, seems to be a part of ordinary life, and does not confront us as an assault against us, or as something we might contain and control. Yet every day in the U.S. millions of citizens—nearly 30 million—drink water from contaminated water supplies; millions more are exposed to the types of air pollution common in urban areas. These people are, on a daily basis, the victims of crime against the environment.

It is our hope that criminologists begin to pay greater attention to the victims of environmental crime and attend to the study of injustice associated with environmental pollution, particularly its differential impacts on people from diverse social classes, races and ethnicities. As we begin to understand the ways in which nature is a victim of these crimes and the interests humans have, even if simply a result of self-interest, we can protect and preserve the environment from the routine and organized assault environmental harms present.

Today, the world is enveloped by environmental harm and crime. It is unfortunate that the discipline devoted to the study of crime and harm, law and justice—to the amelioration of crime and injustice—has ignored these offenses and their perpetrators, the laws and systems of justice that apply to them, and the immeasurable human and nonhuman costs and victims of these activities.

This book is thus both our protest against criminology's treatment of environmental crime, law and justice, and our effort to address and help rectify this situation.

MJL	Tampa, Florida
RGB	Fort Worth, Texas
PBS	Fort Collins, Colorado

CHAPTER 1.

The Scope of Environmental Harm and Crime

INTRODUCTION

A number of widely known environmental problems—exposure to toxic waste, air pollution hazards, species extinction due to environmental degradation, global warming, deforestation, water pollution, the demise of natural fisheries, and the decline of oil supplies, among other issues—have been the subject of scientific studies for the past half century. Today, much is known about the causes and the consequences of many environmental problems (e.g., air and water pollution, global warming, and exposure to environmental toxins). Nevertheless, U.S. policymakers have been slow to address these problems and prefer to privilege business and economic interests over the interests of public and environmental health.

This is not to say that environmental problems have gone unrecognized or unaddressed. For more than three decades scientists, legal researchers and policymakers have endeavored to address a variety of environmental concerns, devising laws and regulations and studying the impacts of those laws and regulations on environmental quality. In recognition of the importance of environmental quality, numerous environmental studies and science and policy programs have sprung up at colleges and universities across the U.S. since the mid-1970s. In other fields including geography, sociology, and medicine, researchers have examined toxic chemical exposure patterns for more than two decades. And, within the past few years, the study of environmental law, crime and justice has begun to penetrate into the field of criminology, though interest in environmental problems continues to lag well behind in this field (Lynch and Stretesky, 2001; Pierce and Tombs, 1998).

We review these facts to illustrate two key issues: first, that the study of environmental harms, laws, regulations and policies have grown significantly over the past half century, and second, to emphasize that the study of environmental problems has been absorbed into a number of different fields and become increasingly interdisciplinary over time. Today, in order to be a knowledgeable environmental researcher, it is necessary to be familiar with

1

research literatures in toxicology, biology, chemistry, environmental science and policy, law, geography, public policy, and sociology.

This book examines one aspect of environmental problems by focusing on environmental law, crime and justice. Today, these topics still occupy a very small space within the criminological literature. Indeed, criminology is one of the social sciences that traditionally paid little attention to environmental studies. Thus, one goal of this book is to promote more extensive study of environmental issues by criminologists. The environmental issues that are ripe for criminological analysis include examinations of laws and policies, the organization and behavior of environmental regulatory mechanisms, the behavior of those who violate and enforce environmental laws and regulations, and definitions of and the process of defining environmental and toxic harms. In order to produce useful studies of these various environmental issues and build a viable criminology of environmental crime, law and justice, criminologists must also integrate research results from environmental sciences, toxicology, chemistry, and biology into their examinations.

Over the past two decades, the scholarly space devoted to documenting and studying environmental problems has increased dramatically. In many disciplines other than criminology where the importance of environmental health has been recognized, the study of environmental problems has expanded at an extraordinarily rapid pace. These disciplines, in fact, have established scholarly specialties in a variety of environmental areas, including law, policy studies, engineering, management, education, and sciences. Criminology remains one of the fields of study that lags behind when it comes to exploring or establishing specialties in environmental matters.

WHY STUDY ENVIRONMENTAL CRIME, LAW AND JUSTICE?

Because so much of our understanding of environmental harms is related to the hard sciences, we might ask, why should criminologists, sociologists and other social scientists be concerned with studying environmental crime? The answer is that studying these issues reveals much about the nature of crime, law and justice in our society. Criminologists typically study street crimes that include murder, robbery, burglary and auto thefts, and the laws and systems of doing justice that apply to this limited set of crimes. However, when criminologists focus on street crimes alone, they ignore a more widespread set of crimes—the crimes of the powerful—which cause much more extensive financial and physical harms than ordinary street crimes (Friedrichs, 2006; Michalowski and Kramer, 2006; Lynch and Michalowski, 2006; Pierce and Tombs, 1993; Reiman, 2005).

Environmental crimes committed by corporations are included among the types of offenses that qualify as crimes of the powerful. It is important to bear this idea in mind because the study of ordinary criminals would seem to preclude corporations or the wealthy people who own them from being among the criminal population. For example, studies of the correlates of crime often point to the idea that criminals are from lower income groups. This characterization would not be true if powerful criminals were counted. And, because criminologists ignore crimes of the powerful and environmental crimes, they also tend to ignore how the social standing of criminal actors or the economic or social significance and power of industries impacts the way in which environmental violators and violations are treated.

Further, consider that unlike ordinary criminal harms, the harms associated with environmental pollution and other negative environmental conditions (e.g., global warming) are tremendous and, as many suggest, pose substantial barriers to maintaining healthy human societies and, potentially, to human existence (Carson, 1962; Colborn et al., 1997; Steingraber, 1997; Wargo, 1998; see image 1.1). These harms are not limited to those that impact humans alone, and many other aspects of environmental harm could be examined (e.g., species extinction, global warming, deforestation, wildlife health and welfare), though we will concentrate our discussion on human harms.

Image 1.1. An extensive fish kill caused by a chemical spill into a waterway.

Fish kills of this nature are widespread and an excellent example of the overlooked impact of environmental crime. We should also keep in mind the fact that chemical spills that can kill fish have the ability to harm other populations that rely on polluted water sources, including humans. (Photograph courtesy of the U.S. Fish and Wildlife Services public image library.)

Moreover, from a justice perspective, we may want to consider the fact that the harms to humans associated with environmental pollution are not evenly distributed across the U.S. population. Residents living in poor and minority neighborhoods are, for example, more likely to be exposed to pollution. The study of the unequal distribution of environmental hazards relative to community characteristics is known as environmental justice, the topic of a later chapter (see Chapter 9). Environmental justice, or the distribution of environmental hazards, tells us much about the nature of justice in a society. Why? Because these studies tell us whether a mechanism of justice is applied equally, or whether justice is modified given certain types of violations, or specific offender or victim characteristics. They also tell us about the kind of injustice a society is willing to tolerate. Since these environmental justice studies indicate widespread racial, ethnic and class injustice, one could conclude that American society is willing to tolerate injustice as long as it is confined to impacts on the poor, relatively powerless, racial and ethnic minority groups.

Finally, there are a variety of laws and regulations that define and control environmental hazards that can be studied to improve our understanding of the operation of law and social control in modern societies. Some of these laws are of interest to criminologists because they are criminal laws. The majority of laws that define environmental harms, however, are administrative, regulatory, or civil in nature. These laws, too, should be of interest to the criminologist, and would be especially relevant to addressing the following types of questions: Why are the dangerous harms presented by environmental pollution typically treated as non-criminal events even though they can lead to widespread injury, disease or death? If environmental harms and ordinary crime produced the same types of outcomes, why are they defined and treated differently? Are regulatory, administrative and civil control mechanisms a more efficient means for controlling environmental harm than criminal law might be? Or do assumptions about the nature of environmental violations (e.g., they are inevitable and not serious or intentional) influence environmental laws and law enforcement mechanisms that apply to environmental harms?

Criminologists should also be interested in the way environmental crimes are investigated, and how the techniques used are both similar to and diverge from techniques used to investigate ordinary crimes. By studying environmental crimes it becomes obvious that the policies used to control this type of crime are dramatically different than the ones applied to ordinary crime. Likewise, it also becomes clear that many researchers and policymakers have offered sound plans to control environmental crime based on theories that are unknown within criminology, such as the theory of sustainable development, which details how our society's assumptions about production and consumption can be reorganized to put less stress on the environment, and in the process, ourselves. This idea—sustainable development—will be examined further later in this book.

EVIDENCE OF ENVIRONMENTAL HARMS AND CRIMES

Let us turn our attention to environmental crimes and harms. To begin this discussion, consider the following facts about the extent of environmental harm in the contemporary world.

Over the past decade a number of important environmental issues have become the focus of scientists and policymakers. One of the most important environmental issues is global warming, which is now so widely recognized by scientists that the majority of the world's nations (with the exception of the U.S. and Australia; for a list of signatory nations see, unfccc.int/parties_and_ observers/parties/items/2352.php) have signed an international treaty, the Kyoto Protocol (the Protocol is available on line at, www.unescap.org/ esd/energy/ publications/compend/ceccpart5chapter2.htm) to reduce the production of global warming gases. The targeted global warming gases are: carbon dioxide (CO_2); methane (CH_4) nitrous oxide (N_2O); hydrofluorocarbons (HFCs); perfluoro-carbons (PFCs); and sulphur hexafluoride (SF_6). Unfortunately, under the presidential administration of George W. Bush, the U.S., which is currently the world's largest producer of global warming gases, has declined to sign the Kyoto Protocol. Recognizing the importance of the Protocol, the 166 nations that are members to the agreement recently (November, 2006) met in Nairobi, and agreed to review its contents and update the agreement in 2008.

Table 1.1 shows the production of CO_2 for the 25 nations that produce the largest aggregate total of this gas. The data used to construct this table came from the Carbon Dioxide Information Analysis Center (cdiac.ornl.gov), which is part of the U.S. Department of Energy. These data may also be accessed through the U.S. Global Change Data and Information System (globalchange.gov).

In 2003, the U.S. produced the most CO_2, in terms of tons, of any nation in the world, with more than 1.5 billion tons, and the greatest tonnage per capita (5.43). In that year, the U.S. produced 40 percent more CO_2 than China, the world's second largest producer of this gas, even though China has a population more than 22 times larger than the U.S. population. Relative to other nations (see "Tons Per Capita" and "Percent U.S. Output", Table 1.1) the U.S. emitted substantially larger quantities of CO_2 than most other nations, with the exception of Canada and Australia. For example, the United Kingdom's per capita emissions were only 47.2 percent of U.S. per capita emissions, while China, which produces a substantial proportion of the word's CO_2, emitted only 15.8 percent of the U.S. level on a per capita basis.

High levels of carbon dioxide pollution have characterized American society for some time (Marland, Boden, and Andres, 2006). By 1890, during the Industrial Revolution, the U.S. topped the UK's CO_2 output; by 1920 U.S. production was 3.5 times higher than England's; and by 1950 it was five times greater. Thus the U.S. has long been the nation that has contributed an excessive level of carbon dioxide to the world's environment.

Table 1.1. Top 25 Nations, Production of Carbon Dioxide, 2003

Country	Total Tons (1000s)	Tons Per Capita	Growth % (since 1996)	Percent U.S. Output Total	Per Capita
United States	1,580,175	5.43	9.5	100	(100)
China	1,131,175	0.86	24.1	71.6	(15.8)
Russian Fed.	407,593	2.85	0.0	25.8	(52.5)
India	347,577	0.33	27.0	22.0	(6.1)
Japan	336,142	2.64	5.5	21.3	(48.6)
Germany	219,776	2.66	- 6.4	13.9	(49.0)
Canada	154,392	4.88	25.1	9.8	(89.9)
U. K.	152,460	2.56	- 2.1	9.7	(47.2)
So. Korea	124,455	2.59	11.8	7.9	(7.7)
Italy	121,608	2.10	10.1	7.7	(38.7)
Mexico	113,542	1.10	12.2	7.2	(20.3)
Iran	104,112	1.57	26.2	6.7	(28.9)
France	102,065	1.70	0.2	6.5	(31.3)
South Africa	99,415	2.23	12.6	6.3	(41.1)
Australia	96,657	4.85	12.5	6.1	(89.3)
Ukraine	85,836	1.80	-20.7	5.4	(33.2)
Spain	84,401	2.03	32.4	5.3	(37.4)
Poland	83,121	2.13	-15.7	5.3	(39.2)
Saudi Arabia	82,530	3.64	10.9	5.2	(67.0)
Brazil	81,445	0.48	7.9	5.2	(8.8)
Indonesia	80,544	0.36	8.7	5.1	(6.3)
Thailand	67,131	1.07	21.4	4.3	(19.7)
Taiwan	62,720	2.77	25.4	4.0	(51.0)
Turkey	60,057	0.84	16.9	3.8	(15.5)
Algeria	44,672	1.40	69.6	2.8	(25.8)
Average	277,744	2.20	13.0		

While the U.S. contribution to the production of CO_2 is enormous and disproportionate to its population and to the contributions from other nations, the problem of global warming would be extreme if other nations, particularly developing nations, began to produce this gas at the same rate as the U.S. For instance, if China alone were to match the carbon dioxide output of the U.S. (5.43 tons per capita), it would add nearly 31 billion tons of this gas to the environment annually, and that figure is not adjusted for population growth! Even if China achieved the world average per capita carbon dioxide output (2.2 tons per capita), it would contribute more than 8.8 billion tons annually to global warming gases.

The problem, however, isn't simply that some countries are developing and adding to the world's carbon dioxide burden; it is also that several developed nations produce much more carbon dioxide per capita than other nations. If the U.S., Canada, and Australia cut their CO_2 output in half, they would still produce more of this gas than the average developed nation (e.g., Germany, 2.66; UK, 2.56; Japan, 2.64; Spain, 2.03; France, 1.70) but also would emit 1 billion fewer tons of global warming gases annually. Unfortunately, the U.S. and Australia have refused to ratify the Kyoto Protocol, signaling to the world a lack of interest in reducing global warming gases.

The George W. Bush Administration's hard-line stance against joining international treaties that limit the production of global warming gases is not, however, widely supported among the U.S. public. Moreover, there is opposition to the administration's position on global warming by both the Democratic and Republican parties. For instance, in July of 2006, California's Republican Governor Arnold Schwarzenegger entered into an agreement with British Prime Minister Tony Blair to become partners in the battle against global warming. Following the signing of this agreement, Schwarzenegger criticized the federal government's lack of response and noted that California will become a leader on this issue: "California will not wait for our federal government to take... action on global warming.... International partnerships are needed in the fight against global warming and California has a responsibility and a profound role to play to protect not only our environment, but to be a world leader on this issue..." New York's Republican Governor George E. Pataki has also become active in the effort to reduce greenhouse gases. At Pataki's urging, nine Northeast and mid-Atlantic states formed the Regional Greenhouse Gas Initiative (RGGI; www.rggi.org), which sought to develop carbon dioxide emission caps and trading allowances. Political leaders from New England have also been actively engaged in forging such agreements in the new millennium. New Jersey, for example, adopted a greenhouse gas reduction program in April of 2000. Moreover, in August of 2000, several representatives from New England states and Eastern Canadian Provinces met at the Conference of New England Governors and Eastern Canadian Premiers (NEG/ECP) and formed the Climate Change Action Program (Resolution 25-9).

In October of 2006, Governors Schwarzenegger and Pataki met to determine how California could support and cooperate with the RGGI. These initial efforts by a handful of prominent political leaders are a step in the right direction, and one that individual states are making despite the position on global warming adopted by the George W. Bush Administration.

Global warming is a major threat to the world. There are, however, a number of other persistent environmental problems that face the world's citizens. Among these problems is solving the growing energy crisis created by the declining availability of crude oil, and the link between burning fossil fuels and global warming. Another important issue is the problem of air pollution, which numerous studies indicate causes a large number of diseases from asthma to cancers to heart ailments, all of which possess the potential to lead to premature deaths, especially in the young and the elderly. Water pollution is also a significant problem in developing nations where inhabitants use local waterways as both sewer systems and fresh water supplies. The water quality in advanced nations is threatened by widespread contamination by pesticides, heavy metals, and other industrial pollutants. In addition, industrial production has created not only elevated levels of air and water pollution, but toxic waste disposal problems. Taken together, the level of injury, disease and death caused by environmental problems far exceeds that associated with the street crimes upon which criminologists typically focus their research efforts (Lynch and Michalowski, 2006; Burns and Lynch, 2004).

**Image 1.2. A Black-Footed Ferret, a severely endangered species,
   emerges from its winter den.**

In the mid-1980s, fewer than 20 of these wild ferrets were known to exist. This population was captured, bred, and reintroduced into the wild over the past decade and a half using stock from captive populations. The black-footed ferret is endangered due to habitat encroachment and poisoning. (Photograph courtesy of the U.S. Fish and Wildlife Services public image library.)

The increased recognition that human activity damages ecosystems, that the kinds of damage humans do to ecosystems are long-term, and that the consequences of human behavior threatens not only ecosystems but all life on earth, has led to the proliferation of laws and regulations designed to control the disposal and storage of toxic waste in order to protect public health. For the most part, these regulations began to emerge in the U.S. in the 1970s, and the vast bulk of environmental law and the majority of the environmental regulatory structure that enforces these laws have been enacted in the relatively short compass of the past three decades. There are a number of ways of measuring and examining the extent of environmental harms. We could, for example, explore species extinction (Wilson 1992; Eldredge 1998; Ehrlich and Ehrlich 1995; see image 1.2) or the issue of deforestation (Chew 2001; see image 1.3). Instead, we examine the extent of toxic waste pollution in the U.S., and focus on three specific indicators of environmental harm: toxic chemicals and waste sites, water pollution, and air pollution.

Image 1.3. This picture demonstrates the impact of clear cut foresting methods.

The clear cut results in all the trees on the side of this mountain being removed. This creates other environmentally related problems, such as erosion during heavy rains or snow melts and the loss of species habitat. In this case, the photograph depicts a clear cut in Oregon within the range of the endangered Spotted Owl. (Photograph courtesy of the U.S. Fish and Wildlife Services public image library.)

TOXIC CHEMICALS IN THE UNITED STATES

Each year U.S. industries must report the quantity of dangerous chemicals (i.e., those that may harm human health and the environment) that they discharge into the air, water and soil to the EPA. Those data suggest that U.S. industry releases approximately *four billion pounds* of chemicals annually (U.S. EPA, 2007). If this reported volume of waste were evenly distributed over the land mass of the entire U.S. (3,537,441 square miles), each square mile of land would receive approximately 1,130 pounds of toxic chemicals annually. As will be demonstrated in Chapter 9, however, these toxic releases are not evenly distributed. Instead, minority and lower income areas tend to be more heavily polluted than White or high income communities (Bullard, 1990).

Toxins are poisonous substances, and the danger presented by any toxin is related to its concentration at exposure. While the EPA does require that the emissions of approximately 650 chemicals be monitored (see *Emergency Planning and Community Right-To-Know Act* sec. 313), it is difficult to know exactly how many environmental toxins there are in the world today. One reason is the sheer volume of chemicals manufactured today, which is estimated by the U.S. Environmental Protection Agency (EPA) to be in excess of 80,000. Many of these chemicals have not been extensively tested to determine whether they are safe to release into the environment.

At lower concentrations, exposure to toxins does not necessarily lead to death by poisoning. Still, exposure to low doses of toxins can cause a variety of diseases and illnesses that may lead to death, neurological damage, and other forms of permanent physical impairment or chronic illnesses, or to acute, short term symptoms. For example, although there are more than 240 known chemical and chemical compounds that are identified as carcinogens (cancer-causing substances; see *The 11th Report on Carcinogens*, 2005, National Toxicology Program, ntp.niehs.nih.gov/ntpweb), these chemicals and compounds make up only a small portion (approximately 2 percent, or 75 million pounds) of the total quantity of toxins reported released into the environment each year. While carcinogens comprise only a small portion of the total toxic pollution burden, 75 million pounds is nevertheless a significant quantity of carcinogenic toxins. In addition, a number of toxic chemicals are quite potent, meaning that very small quantities are sufficient to cause serious negative health outcomes. Chlorinated dioxins (CDDs) are comprised of 75 different chemicals, the most widely recognized of which is 2,3,7,8-tetrachlorodibenzo-*p*-dioxin (TCDD). These chemicals have no commercial use and are inadvertent byproducts of municipal and medical incineration, the production of metals, the burning of fossil fuels, the production of chlorophenoxy herbicides and polychlorinated phenols, and paper milling and bleaching. More importantly, they possess the ability to cause cancer *at extremely low levels of exposure* (Crump et al., 2003; see also the Agency for Toxic Substances and Disease Registry "ToxFAQ" sheet on dioxin, www.atsdr.cdc.gov/tfacts104.html). In recognition of dioxin's extreme toxicity and disease-causing potential, the EPA has set a maximum exposure limit for dioxin of 0.00000003 milligrams per liter of drinking water (www.epa.gov/safewater/ mcl.html#mcls). According to environmental activist Louis Gibbs (1995), these exposure levels do not necessarily mean that dioxin releases are safe. Indeed, variations in exposure and reactions to dioxin and other dangerous chemicals clearly exist. Instead, Gibbs claims that maximum exposure limits merely represent an acceptable level of risk that roughly translates into an industry license to kill a small number of people in the future (e.g., 1 in 1,000,000 or 1 in 10,000,000) in order to make a profit. To put this level of consumption in perspective, we provide a few examples of EPA-regulated maximum exposure levels and *multipliers* (how much more of this chemical you can consume compared to dioxin) for several other known carcinogens in milligrams per liter of water: benzene, carbon tetrachloride, and tetrachloroethylene, 0.005, *166,666*; Chlordane, 0.002, *66,666*; Heptachlor, 0.0004, *13,333*. The quantity of these and other toxins released into the environment as pollution can be investigated using the Toxic Release Inventory.

The Toxic Release Inventory or TRI

How widespread is the problem of toxic releases? What is the magnitude of the problem? These questions can be addressed in part by examining data provided by the federal government through the Toxic Release Inventory or TRI. The TRI was created under the *Emergency Planning and Community Right-to-Know Act* of 1986 (EPCRA), which was designed to inform the public about the toxic hazards facing communities. The TRI was created in response to the 1984 disaster at the Union Carbide plant in Bhopal, India that caused the deaths of thousands of people. United States lawmakers were concerned about a similar accident occurring domestically—especially at the Union Carbide plant operating in Institute, West Virginia which had the same design as the Bhopal plant (Pearce and Tombs 1993). One important goal of the TRI was to reduce chemical emissions. Lawmakers and the EPA believed that pollution reduction would be achieved because an informed public would pressure industry into operating more efficiently (i.e., produce less pollution). Thus, facilities required to report under EPCRA must notify the government concerning the quantities of approximately 650 different chemicals they store on site, transfer, or release into the environment (www.epa.gov/tri). These data provide a somewhat useful estimate of the quantity and location of toxic chemicals in the U.S. despite the fact that TRI reports are often interpreted as being voluntary (see Burns and Lynch, 2004 for discussion) and all polluters are not required to report their discharges. For instance, beginning in 2007 many companies that had in the past been required to report waste discharges into the environment under the TRI are now exempt due to revisions in EPA threshold reporting requirements (revised from 500 lbs/year to 5,000 lbs/year) (Jeffords and Gorte, 2006). Thus, the TRI clearly underestimates the true extent of the toxic waste problem in America.

Figure 1.1 displays the rate of TRI releases for the entire U.S. by year. That figure indicates that the average facility (N=20,214) released nearly 188,000 pounds of chemicals into the environment in 2005. While it is not possible to use the TRI to estimate the degree to which the public has been exposed to toxic chemicals, it is nevertheless clear that the amount of toxins released into the environment leaves considerable cause for concern. Still, as Figure 1.1 indicates, the pollution prevention goal of the TRI appears to be successful, as the amount of toxic emissions has generally been declining (except for the small increase in 2005).

Before examining TRI data in more detail, it should be kept in mind that virtually no location in the U.S. is free from toxins. Environmental toxins are transported across the face of the globe by naturally occurring air currents and climate conditions that transport air borne pollutants, or by waterways. For instance, though there are no industries in the Arctic, chemical pollutants can still be found there. In other cases, environmental toxins are redistributed by design when, for instance, a land fill is created for the purpose of disposing of hazardous waste. Such disposal sites are not secure vaults, and the chemicals stored in landfills and other toxic waste sites may leach from disposal sites over time into ground and surface water. Leaching may be accelerated by natural conditions such as the composition of the ground under and around a land fill, and weather conditions, such as higher than average rainfall, natural disasters including floods, and the presence of other chemicals, especially solvents, in the landfill.

As an example of the widespread distribution of environmental toxins, let us review some data available from the TRI. Table 1.2 contains data on the number of pounds of toxins released in the fifteen most polluted U.S. states. The first half of Table 1.2 ranks states according to the total pounds of TRI pollutants emitted into the environment during the year. The second half of that table shows the ranks of states when TRI emissions are standardized by state land area and presented as pounds of toxins per square mile.

Industrial TRI pollutants are emitted in a variety of forms—gases, liquids and solids. They are emptied into waterways, dumped into landfills and storage tanks, injected deep into the ground, and expelled as air pollutants. Rarely do we think about the volume of these emissions, nor put them into perspective. Table 1.2 illustrates the enormous volume of hazardous waste involved. In Alaska alone, one-half billion pounds of hazardous waste were added to the environment in 2002. In terms of quantity, the top five states add nearly two billion pounds of hazardous waste to the environment each year.

The top fifteen states listed in Table 1.2 produced nearly 4.5 billion pounds of hazardous waste in 2002. And, we must remember that this is the amount that waste industries voluntarily report to the EPA. Unlike the Federal Bureau of Investigation's crime index (i.e., the typical source referenced for street crime data in cities and counties across the United States), the volume of hazardous waste reported in the TRI is not adjusted to correct for non-reporting, meaning that the volume of hazardous waste represented in Table 1.2 substantially under-represents the real level of industrial pollution.

Figure 1.1. TRI On-site and Off-site Disposal, 2001-2005

(per reporting facility)

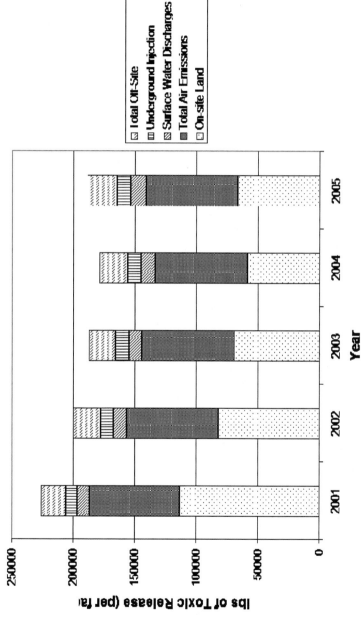

Table 1.2. Toxic Release Inventory, Pounds of Toxins Released, Top 15 States, Total Pounds and Pounds Per Square Mile, 2002

State	Total Pounds per State	State	Pounds per Sq.Mile*
Alaska	547,987,529	Ohio	4,665
Nevada	496,783,772	Nevada	4,493
Arizona	328,676,277	Indiana	3,756
Texas	244,460,208	W.Virginia	3,615
Ohio	209,090,481	Tennessee	3,513
Utah	173,157,779	Maryland	3,356
Florida	151,374,755	Delaware	3,193
Tennessee	148,476,319	Arizona	2,883
Indiana	136,785,790	Pennsylvania	2,410
Georgia	126,580,488	Louisiana	2,320
Louisiana	120,290,949	Florida	2,301
N.Carolina	118,729,088	Alabama	2,208
Alabama	115,716,292	N.Carolina	2,206
Pennsylvania	110,987,443	New Jersey	2,194
Missouri	106,540,505	Georgia	2,131

*Land mass concentration.

The second part of Table 1.2 presents state TRI data per square mile for the fifteen states with the highest TRI emissions. Standardized in this way, TRI data can be used to represent a measure of hazardous chemical concentration. States with the highest hazardous chemical concentrations potentially pose the greatest threat to environmental and human health. In addition, states that produce the most toxic waste may not present the greatest threats to human or environmental health because each state pollutes a different land-mass volume. At 4,665 pounds of reported hazardous pollutants per square mile, Ohio has the greatest land mass concentration of pollutants, even though it ranks fifth in total pounds of toxins produced. Examining this data further, we discover that industries in only one other state, Nevada, report emitting more than 4,000 pounds per square mile into the environment. Further, these data illustrate that New Jersey, often held out as an example of a state with extraordinarily high levels of pollution, has less than one-half the chemical land mass concentration of either Ohio or Nevada.

Other measures of chemical pollution related to human health can be constructed using TRI data. One such measure is the cancer score found on the website *Scorecard* (www.scorecard.org). This measure takes cancer ratings and toxic potency indicators of TRI releases by medium of exposure (air vs. water), and converts them into pounds of benzene equivalents. In this way, different chemical effects are standardized for comparison, and scores from different areas of the country can be compared for purposes of evaluating relative health risks.

Table 1.3 contains *Scorecard's* estimates of the fifteen states with the highest levels of benzene equivalents in 2002. Pennsylvania ranked as the state with the highest level of benzene equivalents in terms of total pounds. West Virginia, however, had the highest concentration of cancer-causing pollutants per square mile. It should be emphasized that the pounds-per-square-mile measure is an average for each state, and that there will be areas within each state that have higher and lower concentrations than indicated in this table. Let us use Texas as an example. Overall, Texas emitted a high level of cancer-causing TRI pollutants—160 million pounds. Because Texas covers a large area, the high volume of cancer-causing output it produces translates into a relatively low average concentration per square mile (596 pounds per square mile)—the lowest level among the states on this list. Nearly half (48 percent) of Texas' cancer-related emissions, however, are found in just one county, Potter County. In Potter County, the pounds of TRI cancer pollutants per square mile is exorbitantly high—more than 85,000 pounds. This concentration level is more than 143 times the state average and more than 8 times the average for the most polluted state on this list in terms of average pollutants per square mile, West Virginia. And, while the population of Potter County is relatively small, its average population slightly exceeds the average population of Texas' 254 counties.

Table 1.3. Cancer Ratings from Benzene-Equivalents from TRI Reports, States with Highest Concentrations 2002

State	Pounds Benzene-Equivalents	Pounds per Square Mile
Pennsylvania	380,000,000	8,251
Nevada	320,000,000	2,894
Arizona	270,000,000	2,368
Indiana	250,000,000	6,865
West Virginia	250,000,000	10,316
Ohio	220,000,000	4,908
Virginia	220,000,000	5,143
Alabama	210,000,000	4,006
Kentucky	200,000,000	4,949
Tennessee	170,000,000	4,034
Texas	160,000,000	596
Missouri	150,000,000	2,152
N. Carolina	130,000,000	2,415
Georgia	120,000,000	2,019
Iowa	110,000,000	1,955

Reported By *Scorecard* (www.scorecard.org).

In further analysis of *Scorecard* data we can see that an additional 43 percent of Texas's TRI cancer-related pollutants are distributed over six other counties (Harris, Jefferson, Camp, Brazoria, Limestone, and Fort Bend), which are home to an additional 20.5 percent of Texas's population. There was an average of more than 11,000 pounds of cancer pollutants per square mile for these counties, more than 18 times the average for the state. Taken together, the approximately 21 percent of Texas citizens who live in these seven counties are exposed to very high concentrations of cancer causing agents; much higher than the average Texan.

In contrast, 75 percent of TRI cancer emissions in West Virginia occurred in only two counties, Grant and Berkeley, where only 4.8 percent of West Virginia's population resides. The TRI cancer concentration in these two counties is extraordinarily high with 232,000 pounds per square mile, or 2.8 times the concentration found in Potter County, Texas, and 22.5 times the West Virginia average.

Above, we provided examples of states and several counties with extra-ordinarily high concentrations of cancer-causing chemical emissions in the U.S. There are, however, several states where the level of cancer-related emissions are relatively low. These states are presented in Table 1.4.

Table 1.4. Cancer Ratings from Benzene-Equivalents from TRI Reports, States with Lowest Concentrations, 2002,

State	Pounds Benzene-Equivalents	Pounds per Square Mile
Vermont	9,100	0.9
Maine	110,000	3
Colorado	450,000	4.3
Oregon	950,000	9.7
Washington	700,000	9.8
South Dakota	1,100,000	13
Minnesota	1,300,000	15
New Hampshire	170,000	18
New Mexico	3,000,000	25
Alaska	20,000,000	30
Hawaii	340,000	31
Montana	6,200,000	42
California	8,600,000	52
Mississippi	2,800,000	56
Wisconsin	5,700,000	87

Reported By Scorecard, (www.scorecard.org).

In contrast to West Virginia, consider that Vermont has an average of less than one pound of cancer-related TRI emission per square mile, and that every state in that table averages less than 100 pounds per square mile. Cross-state TRI cancer concentrations can also be examined by dividing states into four groups with somewhat similar levels of cancer-related TRI emissions. The first group consists of 16 states (Alabama, Arizona, Georgia, Indiana, Louisiana, Kentucky, Maryland, Missouri, Nevada, North Carolina, Ohio, Pennsylvania, South Carolina, Tennessee, Virginia, West Virginia), which contain 80 percent of all cancer-related TRI emissions in the nation. Group 1 states have an average emission per square mile of over 4,300 pounds.

The twelve states that comprise Group 2 (Delaware, Florida, Idaho, Illinois, Iowa, Michigan, New York, North Dakota, South Carolina, Texas, Utah, Wyoming) contain 16.8 percent of total reported cancer-related TRI emissions and an average of 1,130 pounds per square mile—one quarter the average concentration of Group 1 states.

Group 3 consists of nine states (Arkansas, Connecticut, Kansas, Massachusetts, Nebraska, New Jersey, Oklahoma, Rhode Island, Wisconsin) which average "only" 200 pounds of cancer-related TRI emissions per square mile. The states in Group 3 produce 3.5 percent of the total TRI emissions in this class for the U.S. The final group of fourteen states (Alaska, California, Colorado, Hawaii, Maine, Minnesota, Mississippi, Montana, New Hampshire, New Mexico, Oregon, South Dakota, Vermont, and Washington) contains less than 2 percent of all emissions in this class. The average cancer concentration for this group is approximately 18 pounds per square mile—nearly 240 times lower than the concentration in Group 1 states.

Clearly, if you were concerned about being exposed to cancer-causing toxins and you could choose where to reside, these TRI data would be useful in helping you select a safe location. But you must also remember that the groupings presented above displays average concentrations for states, and that the level of pollution varies within each of these states or groups. For instance, while California is in the lowest group for cancer-related emissions, there are a number of locations in California that rank high on cancer-related emissions, including Kern County (major city Bakersfield; 4.3 million pounds benzene equivalents) and Los Angeles County (1.2 million pounds). These counties have far more cancer-related pollution than Lassen County (14 pounds), Monterey County (28 pounds) or 13 other California counties with less than 1,000 pounds of such pollutants. Likewise, you are safer in Delta County, Colorado (16 pounds), than in Pueblo County (160,000 pounds). In Vermont, nearly all the cancer-related pollution (8,400 pounds or 92 percent of all such emissions in Vermont) were reported in Rutland County, while eight of Vermont's fourteen counties report no cancer related TRI pollutants.

The National Priorities List

The TRI measures only one dimension of the toxic exposure problem in the U.S. The worst toxic waste sites known to the government make up the National Priority List, or NPL. The most serious of these sites, known as Superfund Sites, are scheduled for clean-up under the direction of the U.S. EPA as required under the *Comprehensive Environmental Response, Compensation and Liability Act* (CERCLA; 42 U.S.C. §§ 9601 to 9675) and the *Superfund Amendments and Reauthorization Act* (SARA; 42 U.S.C.9601).

Approximately 11 million Americans or 4 percent of the U.S. population live within *one mile* of the worst toxic waste sites in the U.S.—the 1,305 NPL sites identified by the EPA. The typical NPL site is contaminated with an average of thirty different chemicals, and more than half (18) of these chemicals are known carcinogens. The EPA has established that 618 NPL sites contaminate or threaten local drinking water supplies, expanding the number of U.S. citizens threatened by toxic hazards. Moreover, the Agency for Toxic Substances and Disease Registry estimates that nearly forty percent of those living within one mile of an NPL site are children, including approximately 1.1 million children under the age of 6. In the next section we briefly examine the issue of children and exposure to toxic chemicals.

CHILDREN AND ENVIRONMENTAL HEALTH

The proximity of children to hazardous waste is an important issue for several reasons, especially because of biological differences between children and adults (Bearer, 1995). First, because of their reduced physical size, doses of hazardous materials are greatly multiplied in children, and a dose of a substance that may cause illness in an adult may be large enough to kill a child. Second, children often have elevated intake levels of non-food substances, which increases their vulnerability to toxin intake. Third, children may absorb higher concentrations of toxic substances than adults. Finally, numerous toxins interrupt human developmental processes such as cell growth and the production of hormones, which can interfere with the development of the brain and cause learning disabilities, diminished IQ, attention deficit disorder, and a wide range of other learning, behavioral, and developmental problems. Of special concern are the impacts on minority children, who tend to be overexposed to environmental pollutants (Landigren et al., 1999; Metzger, Delgado, and Herrell, 1995; Mott, 1995). In addition, we must recognize that children, unlike adults, cannot determine where they live; they cannot make choices about their residence, and even if they could, they do not possess the economic resources needed to change residences. This is an important point to recognize because it means that populations exposed to toxic waste are not making a choice to live near a toxic hazard, and that for those without economic resources, living near a toxic waste site is not a choice in any respect.

Lead Poisoning

One of the leading environmental health threats to U.S. children is lead poisoning. According to the EPA (2006), lead exposure is "a major environmental health threat for children" (www.epa.gov/envirohealth/ children/ body_burdens/b1.htm). Of special concern are the long-term and multiple health problems childhood lead exposure can produce, which the EPA summarizes as follows: "Studies... have found that childhood exposure to lead contributes to attention-deficit/hyperactivity disorder, ...hyperactivity and distractibility; increases the likelihood of dropping out of high school, having a reading disability, lower vocabulary, and lower class standing in high school; and increases the risk for antisocial and delinquent behavior." In recent years, and following decades of concerted governmental efforts to lower the concentration of lead in the environment, the average concentration of lead in U.S. citizens has declined (Center for Disease Control, 2005). Despite these declines, nearly half a million children, or slightly more than two percent of all children of preschool age, have high enough blood lead levels to cause impaired intelligence, learning disabilities, attention deficit disorders, and permanent brain damage. The problem is exacerbated among minority populations, especially among African American children under 18, who have higher levels of exposure than White or Hispanic children (Center for Disease Control, 2005; to access these data, see National Health and Nutrition Examination Survey, www.cdc.gov/ nchs/nhanes.htm).

WATER POLLUTION

The levels of toxic pollution examined above only touch the surface—literally— since they relate to land-based pollution. In 2000, the EPA prepared a national report on water quality (U.S. EPA, 2000a). This report summarizes studies performed by a variety of state, federal and local agencies examining water quality in the U.S. This report indicates that 39 percent of rivers, 45 percent of lakes, and 51 percent of estuaries in the U.S. are polluted and unfit for human uses, including fishing and swimming. Translated into measures of area, the report indicates that more than 270,000 miles of rivers, 7.8 million acres of lakes, nearly 16,000 square miles of estuaries are so extensively polluted that they threaten human health.

The report also indicated that elevated levels of mercury were a major source of environmental health hazards in U.S. waterways. Mercury is a neuro-toxin that impacts the brain and central nervous system, and accumulates in the kidneys where it may cause renal damage and failure. Prolonged exposure to mercury is toxic. Mercury is also a known teratogenic, meaning that it causes birth defects. In modern industrial societies, mercury has been a component of pesticides, herbicides and fungicides. The most prominent sources of environ-mental mercury in the U.S. are the burning of fossil fuels, especially coal, and the incineration of waste, which taken together account for 85 percent of environmental mercury contamination (www.mercurypolicy.org). In terms of public health, approximately seven million women and children in the U.S. consume mercury at or above recommended levels (www.mercurypolicy.org; see also U.S. EPA 2002 National Emissions Inventory at www.epa.gov/ ttn/chief/net/index. html). In its *National Water Quality Assessment*, the EPA reports widespread mercury contamination in domestic fish populations. Based on assessments of mercury in fish tissue samples, nearly 80 percent of the 2,823 fishing advisories issued in the U.S. during 2000 concerned elevated levels of mercury.

Image 1.4. Illegal point source pollutant being dumped into a waterway.

(Photograph courtesy of the U.S. Fish and Wildlife Services public image library.)

In addition, the EPA water quality report focuses on the Great Lakes, which have been a major concern over the past 40 years. Current data indicate that the Great Lakes remain highly contaminated. Nearly 80 percent of the Great Lakes shoreline exceeds pollution standards designed to protect human health.

Overall, the EPA's *National Water Quality Assessment* paints a picture of concern with levels of environmental pollution and the health of U.S. waterways. A similar picture of extensive water quality problems emerges from

EPA's *Index of Watershed Indicators* (www.epa.gov/iwi; recently converted to the *Watershed Information Network*). Of monitored watersheds, 16 percent had good water quality, 36 percent had moderate water quality problems, and 21 percent had serious problems (there were insufficient data to determine the status of the remaining 27 percent of watersheds). In addition, 1 in 14 watersheds in all areas were described as vulnerable to further degradation from pollution, primarily from urban and rural runoff. The *Clean Water Act* requires surface water quality to be sufficient to support fish and wildlife populations, protect drinking water sources, and allow for human recreation. Nationwide, nearly 40 percent of waterways (rivers, streams, lakes, reservoirs, and estuaries) do not support at least one of these uses.

A study performed on water pollution permits issued under the *Clean Water Act* by *Friends of the Earth* and the *Environmental Working Group* (www.ewg. org/reports/reportcard/cwatext.html) indicates that U.S. waterways are widely threatened by industrial pollutants. The report examined the status of water pollution permits for each state. Of the 6,621 permits examined nationwide, nearly 25 percent (N = 1640) were expired. Furthermore, the study illustrated that the permit violations span significant time periods. For example, 251 (nearly 15 percent) of the 1,690 facilities with expired permits have not had a valid water discharge permit for five years. An additional 770 facilities hold permits that expired two years ago. The likelihood of an expired permit violation varied by state, and ranged from 100 percent (Washington, DC) to 0 percent (Wyoming and North Dakota). Several states had an extraordinarily large number of facilities with expired permits: Oregon (n = 51; 67 percent of facilities); Massachusetts (74; 50 percent); Louisiana (116; 47 percent); Indiana (81; 46 percent); California (85; 36 percent); Ohio (93; 35 percent); and Texas (135; 23 percent). Given the status of their permits, each of these facilities is in violation of federal water pollution laws and potentially poses significant human health risks.

Permit compliance, however, is insufficient to ensure legal behaviors. In a recent (May, 2006) examination of federal *Clean Water Act* permit compliance in Pennsylvania, *Clean Water Action* (cleanwateraction.org/pa/enforcement. html) discovered that more than seventy-five percent of facilities with valid water pollution permits violated the conditions of their permits at least once between 2002 and 2005. Furthermore, one-quarter of violations involved significant noncompliance, the most severe EPA violation classification for such cases.

In response to similar revelations of public health threats related to drinking water supplies and the health of U.S. waterways in the early 1970s, the federal government passed the *Federal Water Pollution Control Act Amendments* of 1972 (later revised to form the *Clean Water Act* (CWA), 1977; 33 U.S.C.A. § 1251). To be sure, water quality has been improved over the past thirty years. But improved water quality does not mean that water quality is sufficiently safe, nor that all Americans are equally protected. Protecting the public from industrial waste is a daunting task. The EPA must ensure that the rules enacted by the CWA are adhered to by nearly 60,000 facilities that discharge waste waters. Recent evidence of a decline in U.S. water quality relates to the refusal of the U.S. legislature to reauthorize the *Clean Water Act* (House Bill H.R. 1356; Senate Bill S 912). Moreover, the CWA has been weaken by the George W. Bush Administration's stance toward wetland and isolated waterways protection, especially as these interfere with the special interests represented by mining industries and real estate developers. Indeed, George W. Bush Administration directives led to a January 2003 announcement by the EPA and Army Corps of Engineers (ACE) which removed CWA protection for many waterways in the U.S. The Sierra Club estimates that these procedures threaten the public health of more than 100 million Americans who obtain their water from sources affected by revised EPA and ACE procedures (sierraclubplus.org/downloads/2006-05/drinkingwater.pdf).

AIR POLLUTION

Today, close to 60 percent of the U.S. population—more than 170 million people—resides in areas with unhealthy levels of air pollution. These people live in counties that have failed to meet federal air quality standards provided by the *Clean Air Act*. An additional 25 percent of the population lives in areas where they experience short-term, intermittent exposure to unhealthy levels of air pollution. As a result, a significant portion of the U.S. population—85 percent—faces increased risk from heart and lung disease and premature mortality. Even short-term exposure to elevated levels of air pollutants can cause deaths due, for instance, to the interaction of pre-existing conditions such as asthma or heart problems with poor air quality and heat waves.

The *Clean Air Task Force* (see various publications at www.catf.us) reports that fine particulate pollution from diesel engines alone shortens the lives of 21,000 people annually (see also, Samet et al., 2000; Pope et al., 2002)—a figure that exceeds the number of people murdered in the U.S. each year. Diesel pollution also contributes to 27,000 heart attacks and 400,000 asthma attacks each year, and leads to an additional 15,000 hospitalizations. Furthermore, the cancer risk from diesel exhaust is more than 7.5 times higher than the cancer risks associated with all other air pollutants. In addition, exposure to some air pollutants has been linked to birth defects (Ritz et al., 2002), low birth weight (Wang et al., 1997) and fetal mortality (Loomis et al., 1998).

To assess U.S. air quality, the EPA closely monitors six criteria air pollutants (carbon monoxide, ozone, sulfur dioxide, lead, nitrogen dioxide, and particle matter), and regulates an additional 188 air pollutants. To produce an air quality measure that is useful to the public, the EPA monitors daily air quality in major urban areas and converts those measures into the Air Quality Index

(AQI). Air quality maps that include AQI measures and forecast are available on a daily basis from the website Airnow.gov.

SUMMARY

Taken together, the pollution indicators reviewed above illustrate that there is widespread exposure to hazardous and toxic pollutants across the United States. These high levels of victimization exist despite the laws and regulations that attempt to protect public and environmental health. How widespread is the problem? To place the extent of toxic pollution exposure in some context, consider that in the 2005 *National Crime Victim Survey*, the U.S. Department of Justice reported there were more than 23.44 million criminal victimizations in the United States. Ignoring the fact that some of these victimizations involved the same individuals, this means that nearly 8 percent of the U.S. population was the victim of a crime in 2005. Even if we assume under-reporting, about 10 percent of Americans were victims of street crime in 2005. In contrast, consider that the EPA reports that 85 percent of Americans—249 million Americans in 2005, or more than ten times the number of street crime victims—were exposed to unhealthy levels of air pollution alone. This comparison allows us to understand the tremendous public health problems posed by toxic pollution. Even if we assume a very large overlap between exposure to air pollution and land and water pollution, it would be safe to say that ninety percent of Americans—260 million people—are the victims of some type of exposure to environmental toxins.

To be sure, the estimates of the extent of victimization we just reviewed are biased because we ignore plants, animals, waterways, and forests and only consider potential victimization to humans (for extended discussion see South and Beirne, 2006; Beirne and South, 2007). As noted above, for example, 40 percent of waterways in the U.S. are polluted in ways that violate the law. How many animals are impacted as a result of these violations? The point here is not to provide an estimate of these harms, but to illustrate that the extensive level of potential victimization associated with toxic pollution eclipses the estimates of harm to humans. There is, in short, a diverse array and an extraordinarily large number of potential victims of toxic crime.

We argue that these victims—human, animal, or other natural forms—have not been the subject of sufficient criminological attention. In some sense, it seems that such victims are viewed as less worthy of study by criminologists. But there are important reasons why criminologists should study these victims. First, it may be that the level of environmental pollution shows a callous disregard for life-forms, and that the level of pollution societies are willing to tolerate may be related to the levels of crime found within societies. That is, societies like the U.S., where nature is seen as a tool and resource, may entail cultural features that promote criminal forms of victimization. Second, pollution, though widespread, is not evenly spread, and the distribution of pollution may contain clues about the kinds of justice and injustice a society is willing to tolerate. Third, some environmental pollutants have the ability to affect behavior, including crime (Stretesky and Lynch, 2004, 2002). Thus, studying environmental pollution may hold answers to causes of crime that criminologists typically neglect. Criminologists can no longer claim that there is a lack of data to analyze environmental harms, because the EPA and state regulatory agencies, for instance, provide a wealth of information for study. Fourth, victims of toxic pollution, like victims of crime, suffer and deserve attention from researchers who may, through their research efforts, produce the types of evidence that leads to social policies that reduce victimization and unnecessary suffering.

This chapter has provided an overview of the issues examined more extensively in the chapters that follow. We begin with an overview of theories about the environment and the need to protect the environment. These theories provide guidance for understanding environmental policies and laws, and the history of environmental movements and regulations reviewed in subsequent chapters. In addition, the basics of environmental crime investigation, environmental justice, and data sources that can be used by criminologists to study environmental crime are reviewed.

CHAPTER 2

Environmental Theories

INTRODUCTION

This chapter examines several theoretical approaches relevant to the study of environmental crime, law and justice that originate in diverse academic disciplines and emphasize unique approaches. These approaches range from traditional free market theory, to moderate sociology of law approaches, to activist grass-roots models and zero-growth economic positions. Elements from each view are useful for developing a broader understanding of environmental crime, law and justice.

Theories play an important role in how each of us interprets environmental law, what we view as an environmental crime, how we define environmental justice, and whether we believe it can be achieved. Theories also have important policy implications that shape how governments respond to environmental issues. Does nature need to be protected from human activity? Can this protection be accomplished by the free market? Or is some form of governmental intervention required? Theories provide assumptions that answer each of these questions.

As an example of how theory impacts environmental crime, law, and justice policy, consider the environmental protections implemented by the first U.S. president to impose such rules, Theodore Roosevelt. Roosevelt believed in an environmental view called conservation which led him to enact legislation protecting America's wilderness. As an avid outdoorsman, Roosevelt did not believe the free market was forward looking enough to protect the environment for the enjoyment of future generations of Americans, and that external market regulations would be needed for this purpose. In contrast to this view, compare the free market approaches of recent presidents such as Ronald Reagan, George H. Bush and George W. Bush. Each of these presidents actively engaged in actions that eliminated laws and regulations that protected the environment from harm. Each also compiled a rather bad environmental record, and under each, indicators of environmental quality declined and measures of environmental pollution rose (for further discussion see Chapter 4).

Special interest groups that represent businesses also believe that free market theories are appropriate mechanisms for protecting the environment. As a result, special interest groups use their economic power to influence political processes that shape environmental regulations. In contrast to the views of special interest groups, scientists believe that rational environmental decision-making guided by scientific studies of the effects of pollution should receive the most weight in environmental policy matters. Scientific studies often illustrate the limitations of free market models of environmental protection when they illustrate that unhealthy environmental conditions and free markets coexist.

The remainder of this chapter reviews several competing environmental perspectives. Given the large number of these approaches, we cannot review all environmental theories here, and those interested in developing more in-depth knowledge of this topic should refer to the work of Manaster (2000), Perman, Ma and McGilvary, (1996), and Merchant (1992). Several traditional environmental theories are also described in the chapter on the history of environmental movements.

THE FREE MARKET AND ENVIRONMENTAL PROTECTION

Free market ideas have a long history in the United States traceable to Adam Smith and his notion of the "invisible hand." The invisible hand is an abstract representation of decentralized market forces where each individual pursues his/her own self interests and in doing so, and without reaching agreement with others, produces the best possible outcome (e.g., "maximized happiness") for social actors.

Free market approaches are among the most conservative economic, political and social theories, and consequentially produce the most conservative approaches to environmental protection. Why? In a nutshell, free market approaches propose that ordinary market mechanisms will protect the environment, and that no special intervention is needed to conserve nature. These approaches are preferred by the business sector and by those who seek to limit government powers.

The primary regulating mechanisms in a free market are supply, demand, and price. In theory, unregulated, free exchange allows producers to adjust supply to meet demand. At the same time, the balance between demand and supply affects price. Using free market models we examine how supply, demand, and price are related to environmental protection.

In theory, there are two primary scenarios. First, if consumers value environmental protection, demand for goods that damage the environment will decline, and manufacturers will reduce production of those goods or innovate new methods of production that supply a good without damaging the environment. Second, if consumers continue to demand goods that have a low natural supply or which produce environmental damage, prices will rise, forcing a decline in demand, which will preserve natural resources. In the second scenario, producers may also create new methods of production to meet demand that utilize a different set of resources. For example, if there is greater demand for raw timber than its supply, the price of raw timber will rise, slowing demand for raw timber, which will protect the environment. In this view, as the supply of a natural resource dwindles, its price rises, negating the need for artificial, external market controls such as government intervention to restrain the market place and protect against outcomes such as over-consumption which can lead to environmental harm. At the same time, other suppliers will introduce alternatives to raw timber, such as the use of steel, concrete block, or other materials for housing construction, which will help preserve the supply of raw timber. If these things happen, then the environment is protected by internal free market mechanisms.

In free market theory, the environment is protected from damage (e.g., pollution, global warming) or species from extinction because the prices of commodities associated with the overuse or pollution of the environment rise quickly and cause a decline in demand. This scenario should be especially true for commodities produced from rare natural resources; in such cases, prices should rise so quickly and so high that environmental disasters are averted by free market mechanisms that change the behavior of consumers (demand is lessen by high prices) and suppliers/producers (commodity production is reduced as prices rise and demand falls). It should also be kept in mind that unregulated markets work in this way if producers and consumers behave rationally, and each individual has knowledge of the marketplace. Let us see how this explanation can be applied to a real circumstance involving an environmental problem.

Around the turn of the 20th century (late 1880s-1920), exotic bird feathers were highly valued as decorative trim on hats and apparel, and there was an extraordinarily high level of demand for bird plumage. This high level of demand led to the widespread harvesting of wild birds as suppliers attempted to take advantage of high profit levels linked to consumer demand. As demand accelerated, the price for bird plumage rose. The price increase should have been extraordinary since there are natural limits to the supply of wild bird plumage. Despite these conditions, demand for plumage continued to rise. The increased demand, however, did not alter suppliers' behaviors, and wild bird harvesting expanded. Despite rising prices and plumage shortages, demand for feathers continued to rise, indicating that the free market failed to balance supply and demand. One reason the free market may fail in such a case is that it does not contain a mechanism for representing non-economic interests such as the value of preserving natural resources. Another reason is that there may be insufficient knowledge concerning the supply of a raw material. A third reason is that supplies of raw materials are often considered to be endless.

Image 2.1. The Great Blue Heron

The Great Blue Heron, which today is commonly found throughout much of the United States, was one of the bird species that became endangered due to the demand for bird plumage. (Public use image by Tom Kelley for the U.S. Fish and Wildlife Service).

Unfortunately, the free market was not protecting wild birds. By the turn of the century it was estimated that in the U.S., 15 million birds were harvested annually (Doughty, 1975), and several species of birds (egrets, herons and grebes) were pushed to the brink of extinction. In response, in 1906 Queen Alexandra of England publicly announced that she would no longer wear attire adorned with wild bird feathers. This announcement had only a minor effect. Several years earlier in the U.S., Harriet L. Hemenway attempted to address this situation when she formed an organization to combat this problem, which eventually became the National Audubon Society.

It became clear that the free market was not protecting bird species. In response, in 1913 the U.S. became the first country to regulate bird plumage when it banned its importation for purposes other than scientific or educational investigations (U.S. Statutes at Large, Vol. 38, Part 1, Chap. 16, pp. 146-52). Similar legislation was passed in Canada in 1915, and in England in 1921 (the British Bill was introduced in 1908, but took 13 years to pass). These actions provided the type of protection for wild birds that the free market could not (for similar modern problems in other animal species see the Kootenai Subbasin Plan, pp. 183-186, www.nwcouncil.org/fw/ subbasinplanning/ kootenai/plan/ EntirePlan.pdf).

Image 2.2. Historical examples of women's hats from the late 1890s elaborately adorned with bird feathers that helped escalate the demand for bird plumage.

(Original color plate from the Millinery Trade Review, February, 1897. Public use image from the Library of Congress, reproduction number LC-DIG-ppmsca-02905 DLC).

The effect of human activities on wild bird populations provides one example of the inability of free markets to protect the environment. Indeed, as we have discussed elsewhere (Burns and Lynch, 2004), environmental regulations often emerged to solve environmental problems *created by free markets*. Indeed, environmental regulations tend to be created in response to the extreme levels of environmental pollution, species extinction, and resource depletion *that occurred under free market conditions.*

Despite the limitations of free market views on environmental protection, this theory can be employed to reveal one reason that environmental regulations often fail. Environmental harms emerge in markets where environmental costs such as pollution are treated as *negative externalities* or as costs paid by entities other than producers, and which, therefore, do not affect market price. Negative externalities may include the costs of *resource depletion* including dwindling supplies of raw materials, which appear as environmental problems such as deforestation, species extinction, or water shortages. In other words, when producers or consumers engage in behavior that has environmental cost, but the cost is not part of the price of producing or buying a commodity, then the cost has been externalized, and the producer/consumer has no reason to alter her/his behavior. Consider, for instance, the numerous costs of air pollution (e.g., a decline in air quality; a decline in pubic health; an increase in diseases; damage to building, roadways and personal property, etc). Under free market conditions, these costs are not part of the costs of producing commodities, and do not become part of the price of a commodity. Consequently, they do not impact consumer or supplier behaviors. Under free market conditions, then, some external mechanism is needed to transform external costs into internal costs of production.

As an example, consider the Corporate Average Fuel Economy or CAFE program created by Congress in 1975 (Public Law 94-163; 49 U.S. Code 329; see Burns and Lynch, 2004, for extended discussion). CAFE requires automobile manufacturers to meet specific fuel efficiency requirements (average fleet miles per gallon) to reduce both U.S. reliance on foreign oil and automobile related air pollution. Manufacturers who fail to meet CAFE standards are fined, which, in theory, transforms the external costs related to air pollution into an internal cost of producing and purchasing inefficient vehicles. If these fines are adequate, there should be a corresponding decline in demand for inefficient vehicles and increased demand for lower cost, fuel efficient vehicles. As a result, manufacturers would be pressured to invent fuel efficient vehicles, which would result in improved air quality and a reduction in oil consumption.

In practice, however, CAFE regulations have had limited impacts on the vehicle market. One reason is that CAFE fines are rather small, and vehicle manufacturers and oil producers have effectively lobbied Congress to keep CAFE fines and efficiency standards to a minimum. For example, under pressure from trade associations, CAFE standards in the U.S. remained stagnant for a decade and a half. Likewise, CAFE fines are quite small on a per vehicle basis ($5.50 for each 1/10th of a mile per gallon under the CAFE standard), and there is a lower standard for the least efficient vehicles, light trucks and SUVs. Consider, for example, that in 2005, the per vehicle fine for a Hummer H2, a very inefficient vehicle that averages 11 miles per gallon (10 city; 13 highway) was $550, or about 1 percent of an H2's suggested retail price. This insignificant fine would not deter consumer interest in an H2 or any other inefficient vehicle since those who purchase these vehicles have high incomes and many also receive tax breaks of several thousand dollars for purchasing these vehicles (see Burns and Lynch, 2004).

To be sure, while an inventive idea, CAFE regulations have not been extraordinarily effective in improving automobile efficiency. As noted, lobbying activity helped keep CAFE standards stagnant and fines small. In addition, automakers discovered methods to avoid stricter CAFE requirements by redesigning vehicles so that they would be classified as light trucks or SUVs rather than as passenger cars. Moreover, because the U.S. government subsidizes U.S. oil producers—a violation of free market principles—gasoline prices in the U.S. remain low compared to other nations, stimulating high levels of demand for less fuel-efficient vehicles.

CRITICISMS OF FREE MARKET APPROACHES

So far, our discussion has illustrated a number of issues. First, a free market, unfettered by external restraints, does not tend to create its own remedies to environmental problems, and instead requires government intervention to establish minimal regulations. Numerous examples of the failure of the free market to respond to consumer interests (a host of other environmental regulations, those related to pure foods and drugs, worker health and safety, etc.) could be provided. These examples are beyond the scope of the present work. Nevertheless, *it should be evident that manufacturers tend to change their behavior in relation to government imposed standards, not solely in response to market forces.* On its own, the free market is unable to recognize or respond to problems that threaten the environment. Rather, the market responds to the economy of buying and selling, and is far removed from broader social concerns such as protecting the environment.

A second issue is that environmental problems are not caused by government intervention. But neither has government intervention always successfully solved these problems. In part, this may be because the level of government intervention is actually quite minimal, and these interventions have little impact on the free market, and certainly much less impact than free market proponents claim. For instance, CAFE standards have been easily met by vehicle manufacturers, and have not been raised—until recently—since 1990. In the intervening years, vehicle manufactures turned their attention to improving horsepower outputs from smaller engines rather than improving vehicle fuel efficiency (Burns and Lynch, 2004).

Third, free market approaches assume that actors have equal abilities to impact the market place to protect their self-interest, and that competition causes self-interested businesspeople to avoid banding together. Of course, this assumption does not fit the real world. In many industries, manufacturers form trade associations, political action committees (PACs) and lobbying groups to promote their interests. These groups also join together to promote overlapping interests (e.g., automobile manufacturers and the oil industry). When joined together, these groups wield tremendous economic power and resources, which they employ to influence political processes to the disadvantage of isolated consumers. Because manufacturers take these actions, it also means that the market is not free; rather, it is constrained by the actions of manufacturers who band together and violate the idea of free competition.

Finally, in order for a free market to operate effectively, participants require access to knowledge and information. Industries, however, tend to keep numerous secrets, and have obtained legal protection of information defined as a "trade secret." Furthermore, industries use trade association and other venues to produce misleading or counter-information (Rampton and Stauber, 2001; Stauber and Rampton, 1998; Fagin and Lavelle, 1999; Markowitz and Rosner, 2003; Davis, 2003; Warren, 2001) that undermines the principles behind a free market.

Even economists who support free market approaches admit that it is only capable of protecting natural resources through self-interest if those resources are privately owned (Gwartney, 1985). But many natural resources either cannot be owned (e.g., air) or are held in common by governments for the benefit of the population (e.g., national forests). Under such conditions, free markets cannot protect the natural environment effectively. Given these limitations, a number of alternative approaches to environmental protection have emerged.

THE SOCIOLOGY OF LAW

The sociology of law consists of a number of different theoretical approaches. Because the sociology of law includes varied theoretical perspectives that bring contrasting views and interpretive frameworks to examinations of legal issues, there is considerable disagreement concerning the functions, purposes and uses of law in society. Moreover, there is no single "sociology of law."

The studies that comprise the sociology of law include research and theory that examines (1) theories of law, and law's uses and justifications; (2) examinations of legal institutions, their organization, and practices; (3) studies of how law is enforced; (4) the social functions of law; and (5) the examination of responses to violations of legal rules (including penal, civil, administrative and regulatory responses). Any area of law, including environmental law, can be analyzed using insights from the sociology of law.

Historically, one of the more influential sociology of law approaches, called sociological jurisprudence, was founded by Roscoe Pound (1908, 1921, 1928, 1967). Pound's approach contained a critique of existing legal ideas based on *natural law*—the idea that humanly created laws are subordinate to and derived from universal legal principles and moral values common to human societies—and *positive law*—the idea that law contains a system of internal mechanisms such as precedent that establishes and affirms values that may overlap with or be distinct from moral values. In contrast to these views, Pound argued that law is a flexible mechanism used to respond to a variety of contemporary social conditions and human needs. Pound also emphasized a comparative approach to legal studies that contrasted "law on the books" to "law in action" (Lasser, 2002). The goal of this comparison is to determine whether the practice of law (law in action) meets its intent (law on the books). This kind of analysis has important implications for the study of environmental law.

Consider, for example, the *National Environmental Policy Act of 1969* (42 U.S.C. 4321-4347). According to this Act (section 101), it is the continuing responsibility of the Federal Government to use all practicable means, consistent with other essential considerations of national policy, to improve and coordinate Federal plans, functions, programs, and resources to:

1. fulfill the responsibilities of each generation as trustee of the environment for succeeding generations;

2. assure for all Americans safe, healthful, productive, and aesthetically and culturally pleasing surroundings;

3. attain the widest range of beneficial uses of the environment without degradation, risk to health or safety, or other undesirable and unintended consequences;

4. preserve important historic, cultural, and natural aspects of our national heritage, and maintain, wherever possible, an environment which supports diversity, and variety of individual choice;

5. achieve a balance between population and resource use which will permit high standards of living and a wide sharing of life's amenities; and

6. enhance the quality of renewable resources and approach the maximum attainable recycling of depletable resources.

Both federal law and federal environmental policies can be subject to analysis following the provisions in the NEPA. For example, consider the controversial "Clear Skies" Amendment to the *Clean Air Act* proposed by President George W. Bush to Congress in 2003. The President's proposal actually weakened existing pollution requirements, proposing, for instance, to raise emission limits from U.S. power plants for mercury, sulfur dioxide and nitrogen oxides. In effect, the proposal is a violation of U.S. law because it ignores the provisions of the NEPA.

To illustrate this point further, we could analyze any number of federal policies using the provisions set forth in the NEPA. Consider, for instance, the construction of federal prisons. Does the NEPA apply to the construction of federal prisons? If so, should these facilities be constructed in accordance with environmentally sound building innovations including the use of solar, wind and geothermal energy, or the recycling of waste into building materials? Since these technologies are available, protect the environment, save money over the long run, and can provide safe and reliable prison facilities, does the building of traditional prison facilities violate the intent of NEPA? Rather than provide an answer to this question here, we direct readers to consider this question on their own.

Sociology of law approaches can also be used to examine other environmental policy and law questions. Consider, for example, Executive Order 12898 (59 FR 7629), issued on February 11, 1994 by President Clinton entitled "Federal Actions to Address Environmental Justice in Minority Populations and Low-Income Populations." This order required all federal agencies to "make achieving environmental justice part of its mission by identifying and addressing....disproportionately high and adverse human health or environmental effects of its programs, policies, and activities on minority populations and low-income populations in the United States..." At issue in sociology of law approaches is whether or not specific agencies have indeed achieved the fundamental intent and specific requirements of Executive Order 12898. Does the law on the books (Executive Order 12898) match the law in action (the procedures agencies adopted, or perhaps failed to adopt, to fulfill the requirements of 12898)?

In sum, the sociology of law provides a guideline for assessing whether specific policies implement the intent of law. This view does not, however, define the conditions for appropriate lawmaking, or whether laws actually protect the environment. A variety of other theories can be employed for this purpose.

MARKETS AND POWER

A number of economic, social, and political theories recognize that economic markets do not provide ideal conditions for free competition because participants have varying degrees of economic and political power. Boyce (2002) argued that power differentials between and contest among people have important implications for understanding environmental pollution and its regulation.

One reason is that law will tend to reflect the interests of the powerful (Chambliss and Seidman, 1982). For example, individuals with similar interests join together and wield their economic and political power to shape environmental laws, influencing the level of protection provided by environmental laws and the application of regulations to communities depending on the social class of a community's inhabitants (Lynch, Stretesky and Burns, 2004a; 2004b). In addition, power affects where hazardous waste and pollution is produced, stored, and disposed. As a result, low-income communities are more likely to be proximate to environmental hazards and pollution, and less likely to be protected from toxic hazards.

Boyce's argument is based on the idea that power differentials are structural, and that in class-based societies, those with economic power can use economic and political resources to impose pollution costs on less powerful social classes. This explanation is also important to the study of environmental justice—the idea that exposure to environmental pollution varies with community race and class characteristics—an idea reviewed in a later chapter.

Boyce also tested the theory that the costs of pollution are unequally distributed and are related to structural inequality. For example, he demonstrated that income inequality impacts exposure to environmental pollution across countries (pp. 47-66), and that power differentials across U.S. states (measured by an index including income distribution, income inequality and percent African American and Hispanic) helps explain the level of pollution and legal responses to pollution.

SOCIAL ECOLOGY

There are a variety of social ecological perspectives that employ theories of economic and social inequality to examine environmental crisis, pollution, policy and public health. Each view shares the assumption that humans are part of the natural world, and that the unique human ability to reason and change the environment produces a special responsibility for environmental stewardship. Further, social ecological views argue that humanly constructed systems that produce social and economic inequality and differential access to power affects the distribution of access to environmental resources as well as the distribution and impact of environmental harms.

Marxists

For Marxist social ecologists, the primary concern is how class inequality and conflict affects the making and enforcement of environmental law, access to natural resources, and the distribution of environmental toxins and pollution (Bellamy, 2000; O'Connor, 1997; Benton, 1996). The primary issues for Marxists is detailing how class conflict is worked out, and illustrating how the working out of environmental conflicts tends to favor the interests of powerful social actors such as corporations (Lynch and Michalowski, 2006; Chambliss and Seidman, 1982; Balbus, 1977; Wright, 1985; Domhoff, 2005; Vlachou, 2005). Thus, it is no accident that environmental rules do not lay out strict penalties for corporations that violate the rules; or that the rules are written to allow elevated levels of environmental damage to occur before penalties are imposed or the polluting activity is mitigated; or that corporations can apply for permits that allow them to pollute the environment. Each of these outcomes has a link to class power and privilege. Moreover, Marxist ecologists point out that the inherent goal of capitalism—profit through growth—is at odds with the preservation and stability dynamics of nature (Vlachou, 1993; Lynch and Michalowski, 2006, Chapter 7).

Other issues relevant to class analysis concern the effect of class structure on the distribution of and exposure to toxic hazards. For example, numerous studies indicate that toxic waste sites are more likely to be found in or near lower income and working class communities rather than in upper income communities (Farber and Krieg, 2002; Carson, Jeon, and McCubbin, 1997; Stretesky and Lynch, 1999; see also Chapter 7). The location of these waste sites is part of the class conflict that characterizes capitalist societies. Class also has important impacts on access to natural resources (Vlachou, 2004, 2002). In class societies, natural resources and access to them are controlled by those with economic power. Many current battles over access to the natural resources located within the boundaries of national parks and other federal lands (e.g., the logging of national forests) serve as excellent examples of these conflicts. So, too, does the controversy over the use of mountain top removal mining techniques.

Mountain top removal (MTR) is accomplished by using explosives to expose underground minerals (see image 2.3). This is a cheap and easy mining method that has extensive environmental costs. Consider, for instance, what happens to the removed mountain top: it is moved and dumped somewhere else. MTR, practiced extensively in Kentucky and West Virginia, affects low-income communities that depend on mining, especially when the mountain tops are dumped in nearby valleys and block waterways such as streams used by local communities for water supplies, as food sources, or for recreational purposes (see image 2.4). For example, in West Virginia, Island Creek Mountain and the nearby Big Branch Creek were destroyed by MTR techniques, impacting not only the environment, but the lives of the largely poor populations who live in those locations. Moreover, because MTR uses detonation equipment to unearth coal, fewer miners are needed, which has led to a significant decline in mining employment in areas where quality jobs that provide good incomes are already limited. In addition, consider that mountain top waste typically contains toxins such as sulfur and heavy metals, and that MTR methods use large quantities of water and produce a toxic coal slurry that needs to be disposed. A common disposal method is to pump this toxic waste slurry into underground wells or old coal mines. The mines, which have not been prepared to serve as toxic waste disposal sites, often leach toxins into nearby underground waterways which can contaminate the local water supply. (For more information, see the Mountaintop Removal Clearinghouse, mtrinfo.wordpress.com).

Image 2.3. The use of explosives in MTR mining

(photograph courtesy of *Appalachian Voices*, www.appvoices.org).

A relevant example of Marxist social ecology is found in the work of economist James O'Connor, founder of the journal *Capitalism, Nature, Socialism*, and well known for his earlier economic analyses of the U.S. economy (1973, 1985). O'Connor (1997) argued that capitalism and nature are at odds with one another for several reasons. First, capitalism's insatiable desire for expansion is confronted by the limits of the natural world and raw materials. This has contributed to a form of mobile capital that uses up local raw materials and moves on, leaving behind depleted natural resources and environmental harms and an abandoned working population that earned its livelihood extracting those resources. Second, capitalism treats environmental resources as commodities, even though no one produces them, and interprets access to raw materials as a right. In the view of capital, natural resources are there to be exploited for the benefit of the corporation, and few provisions are made to recognize the rights of local populations with respect to the ownership and control of local natural resource or the quality of the local environment.

**Image 2.4. This image shows a "valley fill" created after mountain top
removal has been completed.**

Note that the fill impedes the flow of the local stream (photograph courtesy of
Appalachian Voices, www.appvoices.org).

Third, the profit motive has caused the centralization and globalization of
capital. Global capital has few meaningful ties to local ecological conditions.
The result has been a tendency to ignore local environmental problems, to view
these as transient, and has contributed to the failure to develop long term
environmental strategies that respond to the unique concerns of local populations or the preservation of local environments. Once the global corporation has
used up the resources in one area, it is capable of moving its operations on to the
next location. Each of these outcomes has been facilitated by an expansion of
free market assumptions and the decline of market regulations in the political
sphere.

At the same time, O'Connor points out that the ecological problems of
capitalism have not gone unchallenged, and that conditions for various
resistance movements have emerged. One example is the movement that pits
native peoples who live in more ecologically pristine areas of the world against
the global reach of capitalism. Such movements, however, are also evident in
numerous cities and nations around the world. Especially relevant for O'Connor
are the "red-greens," ecological movements that combine class analysis and

environmental consciousness. These movements have had important impacts in U.S. cities such as Berkeley, California, and on national politics in various countries (e.g., the Green Party and the Green Alliance in the U.S.; Green Party UK; Els Verds Esquerra Ecologista in Spain; The Federation of Green Parties of Africa; The European Green Party). The ability of localized groups to confront global corporations remains an open question. In Europe, these groups have been able to expand and provide the basis for trans-European political representation. In much of the world, however, especially in the U.S., such movements carry negative ideological connotations and tend to be unpopular. Despite this tendency, O'Connor holds out the hope that people recognize their common interests in protecting the environment, and that these movements will become more popular and capable of controlling the growth and destructive tendencies of capitalism.

Anarchists

Marxists focus on class conflict, though many have also developed theories of human nature and the relationship between humans and nature, and the responsibility of humans to protect nature (for review see, Merchant, 1992, p. 134-142). These latter views are more widely developed by and central to anarchist social ecology. One prime example is the work of Murray Bookchin (2005, 1988, 1987), founder of the libertarian socialist social ecological approach, which advocated decentralized grass-roots democracy as a form of anarchism. In the mid-1960s, he was among the first to argue in favor of locally organized economies as a mechanism for protecting the environment and human health.

In Bookchin's view (1965, 1971, 1992) local citizens would be better able to organize to protect the environment than corporations, especially since modern corporations were not tied to the local economy or environment. For Bookchin, localized production based on microtechnologies that used renewable energy and resources such as recycling would have less impact on the environment. Bookchin also argued that in an ideal world built on equality and freedom, humans and nature would reunite, leading to a natural state in which human interests and nature's interests would realign. In such a state, humans would "naturally" refrain from damaging the environment.

Deep Ecology

Deep ecology establishes a holistic view of humans and the environment (Devall and Sessions, 2001). The founder of this approach, Arne Naess, sought to describe the spiritual aspects of ecology and derived his inspiration from Eastern religions and philosophers, especially Gandhi. Devall and Sessions extended Naess's view and incorporated science as a core element in deep ecology. The idea behind deep ecology is to provide a basis for reinterpreting the world and human efforts to preserve the natural world.

Deep ecology begins with the assumption that humans are not above nature; rather both are on equal footing. In effect, deep ecologists argue that humans must relinquish the egocentric (person centered) or homocentric (human centered) philosophies of the Enlightenment period or free market economics that justify human plunder of the natural world. In contrast, the deep ecologist substitutes ecocentrism, the idea that when using nature, humans have a duty to maintain ecological unity or integrity and to harm nature as little as possible. In traditional views including free market models, nature is a resource to be used to supply materials for human use; it has no independent interests or value outside of its human uses because it is an economic raw material. For the deep ecologist, nature is not a tool to be manipulated to fulfill human desires or artificially produced wants for commodities. Rather, the interconnection of humans with nature and the dependence of humans on nature must be recognized and become central to human social and economic organization. Thus, in the deep ecology view, humans do not posses a natural right to dominate nature. Rather, humans are required to promote sustainable development—forms of progress that does not harm nature. Central to this idea is determining the "human carrying capacity" of nature, and living within those boundaries (Merchant, 1992). In this view, technology is not an end in itself or a simple means of innovation used to sell more commodities; rather, technology should only be promoted to minimize damage to the natural world.

There are a number of varieties of deep ecology. Some are spiritually anchored (e.g., Native ecological approaches), while others promote scientific ecology. It is beyond the scope of this book to detail these differences, and interested readers are directed to Merchant's (1992) excellent detailed description of these views.

Steady State Economics

Traditional economic theory argues that to be effective, economies must grow. Such growth, an imperative behind capitalism, is believed to provide people with incentives to work and "get ahead," which also stimulate economic growth. Furthermore, economic growth is valued because it provides more goods to more people and allows everyone to live "the good life."

In reality, however, economic growth isn't good for everyone, and not everyone gets to share in the economic pie—especially not equally. To illustrate the latter contention, consider economist Edward N. Wolff's (1995, 2002) analysis of economic growth in the U.S. Between 1983 and 1989, for example, those who were already well off (the top 20 percent of wealth holders) received 99 percent of all newly created wealth, leaving 1 percent of new wealth to be split among the remaining 80 percent of the U.S. population. Such a division is clearly unequal and not beneficial to the majority of the population. Moreover, the trend noted in this portion of the 1980s was not unusual. In 1976 in the U.S., the wealthiest 1 percent of families owned 22 percent of all wealth. By 1992, they owned 42 percent of the wealth, indicating that the share of wealth accruing to those who were already very well off economically escalated much more rapidly than the wealth of the remaining 99 percent of the population. In contrast to conventional or traditional economic wisdom, it should be evident that economically, growth is good for those who are already wealthy; it doesn't necessarily benefit everyone else. What about environmentally? Is growth good for the environment?

Herman Daly (1991, 1993, 1996), former Senior Economist for the World Bank's Environment Department, argues that economic growth has its limits, especially when the benefits of economic growth become restricted, as illustrated by Wolff's research, or when the pursuit of growth damages other aspects of human society or causes extensive environmental decay. Daly criticized orthodox economic views for the suggestion that growth is always good, and that continued growth allows the majority to satisfy their growing bundle of wants. He argues that economists reach this conclusion by considering the benefits *but not the costs* of growth—costs that include pollution, resource depletion, species extinction, and global warming. The problem is that the world does not possess an endless supply of raw material; it cannot absorb toxic waste and pollution endlessly; it cannot supply healthy living conditions if humans continue to contaminate it and use it up at an expanding pace. In short, human society, and American society in particular (Henry, 1963), has developed an endless appetite for expansion and consumption that cannot be sustained by the natural world.

Daly argues that for human societies to continue without dramatic economic and environmental consequences, human values must be reoriented away from endless expansion and consumption as cherished goals, toward environmental sustainability and steady state economics. In contrast to ordinary economic models, steady state economics argues against growth as a desirable or essential measure of economic success. In place of growth as a value, steady state economics places emphasis on environmental preservation, restructuring economies so that produced values are more evenly distributed, escalating material reuse and recycling, expanding product life-cycles, minimizing consumption and population growth, and promoting healthy and achievable lifestyles and levels of economic development. The goal is to create a steady or balanced economy where growth and development are devalued because they destroy the environment and produce more extensive human harm than benefit. As economists such as Wolff have shown, the economic benefits of growth are highly constrained, and affect a small percentage of the population. In contrast, as illustrated in Chapter One, the negative effects of economic growth associated with pollution are widespread and impact a very large percentage of society.

Thus, steady state economics calls attention to the connection between economic growth and the impact of growth on human and environmental health. This view illustrates that economic growth has extensive negatives, and that nature and human health would benefit from a more constrained view on economic growth and development that promoted and sustained healthy conditions for existence.

Green Criminology

As a discipline, criminology has largely ignored studying environmental crimes (Lynch, McGurrin and Fenwick, 2004). It is possible that the seeming disinterest by criminologists with regard to environmental crimes could have stemmed from the lack of available data to study environmental harms. However, environmental crime data is currently readily available (e.g., Burns and Lynch, 2004) and in recent years, criminologists have attempted to remedy this neglect and have established an approach referred to as green criminology (Lynch, 1990; Lynch and Stretesky, 2003; Lynch and Stretesky, 2007; South and Beirne, 2006; Beirne and South, 2007). The perspectives adopted by green criminologists are varied, and focus on non-human species and rights (Beirne, 1995, 1999, 2002), the definition of green crimes and green criminology (Lynch, 1990, Lynch and Stretesky, 2003), the scope of green criminology (see articles in the special 1998 special edition of *Theoretical Criminology*, edited by South and Beirne), and pollution issues from toxic environmental crimes to global warming (Lynch and Stretesky, 2001). Here, we summarize our view of the main theoretical issues.

Green criminology begins with the assertion that environmental harms are to be understood as an outcome of the economic organization and goals of modern capitalism (Lynch, 1990; Lynch and Stretesky, 2007). Like other environmental views, this assertion links the unfettered economic growth promoted by capitalist systems of production to the extensive levels of environmental harm that exist in today's world. Going beyond other environmental approaches, green criminology also asserts that environmental harms, the content of environmental regulations, and the exercise of environmental social control must be examined relative to class, race and gender structures of power.

Unlike other environmental approaches, green criminology examines the content of environmental law, how those laws are enforced, and how those with economic power—especially corporations—exercise their power to influence the scope of environmental law and social control. For instance, corporations use their resources to lobby for less restrictive environmental laws, and to produce research that contradicts findings concerning the toxic harms caused by environmental pollution (Lynch and Stretesky, 2001).

Class and race are important issues for green criminologists who study unequal patterns in exposure to environmental toxins, an idea reviewed in a later chapter on environmental justice. In the United States, for example, a number of studies demonstrate that the areas inhabited by the poor and persons of color are more proximate to toxic waste sites, or are selected as locations for hazardous waste sites. With respect to the enforcement of environmental laws, research has demonstrated that those who violate environmental laws in poor and minority communities received reduced penalties (Lynch, Stretesky and Burns, 2004a, 2004b).

Power structures also play a role in the kinds of harms humans commit against animals. Green criminology examines these crimes by focusing on how economic expansion goals affect environmental conditions that drive species into extinction, damage their natural surroundings, or allow them to be used for animal experimentation (Frank and Lynch, 1992).

Green criminologists have also linked their approach to political activism. Lynch (1990), for example, argued that green views are by their origin, connected to political activism, citing the growth of green political parties in Europe as an example. Lynch and Stretesky (2003) note that greens tend to be aligned with grass-roots movements, which in the U.S. is associated with the environmental justice movement.

In short, this emerging perspective is an attempt to build a unique criminological approach for studying environmental harms, the content of environmental laws, and the enforcement of environmental law, but also for building a political basis for corrective action. By doing so, green criminologists hope to expand the level of attention criminology pays to environmental crime.

Ecofeminism

Marxists examine the relationship between class power and structures and environmental harms, while environmental justice research and green criminology extend this focus to include race-linked power structures. Ecofeminism's unique contribution to the study of the environment is its focus on the inter-relationship between the oppression of women and nature (Sturgeon, 1997). Like Marxist and green ecologists, ecofeminists argue that the growth imperative of capitalism has an important effect on the environment. To this, ecofeminists add the idea that the tradition of patriarchy (male-centered or dominated societies) produces the dual domination of women and nature.

The term ecofeminism was first used by the French philosopher Francoise d'Eaubonne in 1974. d'Eaubonne's argued that men had established the domination and oppression of nature and women, and that women and nature were treated in much the same way in male centered social and economic hierarchies. She offered the revolutionary idea that it was, therefore, up to women to liberate nature as they liberated themselves. In order to do so, women would need to alter the relationship between the sexes, and in doing so, between women and society. This powerful idea formed the basis for the ecofeminism movement in the 1980s (Merchant, 1992).

Ecofeminism replaces the traditional view of women as nurturers with a partnership ethic which depicts humans and other species as sharing in supportive, nondominating relationships. The goal of establishing these relationships is to promote the mutual interests of nature and its inhabitants, and to reduce environmental harm.

In order to promote the idea of mutual interests, ecofeminists critique male-centered theories that tend to proceed on the basis of differentiation: establishing the unique interests of women, men, racial groups, or animals and ecosystems. For the ecofeminist, each group is tied together by its shared interests, and it is by recognizing these shared interests that oppressed groups—women, classes, races, nature—can be liberated and recognized as equals. Achieving this goal requires political action, and ecofeminism cannot be placed into practice without a commitment to activism. But before political activism can become widespread, women's consciousness about their oppression and the oppression of nature must be raised. Merchant (1992, pp. 192-193) notes that cultural ecofeminism gave rise to grass-roots environmental movements in which women became activists in response to local environmental issues, such as the effects of toxic waste sites on the health of children, families and communities. The development of these movements was an important step in this process of moving ecofeminism toward political activism. As Merchant (1995) notes, women are the primary participants and activists in grassroots environmental justice movements.

In addition to its focus on gender parity, ecofeminists emphasize other important dimensions of social and economic oppression related to race and social class. Special attention is provided to the role minority women and women in "third world" nations play in promoting ecological and environmental health.

Given their common interests and connections, ecofeminists argue that women can liberate both themselves and nature simultaneously by opposing unbridled economic growth and promoting equity in all social and natural relations. Further, ecofeminists argue that male power depends on the economic domination of women and nature; nature supplies the raw materials that build men's wealth, while women supply the free labor needed to maintain the working class and to produce the next generation of laborers. Thus, the liberation of women and nature depends on exposing and eradicating male domination of labor and raw materials.

EPIDEMIOLOGY AND THE ENVIRONMENT

Epidemiology is a public health science that examines the causes, distribution and control of diseases in a population. It is based on scientific studies that compare the health of populations to one another, or examining the health of populations over time, or the health of a population before and after exposure to a suspected cause of a disease, including toxic chemicals. As a result, epidemiology is a method of study rather than a theory about the environment. And while epidemiology does not contain a theory of the environment, it does contain a theory of how diseases are spread. One such pathway is through exposure to environmental toxins that become part of the environment as humans produce commodities and discard the wastes from this production process.

Historically, important evidence of disease causes and pathways were established by epidemiological studies as early as the fourth century, B.C., when Hippocrates examined lead poisoning among miners (Daugherty, 1997). Over the next 2000 years, physicians employed epidemiological studies to produce links between chemical exposure and disease, but epidemiology did not become a recognized specialty until the 20th century (Luneberg, 1995).

Environmental epidemiology constitutes an important approach to studying the effects of environmental pollution and hazards on human health. Its uses were recognized in the mid-1800s when the disease theory of germ transmission was introduced to study and contain public outbreaks of communicable disease (Luneberg, 1995). Epidemiology became a field for quantitative study in the 20th century as researchers used cohort studies to establish the causes of occupationally related diseases. Such studies were also useful for estimating the risk of diseases from different forms of exposure to toxic chemicals.

Environmental epidemiology, or the study of the causes, distribution and control of diseases caused by exposure to non-occupational environmentally prevalent toxins, did not really emerge in full until the second half of the 20th century. The first significant discussions revolved around the "killer" fogs in Donora, Pennsylvania (Davis, 2002) and London (Logan, 1953). The *Engineer's Career Planning Handbook* (2003; http://www.usphsengineers.org/handbook/) suggests that interest in environmental epidemiology was also linked to the development of the U.S. Public Health Services in the early 1900s, but more forcefully to the establishment of the Environmental Protection Agency in the 1970s.

One use of epidemiology is the identification of disease clusters (Brown and Mikkelsen, 1997) such as cancer clusters (Kulldorff et al., 1997), birth defects clusters (Brender et al., 2006), heart disease clusters (Yauck, 2004), and a host of other illness clusters that result from living near toxic waste sites. These techniques of analysis are used not only by medical researchers and environmental scientists, but also by social scientists to study the characteristics of populations residing near toxic waste sites (see the Chapter 9 on Environmental Justice). For the social scientist, the issue is whether proximity to hazardous waste sites contains patterns that indicate the existence of class or racial bias in either the siting of such facilities, or in housing markets, or in the type and level of response environmental regulators initiate to known environmental hazards. Building on health effects noted by medical researchers, social scientists seek to determine whether some groups are more likely to be exposed to the deleterious health effects of toxic waste sites simply as a result of the social class or racial characteristics of neighborhood inhabitants. Examined in this way, it is clear that epidemiological studies have implications for discussing issues of justice, especially those related to the relationship between social class, race and human disease and health.

CONCLUSION

There are a variety of theories used to understand the relationship between humans and the natural world, and how and why humans respond to the existence of environmental pollution. Traditional economic theories based on free market approaches posit that economic markets will automatically regulate the environment by balancing supply and demand. Historically, this explanation has not fared well, and the free market often contributes to rather than prevents environmental problems.

In response to the inability of free markets to solve environmental problems, governments created regulations to preserve the natural world. The simplest theoretical justifications for doing so were derived from conservation theories which interpreted humans as protectors of the environment. A number of more complicated theories of environmental protection have emerged over the past fifty years. The majority of these theories suggest that human and environmental health are connected, and that there is a need to preserve the environment in order to protect the human species. Human health cannot be left to the possibility that the free market might respond appropriately, because there is much evidence it does not.

In addition, many recent theories view environmental pollution as an extension of the exploitive relationships humans have constructed between themselves: relationships that, for instance, promote the exploitation of working class labor, women, or people of color. In these views, environmental pollution, deforestation, species extinction, and other environmental problems are viewed as extensions of the kinds of relationships humans have constructed amongst themselves.

Theories that describe environmental pollution as an outcome of various forms of social organization created by human societies also note that environmental harms will tend to affect some groups in society more than others. Thus, efforts to protect the environment often require addressing other social and economic conditions, such as the nature of class, gender or race relationships. These theories also recognize that it is necessary to correct human inequality in order to address environmental problems which are also a form of inequality—inequality between humans and nature, rather than between humans as social classes or races or genders. When connected in this way, efforts to protect the environment not only preserve and protect the environment from harm, they also serve to improve the life circumstances of people.

The study of the causes of disease promoted by epidemiology have produced evidence that human health and environmental health are indeed associated. Thus, the evidence from epidemiological studies supports the contention of environmental theories that link human health and well being to environmental health and well being. In effect, we can say that treating the earth poorly produces a boomerang effect that feeds back on those who produce noxious environmental conditions, and that human societies pay a price for neglecting the health of the environment.

In the following chapter, several of these issues are extended by examining the history of environmental movements. To be sure, such movements are associated with theories that set out justifications for preserving the environment. Environmental theories and movement also have important implications for the development of environmental laws which are examined in a later chapter.

CHAPTER 3

The Environmental Movement and Policy In the United States

Jane was a straight-A student at a competitive university where she studied Biology. She demonstrated concern for animals and the environment dating back to her early childhood days when she wanted to be a veterinarian when she grew up, which prompted her to learn more about living organisms. During her sophomore year in college, Jane became involved with a local grassroots pro-environmental group. Her involvement with the group was marginal at first, although by her senior year Jane had been arrested for disturbing the peace at several mild protests, and three months prior to graduation she was arrested on felony charges of arson, when she and fellow members of her group successfully set fire to three bulldozers that were preparing to clear land for a housing subdivision. Jane was dismissed from the university and is currently awaiting trial.

INTRODUCTION

The above, fictitious scenario exemplifies several things: Jane's actions are atypical of environmental activists; violent protests among segments of the environmental movement are not, however, completely unfathomable. The fact that Jane was willing to surrender her education, and many other things, for the sake of the environment demonstrates, in a most extreme form, the passion maintained by many of those who love the environment. To be sure, violent environmental activism is extreme, rare, and arguably detrimental to environmental causes. Most people who support environmental activism do so in nonviolent ways (Taylor, 2003), even though they evince strong convictions and passions (e.g., Couch and Kroll-Smith, 1997). Indeed, much of the public values the environment and favors actions to protect it from harm.

Public support for environmental issues has fluctuated over time, as have the methods of environmental action and the particular causes of concern. To be sure, the intensity and breadth of activism is influenced by significant events (consider the response to the aftermath of Hurricane Katrina), revelations of the callous and calculating nature of the behavior of those who regularly violate environmental laws, or even in response to presidential administrations where environmental policies tend to undermine environmental health (e.g., the Reagan and George W. Bush administrations).

Recently there has been a resurgence of support for environmental conservation and preservation, two movements that impacted environmental policy in the U.S. for the past century. Moreover, throughout this period, public involvement in the environmental movement has waxed and waned. At different points in history, environmentalism has been a concern of the wealthy, the populace in general, and the poor and minorities in the form of environmental justice. Indeed, various historical and current environmental movements have affected how society conceptualizes harms committed against plants, the environment, and animals (e.g., Theodore Roosevelt's "conservationist movement" in the late nineteenth to early twentieth century [Frank and Lynch, 1992]). Each is important in its own right, and some have had long-term impacts. No period of environmental concern, however, has been as protracted as the movement begun in the 1960s.

Despite its persistence, the modern environmental movement is not a unified whole (Athanasiou, 2002), and even "The roots of the modern environmental movement are as deeply fractured as environmental activism is today" (Edwards, 1983, p. 31). Such a fractured heritage makes it difficult to summarize the history of environmentalism. Nevertheless, the remainder of this chapter provides historical highlights and reviews some current events that have shaped societal efforts to promote the conservation and preservation of our environment. As will become evident, the history of environmental concern is largely shaped by, and closely follows, major developments in society in general. Highlights of major developments affecting environmentalism are provided following the following sections.

THE EARLY HISTORY OF ENVIRONMENTALISM

The significance of the environment cannot be understated. In simple terms, we rely on clean air for breathing and healthy water for drinking. If we look more deeply, we can see how changes in the environment affect our everyday well-being and lives including, for instance, where settlers decided to live. Neimark and Mott (1999) describe how the continental divide between Russia and Alaska contributed to the development of the Western Hemisphere, and how changes in the climate shifted populations around the Americas. They note that as glaciers made their way south, the population drifted into what is now Central- and South America. As the glaciers melted, populations moved north to what is now considered North America. The demographic impact of such drastic changes in the environment are notable, and certainly of concern as we face issues such as global warming.

Environmental Values in the American Colonies

The environmental issues faced by American settlers were much different from those faced today, and were more often of a more immediate, short-term nature and involved immediate survival needs. For the American settler, the environment was an obstacle to be overcome and conquered. In the modern era, the environment has been overly "civilized" and conquered, and the problems modern people face are quite different. The loss of environmental habitat, forests, green spaces, the build up of environmental toxins, and global warming all present persistent, long term threats to human survival.

Early societies relied on the land for farming and hunting, and until the industrial revolution, low population density allowed the land to be used in this way without causing extensive environmental damage. In such circumstances, there was little concern for the environment and little need to be aware of how humans damaged the natural environment. But, even in early America there were conflicting visions of the natural environment, and the role humans ought to play in preserving it. One difference is evident when the practices of Native American people are compared to those of who sought to settle America (Merchant, 1992). Native Americans demonstrated a much greater appreciation for the environment than did the European settlers; the latter demonstrated a much greater interest in using the land for personal benefit and profit, and moving on once the wealth of the land had been extinguished. In contrast, the Native Americans saw the land as eternal and humans as care-takers of the land. The settlers took advantage of ripe conditions in the new land to engage in overseas trade while showing little concern for conservation or preservation of the environment. Moreover, the Native Americans understood that the white European settler had a poor environmental ethic, and treated the environment as a tool, as matter to be exploited, rather than as an integral part of human existence.

Earlier societies recognized the value of the environment in many ways, and ceremonies were often built around paying homage to the environment and spirits of nature. Concern for nature, however, seemed to diminish as humans settled into towns, built cities, and became less nomadic and dependent on the cycles of nature. With respect to human settlements, documented concern for the environment dates back to 1290 when King Edward I of England, disturbed by the smoke-filled air of London, prohibited the burning of coal while Parliament was sitting. Years later, a German researcher noted the detrimental effects of exposure to various gas and metal pollutants (Bellini, 1986).

The attempt to protect lands in the Americas dates back to 1626 when citizens of Plymouth Colony passed ordinances limiting the cutting and sale of trees. Similar efforts were made by William Penn's 1681 forest conservation efforts in Pennsylvania (Nash, 1990). Efforts to protect the American environment expanded once it became free of its colonial status. As a colony, the primary purpose of America was to supply raw materials to expand the wealth of England. Moreover, the vast, uncultivated North American lands encouraged the belief that natural resources were seemingly endless. Independence from Great Britain led to greater development and destruction of the environment as the new country attempted to grow and continuously establish itself.

Industrialization and Environment

Industrialization brought further harm to the environment, as did the increasing need to develop access to the east coast. Roads were developed at the expense of forests, and as the east coast grew, expansion of the west continued. The Federal government and the States showed little support for conservation or preservation as an interest in acquiring lands took precedent over caring for what was already acquired. Neimark and Mott (1999) note that concern for the environment was low, with the sole exception of the writers and artists of the time who documented both the beauty of the lands, and the harms being done to them.

The expansion of industrialization was aided by increased immigration and urbanization. As urban populations grew, so too did sanitation problems and the pollution of local water and air resources. Governments did little to rectify these situations, and urban areas became increasingly polluted. Settlement of the west and the exploitation of its natural resources was facilitated by the first transcontinental railroad in 1869 (Neimark and Mott, 1999). As described in an earlier chapter, it was in the mid- to late 1800s that the first species were driven to near extinction by hunting (e.g., buffalo and certain species of birds). And, while there was a need to respond to extraordinarily adverse environmental problems from time to time, certainly nothing that resembled an environmental movement had emerged.

The Progressive Movement

All of this began to change in the early twentieth century. At that time, Americans changed their focus from the countryside to the cities, spurred largely by the introduction of labor-saving agricultural machinery, burgeoning industry, and a surge in urban populations (Nash, 1967). Cities became host to an expanding number of families, and the countryside was no longer recognized as something that required clearing, but something that could instead be the source of recreation. The pro-environment movement at this time, albeit small in comparison to what would occur late in the twentieth century, involved wealthy individuals who engaged in organized resistance to destruction of the environment (Neimark and Mott, 1999). Various conservation-minded groups actively commented on environmental harms, which spurred the federal government to become more involved.

Historians recognize the turn of the century as the beginning of an actual environmental movement. At this time, conservationism, influenced by events of the Progressive Era (circa 1890–1920), began to take shape (Switzer and Bryner, 1998; Edwards, 1998). The Movement took two distinct directions: (1) the *preservationist movement* which centered around protecting environmental resources because of their intrinsic values and not their economic values; and (2) the *conservation* approach, which was concerned with quality of life and economic issues for future generations. In the long run, it was the economic focus of the conservationists' position that prevailed (Cable and Cable, 1995).

In the early 1890s, the U.S. Census Bureau declared the American frontier closed. This announcement increased concern for preserving the environment (Cable and Cable, 1995) consistent with Americans' perceptions of classical liberalism and the protection of individual rights (Edwards, 1998). But behind these outward and philosophically grounded rationales for environmental preservation lurked important economic interests: A major focus of federal laws passed during this period of history was to secure economic benefits from natural resources (Edwards, 1998).

Numerous writers from this period offered their input regarding how to best protect the environment. Among the preservationists, Henry David Thoreau argued that "humans required wilderness in order to remain civilized. By communing with nature, humans could stay in touch with their spiritual self. For this to happen, though, nature needed to remain undisturbed by human activity" (Edwards, 1998, p. 34). Other preservationists included George Catlin, an artist, writer, and advocate for national parks to preserve the American wilderness; and John Muir, founder of the Sierra Club, who argued that "Humans could only sustain their spirituality through exposure to God's undisturbed creations" (Edwards, 1998, p. 34). Later, in 1949, Aldo Leopold wrote *A Sand County Almanac*, which impacted subsequent environmental movements through encouraging readers to form a better appreciation of our environment. Leopold's work is recognized as likely the most influential of all books written on conservation (Schindler, 1995)

Other notable conservationists include George Perkins Marsh (1801–1882) author of *Man and Nature; or Physical Geography As Modified by Human Action* (1864), who suggested that earlier civilizations perished as a result of destroying their environments; Frederick Law Olmsted (1822–1903), who promoted the development of urban parks for public use and recreation; John Wesley Powell (1834–1902), whose work was influential in the *Reclamation Act of 1902* (Nash, 1976), which established the federal water storage and irrigation policies still in use today (Edwards, 1998); Gifford Pinchot (1865–1946) who impacted environmental efforts through his Washington, DC connections (particularly through his relationship with President Theodore Roosevelt). Pinchot is often credited with focusing American environmental efforts on conservation as opposed to preservation (Switzer and Bryner, 1998). Pinchot's influence is evident, for example, in a White House Conference on Resource Management he organized in May 1908, which drew 1,000 national leaders. The conference resulted in the leaders asking the federal government to develop a National Conservation Commission to document all U.S. natural resources (Switzer and Bryner, 1998).

The Progressive Era was clearly a period of significant environmental concern, particularly due to the efforts of Theodore Roosevelt, who has been deemed "The undisputed political leader of the Progressive Conservation Movement" (Edwards, 1998, p. 37). Roosevelt's conservationist approach led to his support of strong scientific management of environmental resources. To encourage orderly growth that preserved the environment, Roosevelt appointed a Public Lands Commission in 1903 and developed the Inland Waterways Commission in 1907 (Switzer and Bryner, 1998; Edwards, 1998). Similarly, Congress created the National Park Service (1916), established new forests, and passed laws to protect migratory birds and historic sites during the presidencies of Theodore Roosevelt, William Howard Taft, and Woodrow Wilson (Switzer and Bryner, 1998). The Progressive Era is also credited with the establishment of conservation groups such as The Sierra Club (1892), National Audubon Society (1901), the Save-the-Redwoods League (1918), the National Parks and Conservation Association (1919), and the Izaak Walton League (1922).

The 1908 White House "Governor's Conference" on conservation and resources is recognized as one of the earliest formal, politically sponsored, environmentally based gatherings. The conference created extraction rates for renewable resources in addition to policies on water and soil conservation and the general protection of natural lands (O'Riordan, Clark, and Kates, 1995). Hays (1959) noted, however, that the conference was little more than a political gesture to rationalize unacceptable resource use during the late nineteenth century. Despite this appearance, the conference was also recognized as the beginning of a period of federal government intervention in natural resource management and pollution control, similar to practice common to European nations over the past fifty years (O'Riordan et al., 1995).

Progressive efforts to protect the environment did not pass without controversy, as managing natural resources in a scientific manner signaled the end of business as usual, and generated criticism of the conservation movement (Edwards, 1998). Groups in the eastern and western parts of the United States were affected differently by the developing environmental legislation and environmental concerns. Westerners, whose lifestyle and economic subsistence were often impacted by environmental legislation, perceived eastern politicians (whose lifestyle and constituents often were unaffected by environmental policy) to be elitist bureaucrats (Edwards, 1998). These conflicts continued to influence environmental activism and struggles, including the famous Sagebrush Rebellion of the late 1970s, which occurred when western land owners challenged the Federal government's *Land Policy and Management Act of 1976* (Edwards, 1998).

Environmentalism and Economics, 1910–1930s

The presidencies of William Taft and Woodrow Wilson were marked by decreased concern for conservation (Edwards, 1998), and expanded attention to events such as World War I, and economic stability (Switzer and Bryner, 1998). President Franklin D. Roosevelt, elected to office in 1932 shortly after the beginning of The Great Depression, brought renewed vigor to the conservationist approach at the federal level (Edwards, 1998). He created several agencies, including the Tennessee Valley Authority (1933), the Soil Conservation Service (1935), and the Civilian Conservation Corps (1933–1942), with the latter designed to promote the conservationist approach while simultaneously stimulating the economy by employing two million previously unemployed young men (Switzer and Bryner, 1998). Legislation enacted during this period included the *Taylor Grazing Act of 1934*, which provided the federal government regulatory control over public lands in the western United States (Edwards, 1998), and the *Food, Drug, and Cosmetics Act of 1938* which regulated the sales of manufactured goods to the public (Neimark and Mott, 1999).

Population growth, urban and suburban development, increased use of automobiles, and expansion of both the food and chemical processing industries during the 1920s and 1930s had considerable environmental impact. Automobiles added to urban pollution problems while unregulated factories poured additional pollutants into urban air and waterways (Neimark and Mott, 1999).

The environmental practices of 1930s promoted industry interests, and the laws enacted were largely designed to protect, conserve and prolong natural resources for economic purposes (Edwards, 1998). The 1930s also brought the development of two important preservationist groups: The Wilderness Society (1935) and The National Wildlife Federation (1936).

Declining Environmentalism, 1941–1960

The expansive economic growth that followed World War II in America was, in large part, due to the growth of highly polluting industries—especially the synthetic chemical industries—pesticides, synthetic rubber and textiles, and plastics. Americans were more concerned with recovering from WWII than protecting the environment, and in taking advantage of the great economic expansion that had emerged. When environmental issues were raised, they were addressed from a conservationist rather than a preservationist position, or through a concern with the scientific management of the environment (Switzer and Bryner, 1998), With economic expansion, Americans had more disposable income and more vacation time, and as Switzer and Bryner (1998) note, they took advantage of these expanding economic opportunities. It was estimated that over thirty million tourists visited national parks in 1950. Expanded use of these spaces forced the government to update, preserve, and protect federal lands. In response, the National Park Service provided a 10-year improvement program "wish list," that would serve as a guide for the development of national parks and recreational areas. Aside from government-sponsored efforts, several other groups contributed to protecting the environment. For instance, the Defenders of Wildlife (founded in 1947) was concerned with habitat protection, while in the early 1950s The Nature Conservancy began to acquire tracts of land to protect the habitats of endangered species (Switzer and Bryner, 1998).

Schindler (1995) notes that during the 1950s the general public was becoming sensitized and more cognizant of environmental deterioration. Continuous population growth and consumerism resulted in expanded use of commercial (and non-commercial) goods, including automobiles and the roads they drive on, and the rapidly growing number of chemical and food processing plants and their associated (and heretofore largely unregulated) harms to the environment. These warnings began to shift public attitudes toward the environment, eventually culminating in the beginning of the modern environmental movement.

"The Times They Are A-Changing," the 1960s

During the 1960s, environmental conflicts between proponents of industrial growth and environmentalists and their supporters emerged. Expanded concern with environmental preservation (e.g., parks and wilderness), but also environmental pollution, grew rapidly, forming the foundation for many current environmental laws and a substantial growth in environmental group membership (Switzer and Bryner, 1998). Scientists such as Rachel Carson (*Silent Spring*) and Paul Ehrlich (*The Population Bomb*) drew attention to environmental issues in the 1960s, highlighting harms associated with pesticides and the dangers associated with explosive population growth. Carson's work, in particular, motivated research into environmental harms especially those associated with the chemical industry. As evidence of the tension between environmentalists and industry during this period, the chemical industry accused Carson of involvement in a "communist plot" to undermine U.S. agriculture (Athanasiou, 2002). Switzer and Bryner (1998) noted that other widely recognized environmentalists (e.g., Murray Bookchin) offered pessimistic predictions of environmental harms, resulting in a gloomy societal outlook for the environment.

Environmentalists of this time certainly played a role in expanding interest in environmental problems. A notable characteristic of the environmental writing of the 1960s was its frequent "alarmist" tendencies, which either aroused a receptive public to respond or caused skeptics to become more vocal in their criticism (Neimark and Mott, 1999). It was during the 1960s that the environmental movement shifted from conservation toward "environmentalism" (Mertig, Dunlap, and Morrison, 2002: 451; Mitchell, 1989). Environmentalism, like conservation, recognizes human destruction of the environment; however, it recognizes and is concerned for urban areas and the effects of environmental problems on quality of life issues, human health concerns, and social systems (Mertig, Dunlap, and Morrison, 2002, p. 451). Environmentalism is more likely than conservation to encompass scientific research and greater complexity in analyses and responses.

During the 1960s, several incidents drew substantial attention to environmental movements. For example, in 1969, there was a major oil spill less than six miles off the coast of Santa Barbara, California, Lake Erie was declared "dead" as a result of industrial pollution (Markham, 1994), and the Cuyahoga River spontaneously burst into flames due to high levels of chemical pollution (Cockrell, 1992). Each of these incidents, and hundreds more, underscored the need to better protect the environment. Criminologist David Friedrichs (1996) suggests that media coverage of these incidents not only contributed to growing awareness of environmental harms, but also promoted political activity among the American middle class. Faced with media coverage of environmental hazards and greater political consciousness among the middle class, the environmental movement also ushered in the idea that environmental harms ought to be recognized as acts of violence (Frank and Lynch, 1992). Indeed, the social environmental of the 1960s produced the context for significant reformulation of environmental laws. The first *Clean Air Act* (1963; later amended to the *Air Quality Act in 1967*) and the *Water Quality Act* (1965) are two of the hallmark pieces of environmental legislation passed during this period. Along with increased legislation came an expanding number of environmental groups and greater participation in existing groups, which forced the federal government to become more involved in what was beginning to be recognized as "the environmental crisis." The evolving, yet primitive cooperative efforts between the states and the federal government was unable to address what was becoming a global issue (Switzer and Bryner, 1998, p. 10).

Unstable Environmentalism, the 1970s

Society's unstable environmental attitudes are possibly best exemplified by the decade of the 1970s. Environmental concerns at this time were impacted by (1) several significant incidents resulting in harm to the environment; (2) political actions in response to societal recognition of harms to the environment; and (3) the institutionalization of environmental groups. Although societal concerns for the environment were attenuated by frustrations over the war in Vietnam and a struggling economy, public recognition of the environment as a major issue continued throughout the decade. Overwhelming public support for the first Earth Day in 1970 is recognized as solid evidence of the public's concern for environmental protection (Edwards, 1998).

During the first Earth Day, millions demonstrated in support of the environment, citing the harms associated with environmental abuses, and generating support for the passage of landmark environmental legislation including the *Endangered Species Act* (1973), the *Safe Drinking Water Act* (1974) , and the Presidential order that created the EPA (1970). Although widespread public interest in environmental issues quickly dissipated after Earth Day 1970 due to continuing economic problems and the war in Vietnam, the two decades following the first Earth Day evidenced unprecedented advances in domestic and international public awareness, scientific understanding, and government responses regarding environmental issues (O'Riordan et al., 1995).

Politicians seized the opportunity to capitalize on public support for the environment. President Nixon, for example, created the *National Environmental Policy Act* in 1969, recognized as a move to bring the environment and the economy into "productive harmony" (O'Riordan et al., 1995, p. 6). Nixon declared the 1970s "the environmental decade," (similar declarations were made by both George H. and George W. Bush) and urged his staff to expeditiously process new legislative proposals. When Congress failed to implement the legislation needed to create a federal environmental agency to develop and enforce environmental regulations, Nixon established the EPA through executive order (Switzer and Bryner, 1998). Congress, meanwhile, enacted over 20 major pieces of environmental protection legislation. Many refined earlier bills, while others created new areas of environmental protection, including marine mammal protection and pesticide and toxic substance regulation (Switzer and Bryner, 1998). Many of these major pieces of legislation remain in place today.

As in the 1960s, several high-profile events that resulted in substantial harm to the environment elevated public concern with environmental protection during the 1970s. The 1973 Arab oil embargo, the 1979 meltdown at the Three Mile Island nuclear plant, and extensive media coverage of the harm caused by toxic dumping at Love Canal in Niagara Falls, New York were among these incidents (Switzer and Bryner, 1998). These high-profile events continued to occur along with numerous local, less newsworthy events (Couch and Kroll-Smith, 1997).

Aside from high-profile incidents and political posturing over environmental harms, the 1970s environmental movement was also impacted by the continued development of increasingly powerful environmental interest groups. At the same time, larger numbers of individuals were associating themselves with the growing variety of environmental groups, leading Edwards (1998) to comment that the environmental movement had became institutionalized. In Neimark and Mott's (1999) view, radical environmental groups were adopting the tactics of protest groups of the 1960s and creating new tactics, ranging from peaceful protests to sabotage, with the goal of promoting their views and generating changes in environmental policies. While the growth in size and scope of environmental interest groups would seem to result in substantial benefits for supporters of environmental protection, several events during the 1970s (and 1980s) shaped the environmental movement, events which have also impacted modern environmental efforts.

The 1970s saw the beginning of industry and business involvement in environmental issues, which changed the playing field with regard to pro-environmental efforts, legislation, and support. Switzer and Bryner (1998) suggest that the change in the goals of the movement from conservation to environmentalism in the late 1960s and early 1970s affected business and industry, which had never faced such threats. Environmental interest groups were also being affected by the increasingly wide range of environmental topics requiring attention, and the need for extensive financial resources and technical expertise to promote particular causes. These increased burdens resulted in business and industry maintaining a notable advantage over many environmental organizations (Switzer and Bryner, 1998). The resultant fragmentation among environmental interest groups led to expansive interpretations of the term environmentalism.

Such pressures explain why many mainstream environmental groups relocated to Washington, DC and used lobbying as a means of self-promotion. Edwards (1998: 44) notes that these groups were recognized as the voice of environmental policies on Capitol Hill, and the "Washingtonization" of these groups eventually had a notable impact on the environmental movement both within and outside of Washington. Their efforts, however, would soon lead to a split within the environmental movement.

Dunlap and Mertig (1992) note that membership in and financial contributions to mainstream environmental groups continued to grow during the 1970s. By the 1980s, the membership of many environmentally conscious groups had doubled (Dowie, 1995). The increase is attributed to the Reagan administration's move to limit environmental enforcement efforts by reducing the budgets of the EPA and other environmental-based efforts, and appointing people who favored businesses at the expense of the environment to influential governmental positions (Dunlap and Mertig, 1992; Lester, 1989; Switzer and Bryner, 1998). Nevertheless, having succeeded in the nation's capital, and with increased membership, mainstream environmental groups drew the admiration and support of many, and maintained an important place in protecting the environment.

While environmental groups were gaining ground in Washington, they were losing favor at the local level. Individuals felt that localized issues were being ignored by environmentalists in Washington, DC. This feeling eventually created a distrust between local and national environmental groups (Edwards, 1998). Dowie (1995) suggests that environmentalists in Washington, DC became indistinguishable from other political figures, a position supported by Ferkiss (1995), who suggests that in addition to previous accusations of elitism was the claim that DC environmental groups had become another group of well-paid bureaucrats who had lost touch with their constituents.

Perhaps one of the most significant and radical branches of the environmental movement first appeared in the 1970s. According to Athanasiou (2002), the anti-nuclear movement, which drew massive public support and has hard-line environmental connections, was founded in 1974.

Toward the end of the 1970s, newly elected President Jimmy Carter, who had strong environmental tendencies, found it difficult to achieve much on this front as the American economy slipped deeper into recession. A depressed economy would create more difficult times for the environmental movement during the 1980s, especially under the Ronald Reagan White House.

De-Prioritizing the Environment, the 1980s

Switzer and Bryner (1998) suggest that the Reagan administration's (1981-1989) concern for deregulation, budget cuts, downsizing government, and installing people into government posts who held a conservative worldview hampered environmentally-based legislative initiatives, and significantly and detrimentally impacted environmental policy for the next ten years. To be sure, this was a period when policy making in the Executive Office blatantly resulted in negative impacts on the environment. Like many presidents, Reagan was faced with political issues that required a disproportionate amount of attention and resources, and U.S. competitiveness in the global market and the Cold War took precedence over environmental concerns.

Reagan's penchant for deregulation and tax cuts had a tremendous impact on the EPA and its ability to act on environmental matters. Reagan's pro-business, less-government-intrusion approach escalated environmental harms. In fact, President Reagan notably handcuffed the EPA through, among other things, personnel reductions, appointing loyalists to key positions, and restricting the agency's budget. In response, environmentalists reacted to the federal government's neglect for environmental protection and activism notably adopted a grassroots approach. The Reagan administration and other politicians overlooked the substantial growth and potential impact of these groups on efforts to protect the environment (Edwards, 1998). Throughout the 1980s, while Reagan was attempting to deregulate at the federal level, local activists were forcing increased environmental regulation at the local level.

The Reagan administration severely hampered the EPA during his presidency, and the agency still bears some of the scars. Reagan's 1980 campaign, which centered on improving the American way of life through less government intrusion (Landy et al., 1990), signified impending trouble for the EPA and environmentalists. Cannon (2000) notes that in the six-year period beginning with his second term as governor of California and his first term as president, Reagan increasingly relied on his pro-development friends in industry and business, as he had no pro-environment advisers. This "less government, more industry" approach is documented in numerous analyses of the Reagan administration (e.g., Johnson, 1991; Vig and Kraft, 1984; Friedrichs, 1996; Landy et al., 1990; Switzer and Bryner, 1998), and contributed to the administration's "stormy chapter in environmental politics" (Switzer and Bryner, 1998, p. 52).

The EPA budget and personnel reductions during Reagan's first term in office precluded any opportunity for significant second-term accomplishments on the environmental front. EPA Administrators Ruckelshaus and Thomas restored some credibility and funding to the agency, while Reagan, who had underestimated public support for the environment (Flippen, 2000) and lost "the battle of public opinion on the environment" (Vig, 2003, p. 109), tried to recover when he curtailed the assault on the EPA. Perhaps his most significant accomplishment was that his anti-environmental policies increased support for, and membership in, environmental organizations (Vig, 2003). Vig (2003) suggests that it was not surprising that Reagan's successor, George H. Bush, distanced himself from Reagan's environmental policies.

Deeming himself "the environmental president" during his 1988 campaign, George H. Bush Ffaced repairing the damage caused by the Reagan administration (both in terms of public support and actual environmental reparations) and several new environmental problems. Among the problems was global warming, which had important international implications. Despite its reluctance to accept the existence of global warming, the George H. Bush administration is credited with passing two major pieces of legislation (the *Clean Air Act Amendments* of 1990 and the 1992 *Energy Policy Act*), which symbolized a break from congressional legislative actions under Republican administrations (Switzer and Bryner, 1998). The 1980s also ushered in one of the most important and prolonged environmental movements in the modern era: the movement for environmental justice. This movement, discussed more fully in Chapter 9, addresses inequality in environmental protection that disadvantages minority groups and the poor.

In sum, environmentalism in the 1980s was largely characterized by the federal government's neglect of environmental protection, which in turn spurred environmental activism. The decade provides evidence of how federal policies encourage activism, and demonstrates the impact of presidential politics on the environment.

The Environment Returns: the 1990s

Renewed interest in the environment returned in the 1990s; a decade originally termed the "Era of Environmentalism." The 1990s brought about "green political parties" whose platforms are structured by environmental concerns, in many countries, including the United States (Frank and Lynch, 1992; Postrel, 1990; Walijassper, 1990), and recycling programs designed to reduce environmental harms caused by household waste. Frank and Lynch (1992) suggest marketing strategies in some American companies used recycling and environmental concerns to attract consumers.

During the early 1990s, people began to shift their allegiance from large, national environmental groups, to local, grassroots organizations involved in, among other issues, struggles for environmental justice. This movement, captured by Ralph Nader's political position and several groups he sponsored, such as Democracy Rising, influenced the development of the American Green Party.

Several events around this time provided a further boost to environmental activism, including Earth Day 1990 and the 1992 Earth Summit. Compared to the 1970 Earth Day, the 1990 celebration (the twentieth anniversary) was much broader in scope, involved a wider array of groups, such as the business community and ethnic minorities, and generated a more upbeat mood. The 1990 Earth Day is credited with garnering support for legislation that otherwise may not have passed (O'Riordan et al., 1995).

The 1992 Earth Summit, formally titled the "U.N. Conference on Environment and Development," was held in Rio de Janeiro, Brazil and generated increased concern for the environment. This groundbreaking meeting highlighted the need for global responses to environmental issues, and identified the differences between industrialized and developing nations in terms of their contributions to, and expectations about, their response to environmental pollution (Switzer and Bryner, 1998). The Earth Summit was recognized as a starting point for establishing global environmental policies and approaches, and was the second of three United Nations conferences designed to address environmental issues, most importantly, global warming (the others are addressed later in this chapter). Among other accomplishments, these meetings facilitated cooperation between international groups, as well as government organizations and non-government groups (O'Riordan et al., 1995). It was around this time that a change in the American political structure appeared to enhance pro-environmental efforts.

Environmentalists expressed great excitement at the 1992 presidential election of Democrat Bill Clinton, who expressed difference with George H. Bush regarding environmental issues (Kline, 1997), and Vice President Al Gore, who was and is known for his particularly pro-environment stance. Clinton, whose energy concerns focused on conservation and efficiency instead of production (Kline, 1997), soon appointed Bruce Babbitt (former head of the League of Conservation Voters) Secretary of the Interior, Carol Browner to the EPA, and several other pro-environment professionals to various influential positions within his cabinet. Environmentalists believed their hard work had finally paid dividends, as they now had in place one of—if not the—"greenest" administrations ever (Dowie, 1995).

Their excitement would soon diminish, however, when the Clinton administration failed to approach the expectations of environmentalists, primarily due to being caught in the predicament of wishing to appease the interests of both environmentalists and industry (Kline, 1997). The administration would often choose to compromise with congressional opponents on many environmental issues instead of asserting its authority (Ferkiss, 1995). Dowie (1995) cites a diminished environmental influence in Washington, DC as a primary reason behind the Clinton administration passing only one meaningful piece of legislation during Clinton's first two years in office, adding that the administration continuously failed to protest anti-environmental efforts by industry, special interest groups, and Congress, such as failing to provide ample support for Babbitt's move to reassume control of public lands from ranchers (Ferkiss, 1995).

The 1994 election of a Republican Congress once again challenged the historical and notable environmentalist accomplishments painstakingly pieced together over the previous decade. The new Congress drew attention to the financial cost and regulatory burdens associated with environmental protection, and Republican House Leader Newt Gingrich's "Contract with America" echoed Reaganism in that it called for reduced government regulation and the promotion of economic development as opposed to environmental preservation (Switzer and Bryner, 1998). Switzer and Bryner (1998) note that Republicans in Congress attempted to minimize environmental regulation by slashing EPA and Interior Department budgets, attaching riders to appropriations bills that hampered particular protections, and attempting to rewrite important environmental regulations.

The Republican stronghold over environmental regulation, however, did not have the impact many anticipated. Facing attacks from concerned environmentalists across the country, an inspired President Clinton challenged the Republican agenda and subsequently watched his popularity climb. Switzer and Bryner (1998) suggest that Clinton's reelection in 1996 was due in part to his willingness to oppose the congressional Republicans' deregulation approach, adding that Bruce Babbitt was instrumental in the president's newfound concern for environmental issues.

Membership in environmental groups was stagnant in the early 1990s. Environmentalists attributed this lack of growth to the ongoing recession (Dowie, 1995). Dowie (1995), however, argues that the problem was the result of self-inflicted wounds. Specifically, he cites the lack of an effective DC presence as a primary cause. This concern is echoed by others, including Ferkiss (1995) who suggests that mainstream environmental groups often share different views on national politics and poorly coordinate their lobbying efforts. Ferkiss also noted that the struggle over the North American Free Trade Agreement (NAFTA) notably divided mainstream environmental groups. These conflicts remained intact for years. Despite substantial improvements to the environment since 1970 and a substantial increase in donations to environmental groups in the new millennium (donations to environmental groups increased to over $6.4 billion in 2001), the Earth's most serious concerns remain as problematic as ever, leaving environmentalists open to claims that environmental groups have prospered while the earth has suffered (Goldstein, 2002). Goldstein questions whether environmental tactics are appropriate to address pressing issues such as global warming, loss of biodiversity, and marine depletion. The lack of coordination and focus at the national level encouraged a notable shift in environmentalist efforts toward local-level participation. Athanasiou (2002) adds that part of the problem was a change in the strategy of corporations. During the 1970s, corporations strongly opposed environmental groups. By the 1980s, they learned to cooperate with, and contribute to them. By the 1990s, however, corporations had changed tactics, creating their own "environmental front groups," and donating to them instead. These groups have names that make them appear environmentally friendly while their work reflects the nature of their corporate sponsorship (see Karliner, 1997). Table 3-1 includes a selection of these groups.

Table 3.1. Selection of Groups That Sound/Appear Environmentally Friendly, Yet Support Industries Operating in the United States

Alliance for Environment and Resources. Founded in 1985 by the California Forestry Association, this group is supported by the timber industry in its attempts to reduce logging restrictions.

B.C. Forest Alliance. Founded in 1991, this group includes the 13 largest Canadian lumber companies seeking to improve the image of the Canadian lumber industry.

Business Council for Sustainable Development. Founded in 1991 and supported by Swiss billionaire-industrialist Stephen Schmidheiny, this group was created to address environmental policies and weaken treaties and alliances that would be formed at the 1992 Earth Summit.

Citizens for the Environment. Formed in 1990 by the *Citizens for a Sound Economy* and funded by major corporations, this lobby group/think tank has no citizen members. It promotes deregulation of the economy as a means for solving environmental problems.

The Global Climate Coalition. This group, founded in 1989, represents business interests in an attempt to convince people, especially Congress, that global warming is a myth.

Information Council for the Environment. Founded in 1991, this group represents the interests of major coal companies in garnering support for coal power and detracting attention from alternative energy sources by convincing people that global warming is a myth.

National Wetlands Coalition. Founded in 1989 by the law firm Van Ness, Feldman, and Curtis, this lobby group represents miners, utilities, and real estate developers that seek to open wetlands for development and reduce wetland development restrictions.

Source: Greenpeace

The shift from support of national environmental issues to local-level, grassroots environmental concerns is a recent movement within the larger environmental movement (Brown and Mikkelsen, 1990; Goldman, 1991; Cable and Benson, 1993). Community-based grassroots environmental groups, focused on local as opposed to national environmental concerns, tend to draw members from lower educational and status groups, and promote enforcement of existing laws and environmental justice as opposed to seeking the creation of new environmental laws or environmental reforms (Clark, Lab, and Stoddard, 1995). Edwards (1998) notes that these smaller, grassroots groups are often referred to as NIMBY ("not in my backyard") groups that organize to halt environmental degradation in their communities. While most grassroots efforts do not involve the direct action tactics assumed by more radical environmental groups such as Earth First! and Greenpeace, grassroots groups have undoubtedly helped highlight societal concern for environmental harms and have impacted responses to such acts (Cable and Benson, 1993).

Environmentalism in the 21st Century: Renewed and Continued Challenges

Entering the 21st century, grassroots efforts to combat limited concern for environmental issues at the federal level of government continued, and reflected enhanced recognition of global issues, particularly climate change. Efforts to attract historically underrepresented groups into the environmental movement also persisted. The new century has already brought about new challenges and offered direction for future environmentalist actions. For example, international concerns about global warming may be the stimulus for widespread environmental activism and the issue that generates international, cooperative efforts to protect the environment.

According to Van Puten (2005, p. 468) "The most perplexing feature of current federal environmental policy is that public attitudes, compelling science, and pragmatic solutions matter so little." In large part, this attitude toward the environment has been promoted by the policies and politics of the George W. Bush Administration, and his election was seen as a renewed challenge to the environmental movement, which as of 2001 consisted of 30 large organizations with roughly 20 million dues-paying members and thousands of regional and local activist groups (Helvarg, 2001; see Table 3-9 for a brief description of the more prominent environmental groups). Helvarg (2001, p. 5) notes that like Reagan, Bush's stance "...on the environment, including decisions on carbon dioxide, oil drilling, arsenic, mining, forests, oceans and energy, as well as budget cuts that target agencies like the EPA and the Interior Department and laws like the *Endangered Species Act*, is mobilizing the environmental movement in" profound ways. Indeed, Bush's environmental stance has led to widespread agreement that he has the worst record of any president on the environment.

Table 3.9. A Short List of Prominent Environmental Groups

Defenders of Wildlife is dedicated to the protection of all native wild animals and plants in their natural communities. Their programs focus on the accelerating rate of extinction of species and the associated loss of biological diversity, and habitat alteration and destruction.

Environmental Defense Fund links science, economics and law to confront society's most urgent environmental problems.

Greenpeace International addresses the most crucial worldwide threats to biodiversity and environment.

Earth First! takes more innovative and radical approaches to environmentalism than many other groups. Their approaches range from grassroots organizing and involvement in the legal process to civil disobedience.

Friends of the Earth is an international network of environmental organizations in 70 countries. The national groups are composed of grassroots local groups working in their own areas. Friends of the Earth considers environmental issues in their social, political and human rights contexts, and seeks to address the economic and development aspects of sustainability.

Izaak Walton League seeks to conserve, maintain, protect, and restore the soil, forest, water, and other natural resources of the United States and other lands, and to promote public education with respect to environmental resources.

League of Conservation Voters advocates for sound environmental policies and seeks to elect pro-environmental candidates who will adopt and implement environmentally-friendly policies.

National Audubon Society seeks to conserve and restore natural ecosystems, focusing on birds, other wildlife, and their habitats for the benefit of humanity and the earth's biological diversity.

National Resources Defense Council- seeks to safeguard the Earth: its people, its plants and animals and the natural systems on which all life depends primarily through working to restore the integrity of the elements that sustain life—air, land and water—and to defend endangered natural places.

National Parks & Conservation Association protects and enhances, through various means, the U.S. National Park System.

National Wildlife Federation inspires Americans to protect wildlife for our children's future, primarily through connecting people to nature, reversing global warming, and protecting and restoring critical wildlife habitats.

The Nature Conservancy protects lands and waters needed by plants, animals and natural communities in order to maintain diversity of life on Earth.

Sierra Club, America's oldest, largest and most influential grassroots environmental organization, supports the exploration, enjoyment, and protection of the wild places of the earth.

The Wilderness Society uses a combination of science, advocacy and education to provide future generations an unspoiled legacy of wild places.

George W. Bush's term has been marked by persistent conflicts between the Administration and environmentalists (e.g., see Robert F. Kennedy Jr.'s book, *Crimes Against Nature*, which critiques Bush's environmental policies). Environmentalists, for example, pointed out that Bush's "clear skies" policies and suggested revisions to the *Clean Air Act* would produce more, not less air pollution, especially by power plants. In addition, Bush's "Healthy Forests Initiative" increased logging in protected wilderness areas. The Bush Administration has also been behind the effort to open the Arctic National Wildlife Refuge to oil exploration (Helvarg, 2001). In 2001, the Bush Administration announced that the United States would *not* ratify the international agreement on global warming gas reduction, the Kyoto Protocol (which mandates reductions of 6–8 percent in emission levels by the years 2008 to 2012 for industrial countries), stating that the United States cannot afford to reduce carbon dioxide emission (Runyan and Norderhaug, 2002). The anti-environmental stance taken by the Bush Administration has made it difficult, to put it mildly, for environmentalists to continue to move legislation that protects the environment (Kennedy, 2004; Burns and Lynch, 2004). But so too, have changes in the composition of the U.S. Congress. Following the 2002 election, the U.S. Senate was controlled by the Republicans, making it more difficult to pass legislation that protected the environment. In addition, there was a change in directorship of the Environment and Public Works Committee from Independent Jim Jeffords (a supporter of environmental causes) to Jim Inhofe, whose major campaign contributor was the oil and gas industry (Helvarg, 2001).

One might speculate that Bush's anti-environmental stance during his first term would increase voter turnout among members of environmental groups. Polling results, however, suggested that voter participation among the estimated 10 million members of environmental groups was the same as among the general population (Hertsgaard, 2006). According to Motavalli (2005), opinion polls suggest that people overwhelmingly identify themselves as environmentalists; however, it is a secondary concern for them, as security, economic, and values-related issues generate the most interest. In highlighting environmentalists' frustrations with the Bush administration's environmental policies, Van Putten (2005) notes that politics, rather than science or thoughtful solutions drive public policy. He adds that environmental groups have also contributed to their marginalization particularly through failing to generate greater bipartisan support for the environment and their slow adaptation to political, demographic and other changes taking place in the United States.

Hertsgaard (2006, p. 12) reaches the interesting conclusion that the Bush Administration

...with its overt hostility to environmentalism, ...highlights an embarrassing paradox for the environmental movement....Bush and his Congressional allies...pursued the most anti-environmental policies in the nation's history—and escaped without paying... a political price. As popular and wealthy as the environmental movement appears, the Bush era has exposed it as something of a paper tiger. Yet, the Bush years may turn out to be the movement's salvation, for they have led even the national groups based in Washington to recognize that a new approach is needed.

That "new approach" may involve more extensive grassroots efforts, targeting individuals from historically underrepresented groups, and expanded emphasis on climate change issues. As Conca (2000, p. 72) notes, the nature of environmental activism in the U.S. has changed:

> Anyone old enough to remember gas lines, Love Canal, or Three Mile Island will recall a time when the environmental movement focused mainly on domestic issues. To be sure, the idea of a fragile planet was always part of the logic of ecology. But the actual work of lobbying for clean air and water, defending endangered species, protecting wilderness, and challenging toxic polluters was mainly a local and national affair.

The American environmental movement began to adopt a global outlook during the Reagan era in response to issues such as the ozone hole and the loss of biodiversity (Conca, 2000). Environmentalists were largely united in these efforts. Today, however, mainstream American environmentalism is unprepared to address the global environmental problems produced by a global economy (Conca, 2000); these problems can not be solved by localized, isolated environmental movements of place. Rather, there is a need for a broader theory capable of understanding and responding to the dilemma of global environmental, economic and political relations and problems (Brown, 2003, 2005, 2006a, 2006b).

Concern for global environmentalism is evident in the 2002 United Nations' "World Summit on Sustainable Development," held in Johannesburg, South Africa. The Summit focused on the environmental threats impacting the planet while examining the extent of 30 years of efforts to protect the environment and offered a look toward the future. The event drew considerable interest and was well attended; 100 world leaders addressed the Summit, and roughly 22,000 participated (www.johannesburgsummit.org).

Minorities and the poor have been extensively involved in localized environmental groups, especially those addressing environmental justice, but largely absent from membership in larger and more general-issue environmental groups. Conservation and preservation groups have primarily included White membership. This racial division is connected to the ways in which environment, race and class intersect in the U.S.—more economically privileged groups can afford to promote conservation and preservation especially as these relate to leisure activities. In contrast, low-income groups must address environmental pollution in relation to daily life issues, including routine exposure to toxic waste likely to characterize lower class neighborhoods (Hertsgaard, 2006).

CONCLUSION

Support for environmentalism is impacted by many factors described above. As noted, both the federal government and environmental activism play a significant role in influencing environmental policy. Even when presidents (i.e, the Bush or Reagan Administrations) attempt to frustrate environmental protection, they face the possibility that they may escalate environmental activism. A notable example of the intersection of political and public environmental activism is Al Gore's documentary on global warming, *An Inconvenient Truth*, which has been identified as stimulating public environmentalism (Adler, 2006).

Mertig, Dunlap and Morrison (2002: 456) identify a new environmental movement in ecologism, which uses both traditional (e.g., lobbying, litigation, demonstrations) and more aggressive tactics (e.g., boycotts, sabotage) to fight environmental harms on a broader number of fronts. For instance, the Earth Liberation Front, an international underground movement, recently engaged in a series of attacks against people who harm the environment by destroying SUVs and machinery used to prepare land for housing developments. To be sure, this behavior depicts the more extreme form of ecologism. Such behavior may become more prominent as environmental conditions worsen.

As environmental protection movements become more popular, they have been confronted by a growing number of conservative environmental organizations that promote commercial interests. One example is the Wise Use Movement, a coalition representing several free-market groups and think tanks. Mertig, Dunlap and Morrison (2002) argue that these conflicts are likely to alter the nature of the environmental movement in the United States.

Some, like O'Riordan (1995), believe that the environmental movement in the U.S. will continue to wax and wane, picking up momentum only when dramatic events are revealed. Solving the global environmental problems facing the world, however, requires a more sustained environmentalism. To be sure, such a movement is more likely in the contemporary period, especially in response to dramatic environmental problems such as global warming. Only the passage of time will tell whether or not society responds in ways that protect the planet and humans from destruction.

Timeline of Environmental Events

1290—King Edward I prohibits coal burning while Parliament in session

1388—Parliament passes act forbidding the polluting ditches, rivers and waters

1626—Plymouth Colony regulates cutting and sale of trees

1690—Governor William Penn requires Pennsylvania settlers to preserve one acre of trees for every five acres cleared

1700—Rapid industrialization and demand for iron and naval supplies stripped England's forests

1720—Hundreds of protestors die in India trying to protect trees from Maharaja of Jodhpur

1762—Benjamin Franklin leads a Philadelphia committee's attempts to regulate waste disposal and water pollution

1820—World population reaches 1 billion

1851—Conservation of wilderness areas begins with felling of enormous tree; outrage over the act leads to calls for a national park system

1854—Henry David Thoreau publishes *Walden; Or, Life in the Woods*

1869—First transcontinental railroad introduced in U.S.

1872—Yellowstone National Park becomes first U.S. National Park

1872—Arbor Day founded and occurs annually on last Friday in April in the U.S.

1876—*British River Pollution Control Act* makes it illegal to dump sewage into streams

1879—U.S. Geological Survey formed

1890—U.S. Bureau of the Census announces frontier has ceased to exist

1890—Yosemite and Sequoia National Parks established

1892—Sierra Club founded

1901—National Audubon Society created

1903—Public Lands Commission created

1905—National Audubon Society organized

1907—Inland Waterways Commission developed

1908—White House Conference on Resource Management

1909—North American Conservation Conference held in Washington, DC

1916—National Park Service created

1918—Save-the-Redwoods League developed

1919—National Parks and Conservation Association established

1922—Izaak Walton League created

1930—World population reaches 2 billion

1933—Tennessee Valley Authority created

1933—Civilian Conservation Corps created

1934—Dust Bowl drought begins

1934—*Taylor Grazing Act of 1934* established

1935—The Wilderness Society founded

1935—Soil Conservation Service established
1938—*Food, Drug, and Cosmetics Act of 1938* created
1945—Atomic bombings of Hiroshima and Nagasaki
1948—Aldo Leopold's *Sand County Almanac* published
1951—The Nature Conservancy founded
1955—First international air pollution conference held
1955—First *Clean Air Act* passed
1956—*Fish and Wildlife Act* created
1960—World population reaches 3 billion
1961—U.S. Army begins use of Agent Orange during the Vietnam War
1962—Rachel Carson publishes *Silent Spring*
1964—Paul Ehrlich publishes *The Population Bomb*
1965—*Water Quality Act* passed
1966—*National Wildlife Refuge System Act* and the *Endangered Species
      Preservation Act* passed
1967—*Air Quality Act* established
1969—*National Environmental Policy Act* created
1969—Friends of the Earth founded
1969—Cuyahoga River catches fire
1969—Lake Erie declared dead
1970—First Earth Day occurs
1970—U.S. Environmental Protection Agency formed
1970—*Clean Air Act* passed
1971—Greenpeace organized in Canada
1972—United Nations Conference on the Human Environment
1972—*Clean Water Act* passed
1973—Arab oil embargo
1973—*Endangered Species Act* passed
1974—*Safe Drinking Water Act* created
1974—Chlorofluorocarbons are first hypothesized to cause ozone thinning
1974—World population reaches 4 billion
1975—*Energy Policy and Conservation Act* passed
1976—*Resource Conservation and Recovery Act* passed
1977—*Soil and Water Resources Conservation Act* created
1978—Love Canal scandal
1979—Three Mile Island nuclear power accident
1980—*Comprehensive Environmental Response, Compensation and Liability
      Act* (Superfund) passed
1986—Chernobyl, world's worst nuclear power accident, occurs in Ukraine
1987—World population reaches 5 billion
1987—Montreal Protocol on Substances That Deplete the Ozone Layer
1988—Intergovernmental Panel on Climate Change established by United
      Nations

1989—Exxon *Valdez* creates largest oil spill in U.S. history
1990—Twentieth anniversary of Earth Day
1991—World's worst oil spill occurs in Kuwait
1992—The United Nations' Earth Summit held in Rio de Janeiro
1997—The Kyoto Protocol negotiated in Kyoto, Japan
1997—United Nations "Earth Summit" held in New York
1999—World population reaches 6 billion
2001—President Bush rejects Kyoto Protocol
2002—United Nations World Summit on Sustainable Development held in Johannesburg
2005—Hurricanes Katrina, Rita, and Wilma cause widespread environmental harm
2006—Former Vice President Al Gore releases *An Inconvenient Truth*

CHAPTER 4

The U.S. Environmental Protection Agency

INTRODUCTION

Prior to the creation of the Environmental Protection Agency (EPA) in 1970, the federal government made several attempts to manage the environment. A series of environmental acts, including the *Water Pollution Control Act of 1956*, the *Clean Air Act of 1963*, the *Water Quality Act of 1965*, and the *Air Quality Act of 1967* symbolized this effort. These efforts were unsuccessful in defining a clear regulatory role for the federal government in environmental protection, however, as they delegated too much authority to the states (Waterman, 1989; Davies, 1970). The government's efforts to regulate environmental pollution spurred environmental groups to lobby Congress for the necessary legislation and contributed to the expansion of the federal government's role in environmental protection and the creation of the EPA (Waterman, 1989).

This chapter highlights the development and practices of the EPA, the agency most responsible for preventing, detecting, and enforcing environmental crime at the federal level. The EPA is also charged with making environmental enforcement information available to the public. This chapter reviews the origins, objectives, and cooperative efforts of the EPA, and major events that occurred at EPA under each presidential administration. This information helps place environmental crime enforcement efforts into perspective and facilitates understanding the historical and current environmental protection efforts exerted by the EPA.

ESTABLISHING THE EPA

In 1970, President Nixon created the EPA through executive order. On one hand, Nixon's actions were monumental, since he created the EPA through direct presidential action after Congress failed to implement appropriate legislation. Nixon understood that the American people were very concerned with environmental issues and that it was incumbent upon political leaders to recognize and give power to this voice. On the other hand, Nixon fully understood the political implications of creating the EPA. When he undertook this action, he was also attempting to solidify his presidential reelection bid. His challenger, Democrat Edwin Muskie, had a strong environmental record in a climate of increased public concern with environmental pollution. Nixon could solidify his environmental commitment if he helped create a federal pollution regulatory agency.

The EPA was charged with regulating a wide array of environmental protection issues, although its responsibilities would be clarified and redirected over time in response to emerging laws and directives under each presidential administration.

By centralizing environmental enforcement practices within one agency the EPA offered the "integrated management of different pollution sources accompanied by a comprehensive research and development arm." The EPA "established in the federal government a highly visible focal point for environmental concerns and provided a governmental institution to reflect and match the widespread and still growing public concern over environmental problems" (Train, 1996, p. 188).

The EPA adopted a stringent enforcement approach upon its inception, and during its first two months of operation it brought five times as many enforcement actions as the agencies it replaced had brought during any similar period (Landy, Robert, and Thomas, 1990). The newly appointed EPA leadership sensed the importance of enforcing environmental standards, adopted a "fair but firm" enforcement approach, and focused its initial efforts on large corporations and cities in an effort to control pollution from industrial and municipal sources (Mintz, 1995, p. 21).

Early enforcement actions at EPA were primarily *reactive* rather than *preventive* during the first twenty years of its existence, largely in response to the lack of established environmental legislation (Collin, 2006). Yet, even today, the EPA continues its reactive practices, and, as Collin notes (2006), the EPA has ineffectively anticipated environmental problems and has suffered from its failure to proactively address environmental concerns.

Budgetary concerns and the politicization of environmentalism have long impacted EPA enforcement practices. For example, as Collin (2006, p. 122) quipped, "The EPA's legally assigned missions always seem bigger than its resources." In addition, balancing the interests of the environment and industry, among other groups, is a recurring issue for the EPA. For instance, the initially aggressive EPA enforcement approach led conservatives and industry members to view the agency as an anti-business environmental advocate, which in turn initiated a series of White House attempts to influence EPA practices (Landy et al., 1990).

During its early years, the EPA was overwhelmed by its rapidly expanding regulatory responsibilities, a lack of direction from the Nixon and Ford administrations regarding the aggressiveness of enforcement efforts, and creative industry tactics to hamper the establishment and enforcement of environmental standards (Gottlieb, 1993). These and other issues faced by the agency are discussed in this chapter.

RESPONSIBILITIES OF THE EPA

Given its primary role as the watchdog for environmental regulation, the EPA is tasked with many duties which, though they change in priority over time, revolve around regulating air and water pollution, hazardous waste, and hazardous chemicals. To do so, the EPA issues permits, sets and monitors standards, and enforces federal laws. It also issues grants to states to create waste water treatment and related facilities (Switzer and Bryner, 1998). These vast powers are difficult to coordinate, and political processes sometimes impact how they are carried out, even across EPA regions. With such varied responsibilities, it was and is difficult to determine an organizational mission at the EPA. Accordingly, the EPA is often placed in a politically sensitive position. For instance, the Executive Office expects the head of the EPA to balance and integrate environmental protection in ways that support industrial expansion and resource development, while environmentalists expect the EPA to promote environmental values, which may include actions contradictory to those encouraged by the Executive Office (Landy, Roberts, and Thomas, 1990).

Confronted with these conflicting demands, EPA administrators often find themselves in a no-win situation. Regardless of the mission they select or the tactics they employ, one of these groups will not be pleased. For example, in a recent decision, the EPA modestly strengthened fine particle pollution criteria while leaving larger particle criteria unchanged. Despite the fact that these alterations were a compromise between the concerns of environmentalists and industry, the decision simultaneously disturbed medical practitioners, environmentalists, automobile manufacturers, and the coal industry (Gorman, 2006).

The EPA has a broad, non-specific mission statement, leading Rosenbaum (2003, p.179) to argue that absent "an orderly mission statement, the EPA must create priorities according to the programs with the largest budgets, the most demanding deadlines, the most politically potent constituencies, or the greatest amount of congressional attention."

At the same time, it is difficult for the EPA to construct a specific mission statement given the variety of laws and regulations it must enforce, and variations in expectations under various presidential administrations. In addition, the lack of a specific mission statement makes it appear that the EPA has difficulty accomplishing its wide-ranging responsibilities, making the burdened agency a target for overwhelming organizational reform and leaving it absent any sense of direction (Rosenbaum, 2003).

Similar to most federal agencies, the EPA faced new and demanding challenges following the terrorist attacks against the United States in September

2001, such as monitoring environmental issues at attack sites and addressing a slew of new homeland security threats. For instance, the EPA had to assess and address the potential public health effects of burning buildings and public exposure to asbestos and other hazardous materials as well as establish new security protocols at U.S. power plants, reservoirs, and waste storage depots (Cohen, 2004). Following 9/11, the Agency was criticized for its alleged lax response in providing timely information about the air quality in the areas surrounding the World Trade Center (Cohen, 2004).

ORGANIZING THE EPA

The EPA is headed by an administrator who is nominated by the President and confirmed by the Senate (see Table 4-1 for a list of EPA administrators by presidential administration). The White House, along with the EPA administrator, sets the primary focus of the EPA.

Table 4-1: EPA Administrators by Presidential Administration

President	Administrator (Years)
Nixon	William D. Ruckelshaus (1970-73); *Bob Fri (1973) Russell E, Train (1973-74)
Ford	Russell E. Train (1974-77) *John Quarles (1977)
Carter	Douglas M. Costle (1977-81) *Steven Jellinek (1981) *Walter Barber Jr. (1981)
Reagan	Anne M. Gorsuch (1981-83) *Lee Verstandig 1983 William D. Ruckelshaus (1983-85) Lee M. Thomas (1985-89) *John Moore (1989)
G.H Bush	William K. Reilly (1989-93)
Clinton	Carol M. Browner (1993-2000)
G.W. Bush	*W. Michael McCabe (2001) Christine T. Whitman (2001-03) *Marianne Lamont Horinko (2003) Michael O. Leavitt (2003-05) Stephen L. Johnson (2005-)

*Acting Director

William Ruckelshaus, the first EPA Administrator, was tasked with creating an organizational design for the newly created EPA. The original staff, selected from a variety of government programs and departments, possessed various views on environmental regulation. Ruckelshaus adopted an enforcement-oriented approach even though he wished to refrain from antagonizing industry (McMahon, 2006). This approach, coupled with a concern for educating and working with the public, helped the EPA establish itself as a credible, powerful government entity (Collin, 2006).

Ruckelshaus organized the EPA into ten regional offices that continue to exist today (see Table 4.2), using three institutional levels: headquarters, regions, and field offices. The EPA exists within the Executive branch of federal government yet its funding appropriations come from Congress and Congressional statutes, sometimes resulting in the EPA attempting to appease and/or respond to both the executive and legislative branches (McMahon, 2006).

Table 4.2. Organizational Structure of the EPA

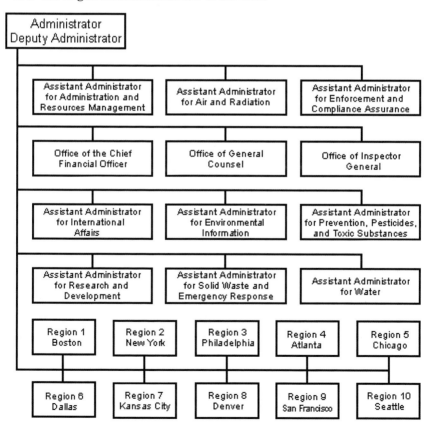

With roughly 17,560 staff members and an annual budget of $7.3 billion (2007), the EPA has certainly grown since its inception in 1970, when it employed 4,084 employees and had a budget of just over $1 billion (Collin, 2006; see Table 4-3).

Table 4.3. EPA's budget and workforce, 1970-2008

Fiscal Year	Budget ($ billions)	Work Force	Fiscal Year	Budget ($ billions)	Work Force
1970	1.003	4,084	1990	5.462	16,318
1971	1.288	5,744	1991	6.094	16,415
1972	2.447	8,358	1992	6.669	17,010
1973	2.377	9,077	1993	6.892	17,280
1974	0.518	9,743	1994	6.659	17,106
1975	0.699	10,438	1995	6.658	17,663
1976	0.772	9,481	1996	6.523	17,081
1977	2.764	11,315	1997	6.799	17,951
1978	5.499	11,986	1998	7.361	18,282
1979	5.403	12,160	1999	7.590	18,375
1980	4.669	13,078	2000	7.563	18,100
1981	3.031	12,667	2001	7.832	18,000
1982	3.676	11,402	2002	8.079	17,500
1983	3.689	10,832	2003	7.616	17,648
1984	4.067	11,420	2004	7.619	17,950*
1985	4.354	12,410	2005	7.800	17,904*
1986	3.664	12,892	2006	7.600	17,631*
1987	5.364	13,442	2007	7.300	17,560*
1988	5.027	14,442	2008	7.200	17,324**
1989	5.155	14,370			

* From annual proposed budget request. Source: EPA Office of the Administrator, "Budgets, Goals and Performance". Available on line: http://www.epa.gov/adminweb/budget-goals.htm
** Projected by EPA

The EPA employs a large number of scientists, attorneys, and other professionals and certainly has an impressive staff that is well-versed on environmental issues (Waterman, 1989). Despite a shared concern for the environment, EPA employees are by no means in complete agreement regarding a specific environmental approach for the agency (Waterman, 1989). In part, these disagreements have something to do with the organization of the EPA (see Table 4.3).

In addition to a national office in Washington, DC, the EPA maintains 10 regional offices (see Table 4.4), each responsible within its region for the execution of EPA programs. Most EPA employees are located in regional offices, while most scholarship on the EPA is directed toward environmental issues and policies originating from the national office in Washington, DC (Waterman, 1989).

Table 4.4. EPA Regional Offices and State Coverage

Region 1	Connecticut, Maine, Massachusetts, New Hampshire, Rhode Island, Vermont
Region 2	New Jersey, New York, Puerto Rico, the U.S. Virgin Islands
Region 3	Delaware, Maryland, Pennsylvania, Virginia, West Virginia, the District of Columbia
Region 4	Alabama, Florida, Georgia, Kentucky, Mississippi, North Carolina, South Carolina, Tennessee
Region 5	Illinois, Indiana, Michigan, Minnesota, Ohio, Wisconsin
Region 6	Arkansas, Louisiana, New Mexico, Oklahoma, Texas
Region 7	Iowa, Kansas, Missouri, Nebraska
Region 8	Colorado, Montana, North Dakota, South Dakota, Utah, Wyoming
Region 9	Arizona, California, Hawaii, Nevada, the territories of Guam and American Samoa
Region 10	Alaska, Idaho, Oregon, Washington

The most recent addition to the EPA's structure is the Office of Homeland Security (OHS). That office was created by Administrator Whitman in 2003 and resides under the Office of the Administrator (see Table 4-2). Among other things, OHS is tasked with emergency response cleanup efforts, infrastructure and building protection; advancing science to more effectively prevent respond to terrorist threats and attacks; centralizing and evaluating communications related to homeland security as they pertain to the EPA's charge; establishing effective technology systems to enhance information processing as it relates to homeland security; and helping EPA personnel adjust to the new tasks associated with concern for homeland security.

INTERAGENCY COOPERATION

To accomplish its task, the EPA relies heavily on state environmental agencies for cooperation. As a result, "the EPA is a curious blend of centralized control by the administrator and decentralized authority over its many functional res-ponsibilities, the other federal agencies with which it shares responsibility, and the intergovernmental component of environmental regulation" (Waterman, 1989, p. 100). Despite its decentralized structure and contending with substantial jurisdictional issues, the EPA is recognized by some as the most important of the major regulatory agencies (e.g., McCormick, 1989).

Prior to the creation of the EPA, environmental policy existed in piecemeal fashion and fell under the domain of a variety of state and federal government agencies. The country's historically limited concern for environmental policy was prevalent in both the Executive Office and Congress (Switzer and Bryner, 1998).

Today, the EPA shares jurisdiction with several other federal agencies on different environmental issues, though it shares primary responsibility over environmental matters with the Department of the Interior (DOI) (Switzer and Bryner, 1998). The DOI has jurisdiction over federal and public lands, including National Parks, and enforces laws on its lands based on policies provided by the EPA (Hyatt, 1998). Other federal agencies that maintain partial jurisdiction over the environment include: the Department of Agriculture (authority over the National Forest Service, grasslands and natural resources); the Department of Justice (responsible for prosecuting all criminal cases related to the environment); the Department of Defense (jurisdiction over military installations, including the disposition of chemical and nuclear weapons); the Department of Energy, Office of Environmental Management; and the Nuclear Regulatory Commission (issues pertaining to nuclear fuel and radioactive materials/waste). A number of other federal agencies have secondary environmental authority (see, Switzer and Bryner, 1998; Hyatt, 1998; Burns and Lynch, 2004). One of the most important agencies the EPA cooperates with is the Council on Environmental Quality (CEQ).

Council on Environmental Quality (CEQ)

Established in 1970 as part of the *National Environmental Policy Act* (NEPA), the CEQ provides policy advice on environmental issues to the president, and coordinates federal environmental efforts, policies, and initiatives (Switzer and Bryner, 1998). Its role is primarily advisory (Collin, 2006). It was perhaps most influential during the Nixon administration, primarily because Nixon staffed the Council with qualified environmental advocates. The CEQ's impact diminished beginning with Nixon's second term as he faced impeachment. Perhaps the greatest damage stemmed from the Reagan administration's attempt to abolish the CEQ (Flippen, 2000).

State Environmental Agencies

By 1990, each state had adopted a regulatory agency similar to the EPA, and each maintains at least one environmental regulatory agency. State environmental regulatory agencies provide invaluable services for protecting the environment and possess a wealth of information on environmental crimes. Like the EPA, state environmental agencies are charged with protecting the environment, although each must address the unique challenges posed by environmental concerns in its respective state. Given its mission, the EPA must cooperate with the 50 state environmental regulatory agencies. This decentralized approach to environmental protection limits the EPA's environmental protection efforts because decision-making authority is spread among multiple levels of government with different focuses, levels of commitment to environmental protection, and financial resources (Bowman, 1984).

In 1995, state and EPA leaders moved to enhance environmental protection through greater, more efficient cooperation via the National Environmental Performance Partnership System (Collin, 2006, p. 198). Many states developed partnership agreements with EPA regional offices, designed to address specific needs within their area. Given the EPA's vast charges and the varied nature of environmental issues throughout the United States, the need for effective federal and state cooperation is essential.

Cooperation between the EPA and the states is evident, for instance, in states being required, by the 1970 *Clean Air Act*, to submit to the EPA a State Implementation Plan (SIP). SIPs describe the processes by which each state will comply with the Act. The EPA, in turn, regulates the plan by determining its adequacy for implementation. The EPA lacks the resources to comprehensively assess each state's environmental protection plans (Waterman, 1989), which ultimately allows a degree of autonomy for the state regulatory agencies.

While the state and federal environmental regulatory agencies rely on each other's cooperation, their association is not without its difficulties. Often states believe the EPA is too intrusive concerning issues that should be considered state matters, yet states also believe the EPA is not aggressive enough in addressing specific issues that adversely affect them (Rosenbaum, 2003).

Industry

Perhaps the most influential group with whom the EPA must interact is the business community or industry, the group with the greatest potential for harming and protecting the environment. Industry is greatly impacted by EPA regulations and enforcement policies. As a result, industries often lobby the White House, legislators, and EPA administrators concerning rule changes and enforcement policy. Industry often laments that EPA regulations cut into profits, and continually seeks to have cost concerns included in legislation and enforcement policy. Recognition of the need to balance environmental concerns with economic considerations are evident throughout EPA history. However, industry often calculates these costs with a primary concern for financial profits. These calculations do not take into account the costs of pollution to the public, government, health care, and the insurance industry.

While industry has expressed concern that EPA regulations impact profits, those interested in environmental protection expressed concern that industry would attempt to subvert the mission of the EPA. Waterman (1989, p. 108), for instance, notes that policymakers were concerned about the EPA becoming "the pawn of the regulated industry," which would influence the authority and discretion provided to the EPA administrator and compromise the EPA's mission.

The EPA is not only affected by its relationship to other organizations, industries, or its organizational structure; it is also influenced by the White House. While the EPA is by no means directly guided by the president, the agency is influenced by the president and there are clear differences in EPA practices across presidential administrations. Such differences, which can be attributed in part to the differing ideologies of Democrats and Republicans, are discussed below.

THE EXECUTIVE OFFICE AND THE ENVIRONMENT

The White House maintains direct control over EPA practices. These influences are well documented (Vig, 2003), and any discussion of EPA practices requires reference to presidential influences and ideology. The president influences the EPA through appointment of the EPA Administrator, though the appointment must be approved by Congress.

The diverse responsibilities of the presidency require the president to balance efforts across many policy matters (Waterman, 1989). In some cases, balancing interests involves the application of the president's personal beliefs about the value of protecting the environment versus, for instance, economic recovery, inflation, unemployment, or international relations. For instance, the Carter and George H. Bush administrations both expressed interest in environmental issues; both, however, were impeded by external crises when it came to making important environmental decisions (e.g., Carter by the oil embargo, Bush by the Gulf War) (e.g. Hyatt, 1998). Environmental concerns are consistently among the most highlighted issues each president faces. These concerns must be addressed in some manner, regardless of anyone's belief in what the president should or should not do.

It is sometimes difficult to clearly evaluate the impact of presidential administrations on environmental policy. For example, the overall merits of the Nixon administration remain under debate decades after he left office. In addition, it is difficult to determine how a president's influence is enhanced or impeded by actions of legislators. To address this issue as it relates to presidential environmental concerns, Vig (2003, p.105) provides a set of indicators that facilitate evaluation of presidential influence on environmental policy: (1) the president's environmental agenda, (2) key presidential appointments, (3) environmental program budgets, (4) presidential legislative initiatives or vetoes, (5) presidential executive orders, (6) White House oversight of environmental regulation, and (7) presidential response to international environmental agreements. The material below examines the impact of presidential administrations on the EPA since 1970 addressing some, but not all or Vig's indicators.

Presidents, Prioritization and the Environment

The federal government, like other levels of government, is constantly challenged by working within the confines of an annual budget. Assessing how the resources within the budget are allocated provides an indicator of presidential prioritization. For instance, President George W. Bush submitted a 2003 budget which proposed eliminating funding for 33 Superfund sites for which a responsible party *could not be identified.* Superfund, a program designed to allow the government to clean up designated hazardous waste locations when no responsible party can be located, requires periodic Congressional reauthorization. The Bush administration's omission of Superfund monies from the 2003 budget ignited protest from many who recognize the significance of Superfund, prompted many groups (particularly the EPA) to figure out how to continue cleaning up Superfund sites, and provided additional evidence of the Bush administration's lack of concern for environmental issues (Cohen, 2004). As an additional example, consider how the pro-business approach of the Reagan administration or the pro-environmental stance taken under the Clinton administration impacted the EPA and environmental policy.

To be sure, volumes have been written on the EPA (e.g., Landy et al. 1990), the presidency as it relates to the environment (e.g., Soden, 1999), and particular presidential influences on the environment (e.g., Flippen, 2000). The following overview sheds light on how the EPA has been affected by presidential practices, societal events, and time, with the amount of discussion devoted to each presidential administration varying according to each president's time in office and impact upon the environment.

Nixon: The Beginning of the EPA

Until Nixon's first term in office, the president, with the exception of Theodore Roosevelt, had limited involvement in environmental policy, and even Nixon was initially reluctant to become involved (Switzer and Bryner, 1998). The Nixon administration, however, is credited with many significant accomplishments in terms of environmental protection, including the creation of the EPA, which is, perhaps, the single most influential environmental action occurring under any administration. Seeking to win public support by appearing pro-environment, Nixon supported the *National Environmental Policy Act* (NEPA) in 1970, declared the 1970s as "the environmental decade," and promoted environmental legislation. While some suggest that the creation of the EPA was politically motivated, others argue that the agency served a clear purpose other than being a political pawn (Hyatt, 1998), and that Nixon era environmental accomplishments were unsurpassed by any subsequent administration (Train, 1996; Kraft, 1996; Whitaker, 1976; and Hoff, 1994).

Nixon appointed William Ruckelshaus, formerly a member of the U.S. Department of Justice, as the first EPA administrator, despite Ruckelshaus's limited background on environmental issues (Switzer and Bryner, 1998; Marcus, 1980). Ruckelshaus initially attempted to convey the message that the EPA would aggressively enforce the newly created environmental policies related to air and water pollution (Gottlieb, 1993; Cohen, 1986). He is credited with demonstrating to Nixon the significance of the 1972 United Nations Conference on the Human Environment in Stockholm, to which Nixon subsequently persuaded Congress to make notable contributions (McCormick, 1989).

Ruckelshaus left the EPA in 1973 to become acting director of the FBI where he later oversaw impeachment proceedings against Nixon. His replacement, Bob Fri, played a major role in creating automobile emission standards, which ultimately led to the phase-out of leaded gasoline. Fri was replaced by Russell Train, who previously served on the CEQ, and was more appealing to environmentalists (Waterman, 1989). While Train (1996) became frustrated with the Nixon administration, he argued that many tend to overlook the positive environmental contributions of the Nixon administration, especially fostering international cooperation to address environmental concerns (Barkdull, 1998).

The accomplishments of the Nixon administration should not, of course, be attributed solely to Nixon, who was actually lukewarm to most environmental issues (e.g., Switzer and Bryner, 1998; Landy et al., 1990; Stine, 1998; Davis, 2002). Devra Davis (2002, p. 95) noted that Nixon once told Ruckelshaus to "watch out for these crazy enviros... They're a bunch of commie pinko queers!"

Some question Nixon's direct contributions to the environmental progress experienced during his administration and suggest that other factors were behind the progress (Barkdull, 1998; Genovese, 1990; Flippen, 1995; 1996; 2000). Flippen (2000), for instance, notes that Congress and Nixon's staff played significant roles in environmental progress during Nixon's second term, when he redirected focus away from environmental issues and toward the nation's economic concerns. Indeed, Flippen (2000, p. 227) stated that during Nixon's second term, he attempted to undermine the EPA (see also Waterman, 1989). Following Nixon's resignation, President Ford inherited a troubled economy, which contributed to a continuation of Nixon's second-term retreat on environmental issues (Flippen, 2000).

The Ford Administration's Limited Response to the Environment

Completing Nixon's second term, Gerald Ford made few significant contributions to environmental issues, and is not recognized for influencing any environmental initiatives. The only notable environmental legislation to emerge from Ford's time in office was the *Federal Lands Policy and Management Act of 1976* (Flippen, 2000). The empty environmental slate of the Ford administration can be explained, in part, by three circumstances (Switzer and Bryner, 1998, p. 51): (1) a focus on responding to the 1973 Arab oil embargo; (2) growing industrial concern with the costs of complying with EPA regulations during an economic recession; and (3) the waning environmental movement. Ford retained Train as EPA administrator, which reemphasized the EPA's image as a strong advocate for the environment (Landy et al., 1990). Concern for environmental issues would reappear within the Executive Office with the 1977 election of Jimmy Carter.

The Carter Administration: Environmental Optimism

In contrast to Gerald Ford, Jimmy Carter arrived at the White House with a sincere interest in protecting the environment (Flippen, 2000). Prior to his election, Carter received recognition from the League of Conservation Voters for his environmental record as governor of Georgia, even though his presidential campaign focused more directly on issues other than the environment (Switzer and Bryner, 1998). Carter recognized the importance of courting environmentalists, benefited from societal concern for the environment, and became the first U.S. presidential candidate to campaign successfully on environmental issues (Stine, 1998).

Carter replaced Russell Train with Douglas Costle as EPA Administrator, a controversial appointment at best despite Costle's role in establishing the EPA (Switzer and Bryner, 1998; Landy et al., 1990). Costle would maintain the agency's image of environmental advocacy, form a strong team of EPA administrators, and redefine the mission of the EPA to focus on public health in place of the earlier mission that focused on the maintenance of ecological balance (Landy et al., 1990). Costle also played a major role in influencing Congress to pass the 1980 *Comprehensive Environmental Response, Compensation, and Liability Act* or Superfund Act—a $1.6 billion trust fund, financed primarily by a tax imposed on industrial feedstock chemicals, that allowed the EPA to sue offending companies and individuals for cleanup costs associated with illegal hazardous waste disposal (Flippen, 2000). The agency now shifted its focus from pollution to toxins and in doing so increased the presence of the organization such that it received a 25 percent budget increase during a time of financial austerity (Switzer and Bryner, 1998).

Carter's election heightened the expectations of environmentalists. But runaway inflation, a stagnant economy, and an oil embargo, among other issues, detracted from Carter's ability to address environmental matters (Switzer and Bryner, 1998) Carter's policy differences with the EPA, which included several attempts to reduce regulatory costs to businesses to stimulate the economy (Waterman, 1989) and his institutionalization of cost-benefit analysis to control government regulation, also aroused questions of Carter's concern for environmental issues.

Several notable environmental accomplishments have led some to rank Carter along with Theodore and Franklin Roosevelt as the presidents most concerned with conservation (Stine 1998, p. 196), Moreover, his recognition of global environmental issues led to the conclusion that "Carter was ahead of his time" (Stine 1998, p. 195).

Despite its accomplishments, the Carter administration fell short of meeting the "unrealistically high expectations" of environmentalists (Stine 1998, p. 179). But, if environmentalists were disappointed with Carter, they were enraged by the Reagan administration.

Deregulation and Reform: The Reagan Administration

Reagan's environmental agenda centered on: (1) regulatory reform, (2) heavy reliance on the free market to distribute resources, (3) encouraging states to accept increasing responsibility for environmental issues, and (4) extensive personnel and budget cuts (Vig and Kraft, 1984; Landy et al., 1990). By 1986, Reagan had slashed EPA's budget by nearly 25 percent, accomplished largely through personnel reductions (Lash, Gillman and Sheridan, 1984; Mintz, 1995). Upon entering office, Reagan implemented a hiring freeze, and fired twenty senior EPA officials before he left office (Johnson, 1991). Stine (1998) suggests that Reagan was moderately successful in attempts to dismantle the environmental progress of the Carter administration, with some critics suggesting that the Reagan administration was almost solely responsible for destroying the accomplishments made with regard to pollution control (Switzer and Bryner, 1998).

Reagan's environmental record is marked not only by his dismantling of environmental agencies, but also poor choice in environmental appointments. For example, Reagan appointed James Watt as Secretary of the Interior, a move that ultimately backfired after Watt's anti-environmentalist approach and thoughtless comments led to his Reagan-coerced resignation (Cannon, 2000, p. 530–531; Lash et al., 1984, p. 231). Reagan EPA appointee Anne (Burford) Gorsuch created an extensive public scandal described below.

The pro-business approach adopted during the Reagan era resulted in decisions to shift EPA regulatory practices from a confrontational approach to voluntary compliance. The administration argued this approach would generate enhanced compliance from the business community (Hyatt, 1998). EPA Administrator Anne Gorsuch, a conservative who embraced the anti-regulatory approach to government, made voluntary compliance standard operating pro-cedure at the EPA. Hyatt (1998) suggests that the decision to seek voluntary compliance was among the most controversial actions taken by the EPA throughout its contentious history. The move brought about a reduction in the number of enforcement actions taken against those found guilty of envir-onmental harms. After years of controversy surrounding the enforcement program, and the reappointment of William Ruckelshaus as EPA administrator, the EPA shifted toward a more enforcement-oriented approach (Friedrichs, 1996; Hyatt, 1998) with positive results. Barnett (1993), for example, found that the pro-regulatory approach was notably effective in responding to Superfund offenses.

The greatest controversy faced by the EPA in the Reagan years were allegations directed toward EPA Administrator Anne Gorsuch and the individual who headed the hazardous waste program, Rita Lavelle. Gorsuch began her appointment at the EPA by eliminating the Office of Enforcement and the EPA's regional enforcement offices, transferring their duties to various programs and offices, including the newly created Office of Legal and Enforcement Counsel, which lacked identifiable boundaries of authority (Landy et al., 1990). Gorsuch's efforts resulted in lapsed promotions and even demotions for EPA employees, which left EPA careerists feeling demoralized (Switzer and Bryner, 1998). Nevertheless, her actions were consistent with the Reagan administration's concern for deregulation.

In the autumn of 1982, Gorsuch became the focus of an investigation initiated by John Dingell, chairman of the House Committee on Energy and Commerce, concerning possible abuses in Superfund enforcement. It was alleged that the Superfund was being used to reduce the federal deficit as opposed to cleaning up hazardous waste sites, and that the EPA had become overly accommodating to corporations involved in illegal toxic waste disposal procedures (Friedrichs, 1996). Gorsuch was subpoenaed to appear before the Committee to provide requested documents; however, she refused to do so, citing executive privilege. With the support of the Justice Department, Gorsuch avoided an appearance before the Committee, despite a vote by the House to declare her in contempt of court (Switzer and Bryner, 1998). The effort of the Department of Justice to protect Gorsuch lapsed following the discovery of a major industry-created environmental hazard in Times Beach, Missouri, which drew substantial press coverage and additional charges of EPA mismanagement of cleanup operations (Switzer and Bryner, 1998). The director of the project, Rita Lavelle, was eventually convicted of charges of perjury and obstructing a congressional investigation, sentenced to six months in prison and a $10,000 fine, and ultimately fired by Reagan (Switzer and Bryner, 1998).

The Times Beach incident and White House disinterest in her well-being (Lash et al., 1984) led Gorsuch to resign in March 1983. In August 1984, a House Energy and Commerce Oversight Committee noted ethical concerns in the EPA, and suggested that between 1981 and 1983 "top level officials of the EPA violated their public trust by disregarding the public health and environment, manipulating the Superfund program for political purposes, engaging in unethical conduct, and participating in other abuses" (Johnson 1991, p. 171). Following the Burford/Lavelle fiasco, a sense of stability would once again appear at the EPA upon the return of William Ruckelshaus, whose primary concern was to restore stability and credibility to the agency (Cannon, 2000). Under Ruckelshaus, the EPA made notable progress in substantially reducing lead in gasoline and removing ethylene dibromide, a major pesticide, from the market (Hyatt, 1998). Yet, despite such progress, Reagan and his staff refused to commit to environmental issues once the scandals were no longer prominent in news coverage (Cannon, 2000). The insignificance of Ruckelshaus's role became evident during a key 1984 meeting in which Ruckelshaus stressed the need for resources to reduce acid rain. During the meeting, Reagan confused Ruckelshaus with Middle East special envoy Donald Rumsfeld, twice referring to his EPA Administrator as "Don" instead of "Bill" (Cannon, 2000). Ruckelshaus became increasingly frustrated with the Reagan administration, and resigned within 18 months (Cannon, 2000). His replacement, Lee Thomas, sought to encourage public and scientific awareness of the dangers posed by ecological threats, and global concerns and international cooperation (Landy et al., 1990), and returned the agency's reputation for strong enforcement with the intent to discourage abusers of environmental policies (Hyatt, 1998; Switzer and Bryner, 1998).

Reagan's environmental record was poor, at best, and many of the environmental advances made during this era were the result of legislative accomplishments (Lash et al., 1984). Twenty years later, Reagan's negative environmental record would be eclipsed, however, by events that occurred under George W. Bush's administration.

Not Really "The Environmental President:" George H. Bush

George H. Bush's election provided some hope to environmentalists since Bush had declared himself "the environmental president." Bush supported his declaration by appointing William Reilly as EPA Administrator. Reilly, previously of the World Wildlife Fund, was the first environmental professional to serve as EPA Administrator (Switzer and Bryner, 1998). Bush's tenure in office was marked more by rhetoric than action, especially on the environment (Flippen 2000, p. 230). The result was an inconsistent environmental record that sometimes favored industry, and at other times favored the environment. Such wavering resulted in the Bush administration facing criticism from both environmentalists and conservatives (Switzer and Bryner, 1998).

Reilly and Bush did influence Congress to approve the first revision of clean air legislation in thirteen years (Switzer and Bryner, 1998). At the same time, Bush undermined environmental protection by helping to open protected wetlands for real estate development purposes, permitting strip-mining to continue, promoting logging in national forests, and abandoning the global warming treaty (Daynes, 1999). Similarly, the reluctance of the Bush administration to address global environmental concerns left the United States "isolated and embarrassed in international environmental diplomacy" (Vig, 2003, p. 110). Bush's record produced a defensive stance during his final year in office (Vig, 2003), and emphasized an anti-regulatory tone reminiscent of the early Reagan administration. His failure to win re-election once again brought a sense of optimism to environmentalists, who believed Democrat Bill Clinton would restore credibility and support to the EPA.

Renewed Optimism and the Clinton Administration

The 1992 election of William Jefferson Clinton provided environmentalists with a level of optimism unseen during the twelve years of the Reagan and Bush administrations. While Bush's campaign focused on protecting jobs and the *Endangered Species Act*, Clinton provided an appetizing platform for environmentalists that included efforts to prevent global warming, an issue Bush had failed to take seriously (Switzer and Bryner, 1998). Despite Clinton's unimpressive environmental record as Governor of Arkansas, environmentalists were frustrated with the Reagan and Bush administrations and had high expectations for Clinton and his "green" vice president, Al Gore (Daynes, 1999).

Clinton entered office with the intent to balance jobs, stimulate the economy, and enhance environmental protection (Daynes, 1999), although he found devoting ample attention to these tasks difficult, often frustrating optimistic environmentalists. Clinton's credibility among environmentalists was challenged when he reduced the EPA research staff (Switzer and Bryner, 1998). He reestablished some credibility when he helped establish the Office of Environmental Justice to address alleged inequities in environmental protection, and opposed anti-environmental Republican initiatives that emerged during the latter part of his presidency after Republicans gained control of Congress in 1994 (Hyatt, 1998; Switzer and Bryner, 1998). McCarthy, Thompson, and Thornburgh (2000) noted that Clinton had a muddled environmental record, in that he did more for the environment than any other President since Theodore Roosevelt; however, he also missed opportunities that may never appear again, particularly due to the irreversibility of much environmental damage.

Clinton appointed Carol Browner as EPA Administrator, who would become the longest-serving head in the agency's history. Following work as an environmental official in Florida, Browner adopted a pro-regulatory stance that infuriated industry and Republicans in Congress (Nash, 2000). Browner was accused of allowing environmental "zealots" to run EPA, leading to the neglect of scientific research (B. Cohen, 1998). Indeed, EPA research microbiologist David Lewis chastised Browner for disproportionately focusing on regulation rather than developing the necessary science (B. Cohen, 1998).

The EPA and took notable steps to protect public lands and endangered species during the latter part of Clinton's terms in office, and Browner is credited with strengthening and enforcing existing regulations and issuing new regulations, particularly tighter air quality standards (Vig, 2003). Most of the Clinton administration's significant contributions to the environment came late in his second term, including several new regulations addressing various forms of pollution and several unilateral actions to protect vulnerable public lands; tighten limits on air particulates, arsenic, and lead; and several other pro-environmental actions (Daynes, 1999; Cohen, 2004). Consequently, environmentalists believe Clinton waited too long to address serious environmental issues. In their evaluation, McCarthy and colleagues (2000) note that Clinton sought to be the new Teddy Roosevelt, but his attempts to help preserve the environment may have been too little, too late.

George W. Bush, Anti-Environmentalist

George W. Bush entered the Oval Office amidst political controversy, and, like his father, touted himself as environmentally friendly. His true environmental stance was made clear soon after taking office when his administration made several anti-environmental policy decisions. First, Bush placed a sixty-day moratorium on Clinton administration rules which had yet to take effect, which impacted several very important environmental policies. Second, Bush reversed a campaign pledge to control carbon dioxide emissions from power plants, announced that the U.S. would withdraw from the Kyoto Protocol on climate change, and sought to open the Arctic National Wildlife Refuge ("the crown jewel of America's refuge system" [Collin, 2006, p. 88]) to oil exploration. On other fronts, Bush had the EPA withdraw its new arsenic-in-drinking water standards, and had the boundaries of 19 National Parks redrawn to encourage oil exploration (Vig, 2003). Adding further insult and injury on the environmental front, Bush called for increased fossil fuel exploration, minimized rules against strip mining, and encouraged the Justice Department to drop EPA-initiated lawsuits against coal-fired power plants.

More than anything else, Bush's clear anti-environmental policy stance has been encouraged by the fossil fuel industry. In 2004 alone, the fossil fuel industry donated more than $20 million—80 percent of donations—to Republicans. As a result, many of the Bush's administration's environmental policies have favored oil industry interests over public interests in environmental protection. To a significant extent, the Bush administration has been staffed with fossil fuel industry representatives (see Table 4.5).

Table 4.5. Name, Position, and Former Employment of Key Political Appointees of the Bush Administration

Spencer Abraham, Energy Secretary. The former, one term, Michigan Senator has taken a clear anti-fuel economy standards position. He received more money from the automobile industry than any other politician.

George W. Bush, President. Former owner *Abrusto Energy;* CEO *Spectrum 7,* Board of Directors, Harken Energy.

Andrew Card, White House Chief of Staff. Formerly chief lobbyist for General Motors, and CEO of the American Automobile Manufacturers Association, Card opposes fuel-economy standards.

Vicky Bailey, Assistant Energy Secretary, International Affairs and Domestic Policy. Bailey is the former President of PSI, a subsidiary of Cinergy Gas.

Kathleen Cooper, Under-Secretary of Commerce, Economic Affairs. Former chief economist at ExxonMobil.

Don Evans, Commerce Secretary. Former Chairman and CEO of the oil/gas
company, Tom Brown.

Cam Toohey, Interior Specialist, Alaska. Former Director of Arctic Power, a
lobbying group solely designed to obtain the rights to drill for oil and gas in
the Arctic National Wildlife Refuge.

Gale Norton, Interior Secretary. An understudy to James Watt, Norton has served as
legal counsel to mining industries and other anti-environmental groups.

Lawrence Lindsay, Presidential Economic Advisor. Before his appointment,
Lindsay was a consultant on natural gas issues to Enron.

Clay Johnson, Director, Presidential Personnel. Advisor on appointments to the
Federal Energy Regulatory Commission, Johnson was a major stockholder
($250,000) in El Paso Energy Partners, a Texas gas/oil company.

Lewis Libby, Vice President Cheney's Chief of Staff. Large stockholder in
ExxonMobil, Texaco, Chesapeake Energy, and Enron.

Karl Rove, Senior Presidential Political Advisor. Large shareholder in Amoco,
Royal Dutch/Shell, and Enron.

Condoleeza Rice, National Security Advisor. Former board member at Chevron. An
oil tanker was named after her.

Bush's environmental record as president should have come as no surprise
given the record of environmental degradation he achieved while governor of
Texas. For example, one of Bush's first actions as Governor of Texas was to cut
the budget of the state's environmental protection agency (the Texas Natural
Resource Conservation Commission, TNRCC; now called the Texas
Commission on Environmental Quality, TCEQ) by 20 percent. Bush appointed
Ralph Marquez, formerly with Monsanto Chemicals and the Texas Chemical
Council, as the first appointee to the TNRCC. Marquez responded by helping
Houston businessmen suppress smog advisories and smog data from public
view. Bush also appointed Barry McBee, an opponent of the Right-To-Know
legislation, to TNRCC. Having been turned into a voice for industry rather than
public health, TNRCC opposed new EPA air quality regulations on several
occasions over the next few years, and refused to meet federal standards.

Bush also gutted other environmental legislation that protected public
health, such as the vehicle emission inspection program. The governor was sued
for this action because it violated a contract with a private business entity (not
because it violated *Clean Air Act* requirements for designated non-containment
areas). The private contractor won the suit, which lead to a $140 million
settlement against the state of Texas. To make the settlement payment, Bush cut
the TNRCC's budget by an additional 18 percent ($125 million).

The Bush administration's lack of concern for environmental issues was
further evident in its 2001 proposed energy plan, which requested substantial
increases in future domestic oil and gas production during an era of significant
climate change. The plan called for streamlining environmental regulations with
the intent to accelerate the production of new energy (Vig, 2003; Sanger and

Kahn, 2001). Bush's first budget proposal reduced the EPA's budget by 6.4 percent (Vig, 2003, p. 118). The Bush appointed former New Jersey Governor Christie Todd Whitman as EPA Administrator, even though some believed that "Whitman has been an unmitigated disaster for New Jersey's environmental protection" (Ireland, 2001, p. 18). While Governor, she cut the state Department of Environmental Protection (DEP) staff by 738 employees during the first three years she was in office, reduced the remaining staff's workweek by five hours, eliminated fines on polluters as a source of DEP revenue, and made notable cuts in the agency's budgets (Ireland, 2001).

As EPA Administrator, Whitman was recognized as being sympathetic to environmental issues, yet also powerless or unwilling to address environmental concerns (Greene, 2003). She faced a difficult challenge in balancing the interests of the environment with a pro-industry Bush administration. Perhaps the challenge was best exemplified in her attempts to persuade President Bush to sign the Kyoto Protocol on global warming, only to have the President dismiss the idea.

To replace Whitman, Bush nominated Utah Governor Michael O. Leavitt as EPA Administrator to balance environmental concerns and business interests. Republicans favored Leavitt's anti-regulatory stance, while Democrats dismissed Leavitt as being similar to other ineffective EPA administrators (Allen and Milbank, 2003). Philip Clapp, president of the National Environmental Trust, suggested that Leavitt's philosophy centered on decreased regulation, regardless of the costs to public health and the environment (Allen and Milbank, 2003). Spangler and Dougherty (2003) noted that, if confirmed, Leavitt would regulate many of the same companies that strongly supported his political campaigns as governor of Utah.

Virtually all of Bush's other appointees were considered anti-environment (Vig, 2003), leading some to recognize the administration as more conservative than the Reagan administration (Milbank and Nakashima, 2001). In a scathing, public resignation from his position as director of the EPA's Office of Regulatory Enforcement, Eric Schaeffer (2002), a career EPA employee, cited the Bush administration's disregard for environmental issues, particularly pollution control, the administration's failure to fill key vacancies in the agency, its practice of slashing enforcement budgets, and its overall destruction of years of environmental progress.

Following pressure resulting from his decision to revisit the numerous environmental regulations put forth by Clinton during his last few weeks in office, President Bush apparently took heed of his developing reputation as one who disregards environmental issues. In response, he attempted to improve his image by offering several environmental regulations of his own, including extensive paperwork for small users of lead and an efficiency standard for new washing machines ("Green Bush," 2001). Bush also agreed to tighten the standards for arsenic in water, although not to the extent proposed by Clinton

("Green Bush," 2001), and further showed support for environmental regulation by deciding to maintain the cabinet rank of the EPA administrator (Nash, 2001). Some suggest that Bush's largest mistake since assuming office is his lack of communication, particularly with regard to his decision to repeal, yet not discuss, many of the proposed Clinton regulations ("Green Bush," 2001). Perhaps the most indicting comments offered in response to the Bush administration's approach to the environment came from six former EPA administrators who notably criticized the Bush administration for its failure to effectively confront global warming (McGowan, 2006).

Like other presidents, George W. Bush has had to juggle several pressing issues during his time in office, not the least of which are terrorist threats, homeland security, and wars in Iraq and Afghanistan. However, some suggest Bush, like several presidents who served before him (e.g., Nixon and Clinton) is responsible, in part, for creating and/or perpetuating these concerns. Regardless of responsibility, it remains that the Bush administration has provided environmentalists and the EPA a constant flow of challenges in various forms and its ongoing anti-regulatory approach to environmental protection conjures images of the Reagan administration.

Bush's anti-environmental agenda runs so deep that it is difficult to review completely here. The most devastating and thorough critiques of Bush's environmental policies have been written by Robert F. Kennedy Jr., and Carl Pope (for review see Burns and Lynch, 2004). Pope, the Executive Director since 1992 of the oldest environmental group in the U.S., The Sierra Club, offers a well-rounded critique of the Bush Administration in his book, *Strategic Ignorance: Why the Bush Administration is Recklessly Destroying a Century of Environmental Progress* (Sierra Club Books). Perhaps more than any other individual, Robert F. Kennedy Jr. has delivered the bad news about Bush to Americans in the form of public addresses, radio and news interviews, magazine articles and books. Kennedy is an environmental lawyer, professor of environmental law at Pace University, senior attorney for the National Resource Defense Council, and President of the *Waterkeeper Alliance*. His article "Crimes Against Nature" (www.rollingstone.com/politics/story/ 5939345/ crimes_against_nature), which appeared in *Rolling Stone Magazine* (November 2003), laid the background for his more extensive work, the book *Crimes Against Nature: How George W. Bush and Corporate Pals are Plundering the Country and Hijacking Our Democracy* (HarperCollins, 2005).

LOOKING FORWARD

The short history of the EPA demonstrates an agency with an incredibly large mandate, fluctuating support, and limited direction. Rosenbaum (2003) suggests that there is extensive dissatisfaction with the agency despite its significant achievements. The EPA often faces a no-win situation when trying to balance public health with business interests.

Presidential influence over the EPA contributes to its unstable nature, objectives and evaluation. Oval Office directives that change agency focus, impact its direction through the selection of an administrator, and affect budgetary support issues can severely alter the tasks the EPA undertakes. The need to battle Congress, which consists of individuals maintaining their own agendas, results in further difficulties for an agency dependent on governmental/political support.

In looking ahead, the EPA faces many challenges; some old and some new. Among the existing challenges are competing for resources, answering to various powerful groups, and confronting a wide array of harms to the environment, including community-based environmental planning, environmental justice, sustainability, cumulative impacts, and ecosystems approaches (Collin 2006, pp. 231-272). Unfortunately, "While many of the world's most advanced countries have made earnest strides over the past decade to embrace sustainable development, the United States is steadily moving backward in time" (Cohen 2004, p. 84).

Despite the notable efforts of many career EPA employees who maintain sincere concerns for environmental protection and numerous significant accomplishments, the level of disorganization and inconsistency characterizing the history of the EPA led to piecemeal progress and limited efficiency with regard to environmental regulation. The EPA remains, however, the primary agency charged with regulating the environment, and historical inconsistencies do not necessarily imply future problems.

The following is a list of significant events in the EPA's history (see Collin, 2006).

THE ENVIRONMENTAL PROTECTION AGENCY CHRONOLOGY OF KEY EVENTS

1970—*Clean Air Act* passed

1971—*National Air Quality Standards and Ocean Dumping Act* passed

1972—DDT banned

1973—First Wastewater Permits issued; phase-out of leaded gas begins

1974—Fuel Economy Labeling; *Safe Drinking Water Act* passed

1975—Pollution control on cars required

1976—*Toxic Substances Control Act* and *Resource Conservation and Recovery Act* passed

1977—*Safe Drinking Water Standards* set; *Clean Water Act* passed; Coal-fired power plant scrubbers required

1978—Lead is regulated; aerosol fluorocarbons banned; Great Lakes Water Quality Agreement passed

1979—PCB manufacture banned; United States sues for Love Canal cleanup; EPA establishes Hazardous-Waste Enforcement and Emergency Response System

1980—Three Mile Island cleanup; Superfund authorized

1981—First State Hazardous-Waste Program authorized; first Superfund sites identified

1982—*Asbestos School Hazard Abatement Act* passed; Superfund pays for Love Canal cleanup

1983—EPA relocates Times Beach residents; Olin Corporation agrees to clean up DDT in Triana, Alabama

1984—Chesapeake Bay cleanup; Hazardous-Waste and Solid-Waste amendments passed

1985—Revised gasoline-lead limits passed; Air Toxics Program expanded

1986—The *Superfund Amendments and Reauthorization Act* (SARA), *Safe Drinking Water Act* amendments and *Emergency Planning and Community Right-to-Know Act* passed

1987—EPA mandates sanctions against states not meeting air standards; *Hazardous Chemical Reporting Rule* passed

1988—Standards set for underground storage tanks; *Federal Insecticide, Fungicide, and Rodenticide Act* amendments and the *Ocean Dumping Ban Act* passed

1989—Medical waste tracking established; EPA responds to *Exxon Valdez* oil spill; Alar banned for food uses; Toxic Inventory Data released

1990—*Clean Air Act* amendments; *Pollution Prevention Act* passed; land disposal of hazardous wastes restricted

1991—Acid Rain Emission Sales Rule passed

1992—New drinking water contamination standards introduced; EPA and New York City mark end of sewage sludge dumping; EPA commits to reducing environmental risks to minorities

1993—Federal facilities ordered to reduce toxic emissions; CFCs and other ozone depleters phased out; passive smoke designated as a human carcinogen

1994—Federal Environmental Justice Order signed

1995—Refinery Air Toxics Rule passed; EPA expands acid rain emissions trading

1996—EPA implements *Lead-Based Paint Right to Know*; EPA finalizes leaded gas ban; *Safe Drinking Water Act* revisions

1997—EPA implements *Food Quality Protection Act*

2000—Cleaner Diesel Fuels Plan; most Dursban uses banned

2001—EPA responds to September 11 terrorist attacks

2003—EPA issues a strategic plan for homeland security

2005—EPA awards Brownfield grants to clean up contaminated properties; EPA responds to Hurricane Katrina

2006—EPA issues new methods to determine mpg estimates on new vehicles

CHAPTER 5.

Environmental Law in the United States

INTRODUCTION

In the United States, environmental laws vary from state to state, and sometimes even within states. California, for example, has stricter air pollution standards than all other states (see "California Environmental Law" and "Suing California" highlights). While environmental laws vary across states, the legal minimums for environmental protection standards that each state must met are often defined by federal laws and regulations. Because most environmental laws work this way—the federal government's laws and regulations set the minimal requirements for standards of protection—this chapter provides an overview of relevant federal environmental regulations. As noted, the departures from this tendency involve states or even local governments that pass more restrictive environmental regulations.

Before beginning, it should be kept in mind that environmental laws are complex and that much of this complexity has to do with the scientific aspects of identifying toxic harms and damaging levels of pollution, and the process involved in translating scientific knowledge into legally binding rules. Environmental laws must not only specify the violation, but the specific exposure standard or concentration for each regulated pollutant, and, when applicable, the appropriate testing requirements, equipment, and protocols. The exposure standard for each pollutant varies because each causes human or environmental harm at different concentration levels, or depending on the length of exposure. As a result, laws regulating pollution sometimes also include rules related to maximum exposure over an identified period of time.

It should also be noted that the construction of environmental law is complex because it involves a political process, and is not simply an effort to codify scientific knowledge (e.g., Lazarus, 2006). Indeed, proposed environmental regulations are often the subject of intense debates between sides with opposing interests, such as the public on the one hand, who desire protection from hazardous pollutants, and corporations on the other hand, who desire few restrictions on production so that expenses remain low. In this context, chemical exposure limits become the subject of political processes and conflicts, and regulated industries often challenge threshold and exposure limits by offering counter-evidence about chemical safety that is often produced by company scientists or industry sponsored scientific research groups (e.g., the Chemical Manufacturers Association, American Chemistry Council, American Crop Protection Association, Phthalate Esters Panel, Chlorine Chemistry Council, Society of Plastics Industry, American Council on Health and Industry).

In addition, applying environmental law is complex because these laws often overlap, and more than one kind of law may come into play in a given situation, a very different circumstance when compared to ordinary crimes defined in penal law. Environmental law violations are spread across numerous jurisdictions' codes (i.e., federal, state and local) that may apply to specific kinds of pollution (e.g., solid waste, water pollution, air pollution) or to the pollution of a specific environmental medium (e.g., air, water, soil).

The construction and use of environmental laws can also become complex when specific issues are examined because of the role played by case law. Case law or the modification of law as it is applied occurs as courts interpret the law and even the meaning of specific words within laws and regulations. Because this chapter provides an overview of federal regulations, little emphasis is placed on case law.

Furthermore, environmental laws are relatively new compared to other legal forms. Many key environmental laws are less than two decades old, and the fine points of these laws have not been completely resolved in the courts. Challenges to these laws emerge on a routine basis, and environmental law is in a constant state of flux. Because these laws are constantly evolving, current laws may supersede the discussions that follow.

Discussion Box 5.1. California Environmental Law

California has passed and proposed an extraordinary number of laws designed to protect the environment. These laws are important because they exceed the environmental protection standards established by federal law. Several examples are found below.

AB 32, The Nunez-Amendment or the California Global Warming Solutions Act of 2006. Faced with President Bush's refusal to sign the Kyoto Protocol, an international treaty designed to reduce the emission of global warming gases, California representatives introduced a bill to meet the general intentions of the protocol. The Bill has passed the Legislature and is awaiting the signature of Governor Schwarzenegger to become law.

AB 1493, the "Pavley Law." In July of 2002, California became the first state to regulate the emission of global warming gases by passenger vehicles and light trucks. This significant piece of legislation, which takes effect in 2009, requires a 30 percent reduction in vehicle greenhouse gas emissions by 2016.

.

California Vehicle Emission Control Act. In 1963, California legislators passed this act to regulate vehicle emissions beginning in 1966. In doing so, California became the first government in the U.S. to regulate vehicle emissions and to set emission limits. The California Highway Patrol used random roadside testing to enforce the regulation. At the national level, similar federal regulations became effective in 1968.

Zero emission vehicles (ZEV). In 1990, California became the first state to regulate the composition of the market of vehicles sold within the state by requiring automakers to ensure that 2 percent of automobiles sold by 1998 were zero emission vehicles, and that this figure increased to 10 percent by 2003. By 1994, 12 other states had adopted California's model ZEV legislation

THE EMERGENCE OF CONTEMPORARY ENVIRONMENTAL LAW: A BRIEF HISTORY AND CONTEXT

Prior to the implementation of federal environmental laws and the creation of the U.S. EPA in 1970, few laws defined or dealt with environmental crimes. Many activities now regulated by environmental law previously fell under the purview of common law, which meant that each assertion of an environmental harm had to be litigated and regulated on a case-by-case basis. What led to the emergence of environmental law?

With few exceptions, there was little concern with environmental pollution and damage to ecosystems as these related to human and environmental health or species extinction before the 1960s. As noted, before this time, environmental hazards were addressed through common laws related to the creation of nuisance, and were resolved on a case by case basis. Such a system was inefficient, and did not provide a systematic set of regulations that could limit environmental pollution and improve environmental quality.

Before the 1970s, there were relatively few federal or state environmental laws even though some of the major environmental problems of the contemporary world had been identified by the late 1800s. For example, during the 1860s, French scientist Augustine Mouchot linked the use of coal to high levels of pollution found in industrialized cities. In response he created the first solar energy converter in 1874. In 1894, Swedish scientist Svante Arrhenius was the first to study the impacts of increased atmospheric carbon dioxide on the climate (i.e., today called global warming). Despite increased scientific knowledge of how human activities harmed the environment and evidence of these effects related to air pollution in industrial cities around the world, little effort was made to protect the environment. Moreover, until the latter half of the 1900s, efforts to protect the environment, while laudable, were sporadic and not part of a larger environmental plan.

Discussion Box 5.2. Suing California

After passing legislation limiting the emission of global warming gases by motor vehicles, California was sued by the Alliance of Automobile Manufacturers (AAM) and thirteen new car dealerships in December 2004. AAM represents the interests of nine major automobile manufacturers (BMW, DaimlerChrysler, Ford Motor Company, General Motors, Mazda, Mitsubishi Motors, Porsche, Toyota and Volkswagen). In objecting to the California law, AAM argued that California did not have the right to regulate fuel economy standards, that the law violated free market principles by increasing vehicle costs and restricting consumer choices, and that because global warming is not a localized phenomenon, Californians would not receive any direct benefit from the legislation. In February of 2005, the Association of International Automakers (AIA), a trade association representing Aston Martin, Ferrari, Honda, Hyundai, Isuzu, Kia, Maserati, Mitsubishi, Nissan, Peugeot, Renault, Subaru, Suzuki and Toyota, joined the suit, which was scheduled for hearing in January, 2007.

In part, the suit results from a 2003 U.S. EPA ruling that it did not have the authority to regulate carbon dioxide or other global warming gases, and as a result could not transfer this right to California. The EPA was sued unsuccessfully over this ruling by thirteen states. More recently, Massachusetts, California, 10 other states, and several major environmental groups filed a new suit against the U.S. EPA claiming that both the EPA and California have the right to regulate greenhouse gases. In a close 5-4 vote, that suit was decided in favor of the petitioners and against the EPA by the U.S. Supreme Court (Massachusetts vs. EPA, 05-1120; April, 2007), which ruled that the *Clean Air Act* gives the EPA the authority to regulate emissions of carbon dioxide and other greenhouse gases.

In September, 2007, the State of California sued the six major automakers, claiming that by failing to produce efficient vehicles and ignoring global warming, the automobile industry has cost the State of California billions of dollars. These losses relate to reduced snow pack and water supply issues, beach erosion, ozone pollution, deterioration of farming conditions, and impacts on endangered animals and fish. The AAM issued a statement claiming that the suit was frivolous and was nothing more than an attempt by California's Attorney General to advance his political career. Yet California is particularly concerned about greenhouse gases since it is the largest producer of such gases in the U.S., and localized effects, including environmental damage and continual smog conditions in some California cities, have particularly disadvantageous effects for California, as demonstrated by a report produced by the California Climate Change Center and the Union of Concerned Scientists ("Our Changing Climate: Assessing the Risks to California," http://www.ucsusa.org/clean_california/our-changing-climate.html).

For example, the first federal effort to preserve wilderness occurred in 1864 when President Lincoln deeded Yosemite Valley to the State of California as a public trust. Several years later (1872), President Grant created the first national park at Yellowstone when he set aside more than 2.2 million acres for preservation. Grant's inconsistent environmental position, however, led him to veto a national buffalo protection act in 1875, and the buffalo nearly became extinct. In 1891, Congress expanded the federal government's rights to preserve the environment when it passed the *Forest Reserve Act*. During the interim period, the federal government created the *U.S. Fish Commission* (1871) to study the decline in coastal fish populations; Iowa passed the first hunting "bag limit" law to protect game birds in 1878; in 1879, the federal government established the *Division of Forestry* (later renamed the *U.S. Forest Service*); Chicago became the first city to regulate smoke discharges in 1881; and in 1885, the *U.S. Biological Service* was created to help protect wildlife after the buffalo and passenger pigeon neared extinction. Each of these acts, however, addressed a limited environmental issue affecting a specific species or a very limited environmental problem or region (e.g., pollution in or the preservation of a specific place).

This piecemeal approach to environmental protection began to change in 1899, when the U.S. Congress passed the *Rivers and Harbors Act*, the first national environmental legislation, which made it illegal to dispose of pollution without a permit (in this case, to dump waste into waterways without a permit issued by the Army Corps of Engineers). Over the next fifty years, with the exception of the establishment of Federal parks by Theodore Roosevelt and their extension under Franklin D. Roosevelt, few important federal environmental laws were created.

During the 1950s and 1960s, as the damage associated with environmental pollution became more protracted and visible, the push to protect the environment was accelerated and expanded. The visible signs of extensive environmental damage were reported in newspapers across the nation. For many, the conspicuous evidence of environmental pollution was gathered first-hand. Smog, a problem in California since the 1940s, became more noticeable in other American cities. The health threat posed by smog became all too real in 1948 when a smog bank enclosed the small steel town of Donora, Pennsylvania, and caused 20 deaths and several thousand illnesses (Davis, 2003). Waterways across America became increasingly polluted, and some rivers, such as the Cuyahoga River in Ohio, caught fire several times between 1950 and 1969. Large fish kills also became noticeable as pollution in American waterways continued to rise. By the late 1960s, water pollution in Lake Erie was so extensive that environmentalists declared the lake dead (Kormondy, 1970). Other major events such as the Love Canal disaster, where a community in Niagara Falls, New York was found to be so polluted as to be uninhabitable, added to growing public concern about environmental pollution (Brown, 1982).

Public concern with pollution and environmental damage was also stimulated by the publication of the most important environmental book of that era, Rachel Carson's *Silent Spring* (1962). Carson was the first to link chemical hazards and especially the use of pesticides to threats to the health of wildlife. The book, which was excerpted in the *New York Times*, created a national controversy concerning the safety of synthetic chemicals such as pesticides.

THE MOVE TO REGULATE POLLUTION: THE LIMITS OF THE FREE MARKET

By the mid-1950s, it became increasingly clear that there was a need to create legislation to protect the public and environment from the extensive levels of pollution produced and dumped into the ecosystem by manufacturers. This realization was a blow to free market economic theories which had held that a free, competitive marketplace served the best interest of the public. In this view, competition between producers, the choices made by informed consumers, and rising prices caused by scarcity, should have provided a "natural" economic barrier that would protect the environment from extensive damage. The history of environmental damage from the late 1800s through the 1960s *proved that this theory was inaccurate;* across America air and waterways had become so polluted that they could no longer sustain life, and posed a threat to both animal and human populations; animal populations were destroyed and driven to near extinction by industries that turned animal parts into commodities; and natural resources became more and more scarce as the American culture of consumption was pushed to new heights.

Why didn't the free market protect the environment? Findley and Farber (2000, pp. 81-84) argued that free markets fail to protect the environment because corporations are able to minimize the internal costs (i.e., costs to self) of polluting by maximizing their external costs, that is by shifting the costs of pollution onto others such as consumers or taxpayers. In economist James O'Connor's (1973) view, externalization expanded rapidly in the 1960s, as corporations learned to increasingly socialize the costs of doing business, and the U.S. government facilitated this tendency. External costs include, for example, the costs of cleaning up the environment, which will tend to be shared by the government and taxpayers. Based on this observation, Findley and Farber (2000, p. 83) conclude that "because the free market provides inadequate incentives [to reduce polluting behavior], the government must intervene to limit external costs and facilitate production of external benefits and collective goods." But, how?

Theoretically, the answer is easy. Because corporate behavior is economically motivated, penalties (including fines or prison sentences) applied to polluting behaviors increase internal costs and lower the incentive to pollute. Typically, environmental laws internalize environmental impacts through penalties and fees; taxes and subsidies; and flexible market incentives (Ferrey, 1997, pp. 8–11; Findlay and Farber, 2000, pp. 83–84).

Penalties and Fees

Penalties and fees require polluters to pay at least some (but usually not all) of the costs associated with polluting activities, and internalizes some of the costs of polluting by producing losses for businesses. If, for instance, a corporation must pay a $1 penalty or fee for each pound of pollution it released into the environment, and the corporation produces a millions pounds of pollution a year, then it will incur an additional $1 million expense. It does not really matter to the corporation whether this economic loss is a penalty (e.g., a fine for an activity) or a fee (e.g., the cost of disposing of waste into a river). What matters is that the government's response causes the corporation to log a loss against its profits. In response, the corporation should seek methods to minimize the government's imposed costs for polluting, which may lead to innovations in commodity production methods or the invention of pollution control devices. By limiting the free market, the government not only produces conditions that will limit environmental pollution, it also stimulates the development of new industries that expand economic growth and employment in these new industries.

Penalties and fees appear to make logical sense as mechanisms for controlling polluting behavior. Nevertheless, these methods of control have less effect than intended for three reasons. First, penalties and fees tend to be small relative to profits or alternative pollution disposal methods and, consequently, have not become an effective means for internalizing pollution costs. These penalties and fees, for instance, rarely approach the $1 million mark used in the earlier example. Moreover, corporations often use their economic power to lobby rule-makers to keep penalties and fees to a minimum.

Second, environmental regulations are not often enforced stringently, or are often enforced irregularly, resulting in a low apprehension rate or probability of detection. Because they are unlikely to get caught, corporate executives can assume that the penalty or fee is unlikely to impact their business's profits.

Third, corporations have the ability to shift penalties and fees onto consumers, who end up paying the corporation's pollution liabilities. Because the fines are small and spread across a large number of consumers, they have little impact on consumer choices or the price of the commodity the offending corporation offers for sale. Furthermore, when the price of a commodity rises, consumers are not told that the increased product cost resulted from an environmental penalty. If they were, consumers might use this information as if the market were really free and competitive, and alter their buying behaviors to purchase commodities from more environmentally friendly producers.

Taxes and Subsidies

Taxes and subsidies are used to internalize pollution costs and to reward efforts at pollution reduction (Ferrey, 1997, p. 8). Taxes internalize pollution costs by assessing fees for polluting. One of the limitations of this approach is that its use has been restricted to pollutants that exceed a specified threshold or amount. These "threshold taxes" allow manufactures to produce a certain level of pollution without incurring a penalty; consequently, the tax only deters excessive levels of pollution and only if the tax is sufficiently large. If pollution taxes are large enough, these might also encourage pollution generators to seek alternative means of production that reduce pollution outputs. But it can be argued that high pollution taxes might also encourage corporations to employ illegal means to dispose of pollutants, or to hide the amount of pollution they produce. To address these problems, additional enforcement mechanisms become necessary to punish violators.

Subsidies can also be employed to reduce pollution by, for example, providing payments for the installation of pollution control devices. Government subsidies come in a variety of forms, including grants to cover the costs of installing pollution control devices, tax breaks that provide rebates for costs, and low- to no-interest loans.

When applied, taxes appear to be similar to penalties, while subsidies serve the same function as rewards for pollution reduction. One argument favoring taxes and subsidies over penalties is that they can be more easily adjusted and controlled (Ferrey, 1997). Like penalties, however, tax and subsidy systems also have limitations. The primary problems are establishing an effective external control or monitoring mechanism, and translating pollution related harms into monetary costs or determining the level at which a tax or subsidy will accomplish its stated goal (Ferrey, 1997, p. 9). How large does a tax (or subsidy) need to become before polluters change their behaviors? This often requires trial and error. But, similar problems are encountered when deciding other types of penalties. How long, for example, does a prison term need to be before it deters criminal offenders? Given these difficulties, the EPA also uses a program of flexible market incentives.

Flexible Market Incentives

Flexible market incentives (FMIs) are similar to a credit and debit system. Corporations can earn pollution credits by generating less pollution than environmental regulations specify. They can also accumulate pollution debits when they exceed their pollution limit. The corporation must pay off pollution debits with either cash or pollution credits, which may be earned or purchased.

FMIs are typically constructed on a regional basis and reflect local pollution problems that vary from one region to the next. Thus, in contrast to some EPA rules which are standardized for the nation, FMI rules contain flexible standards and criteria that depend on the location of pollution emitters and levels of pollution in the region in which a manufacturer is located. In this type of *flexible market scheme*, the EPA may, for example, determine that a given pollutant is a problem in one specific area of the country because of the threat it presents to public health there, while the same pollutant does not need to be so strictly regulated in other areas of the country.

One FMI approach is the *general market trading allowance* (GMTA). GMTAs establishes a pollution reduction target within a region, determines the current level of the targeted pollutant, the estimated health consequences and environmental damage associated with the current level of pollution, and the benefits that would accrue from reducing pollution. After EPA determines the new target level for a pollutant, the total allowable pollution level is divided among all the individual manufacturers who emit that pollutant within a region. Each pollution emitter then receives a pollution allowance. Using this procedure, the EPA determines how much pollution is permitted by assessing the effects on public health, and who can emit the pollutant and at what level.

The EPA employs free market principles by allowing each individual company to determine how it uses its pollution allowance. Some companies may decide to close a plant or limit production to stay within their assigned pollution limit. Other companies may terminate all manufacturing that produces the pollutant, in which case they will have an excess of pollution credits. Still other companies may install new manufacturing equipment or pollution control devices that reduce the level of pollutants emitted. Companies that choose one of these alternatives will have an excess of pollution credits. The EPA allows companies with excess pollution credits to sell them to companies that are expanding and producing an elevated level of the regulated pollutant, or to accumulate these credits for future use.

The problem is that this type of FMI does not necessarily reduce the overall emission of a pollutant within a region *unless* EPA significantly lowers the pollutant target, and the target continues to be reduced over time, requiring industries to adapt to the new limits. In theory, the general market trading allowance does, however, establish incentives for some companies to reduce their pollution outputs because they can profit by selling their pollution credits.

The FMI approach outlined above cannot work, however, unless there are also penalties for failing to stay within assigned pollution limits. When a company exceeds its assigned pollution limit, it begins to accrue pollution debits. The EPA translates pollution debits into fines, and the company must pay these fines either in cash or with pollution credits it purchases from other manufacturers.

Pollution Offset Requirements

Pollution offset requirements are an alternative FMI procedure that restricts the trading of pollution credits to within a company and within a region. For instance, a fictitious company, Growth Development, wants to add a new factory that will increase its output of a pollutant regulated under an offset requirement. To do so, Growth Development must offset the additional pollution it will create by eliminating pollution at one of its other facilities. This can be accomplished in a number of different ways. Growth Development could close an older plant that produces higher levels of the pollutants because it is equipped with outdated manufacturing technology. Or it might offset the expanded level of pollution by reducing the output of that pollutant at all or some portion of its other facilities; or, in some cases, the company may be able to offset the pollution increase by lowering the production of a comparable regulated pollutant (what the EPA defines as a "pollution equivalent"). Offset requirements are more stringent than GMTA because they force pollution producers to reduce emissions without recourse to pollution credits that may be available in the broader regional marketplace.

FMIs, like subsidies, provide *incentives* for complying with the law or for exceeding pollution reduction limits. The incentive structures used to control pollution levels are a unique type of social control response that differ dramatically form the criminal law penalties criminologists tend to study. The criminal law, for example, does not provide incentives to conforming individuals; does not establish a target level for an acceptable number of burglaries; nor does it allow offenders to sell unused "crime credits" to other offenders. Thus, it should be clear that corporations that violate rules and regulations are not treated in the same ways as ordinary criminals. What is similar across these two groups of violators (criminal law and environmental law violators) is the idea that law uses several different mechanisms to obtain compliance with the law. Both approaches tend to use mechanisms that are designed to deter offenders from engaging in socially disapproved behaviors.

DETERRENCE AND COMPLIANCE

Deterrence and compliance are the primary social control mechanisms employed to reduce pollution levels. To some degree, compliance and deterrence are opposing means for carrying out the intentions of environmental law. Compliance, for example, is often achieved by offering incentives or rewards for fulfilling obligations stated in law (e.g., subsidies and FMI structures), while penalties for violations of rules, such as fines, taxes, or imprisonment are used to achieve deterrence.

Compliance and deterrence mechanisms are related to the theory of utilitarian calculus set forth by philosopher Jeremy Bentham, which is based on the idea that rational actors will modify their behaviors based on the costs and rewards associated with the various choices they can make. In theory, then, society can manipulate the behavior of actors by altering the costs and rewards derived from different behavioral choices. A similar idea informed the work of an economist and Enlightenment philosopher who emphasized the idea of "rational man" economics. Adam Smith's (1776) *The Wealth of Nations*, which blends free market and rational man models, is an excellent example of this view. Smith argued that external regulations were unnecessary in free market capitalism because the choices made by competing individual decision-makers who based their behaviors on rational self-interest would produce long term market stability and the greatest good. For more than two centuries, this view dominated the way U.S. economic markets were understood, which explains why there were, until recently, few environmental laws or external market regulations.

Let us take a moment to reconsider Smith's theory and free market theories more generally in light of the history of environmental destruction evident in the U.S. since the mid-1800s. Throughout this period, the U.S. environment was continually threatened; waterways and airways were polluted; toxic pollutants were dumped into landfills to create hazardous waste sites that threaten human health; numerous species have gone extinct or were driven to the brink of extinction; forests were depleted; coal was mined in environmentally destructive but economically efficient ways; and other natural resources, such as the U.S. oil reserve, were rapidly depleted. Each of these outcomes illustrates the flaws of free market economics; in none of these cases does a free market protect the environment. Indeed, it was the failure of the free market to protect the environment and human health that led to external market controls such as environmental law.

Deterrence

Like the free market, deterrence has also not worked well as a mechanism for protecting the environment. Deterrence is based on the idea that human behavior can be steered by raising the costs of specific behavioral choices we don't want people to make. This is typically done by attaching a penalty to specific behavioral choices. Based on these assumptions, Bentham argued that criminals could be deterred from committing socially harmful acts by increasing the costs of acts until they outweighed the act's rewards.

Similar arguments have been made with respect to polluting behavior: by attaching penalties to polluting activities, polluters could be deterred. The problem with this approach is determining the appropriate magnitude of the penalty. Because environmental crimes such as pollution are very cost-effective for corporations (remember, pollution externalizes costs), the penalties must be extraordinarily high to deter polluters. Historically, penalties for pollution and other environmental crimes have not been extraordinarily high, and it could be easily argued that they have been extraordinarily low.

Nevertheless, deterrence has the potential to be a useful mechanism for controlling corporate behavior, given that corporations are rational actors that calculate the costs and rewards of their behaviors. Indeed, these kinds of calculations are an integral part of planning in a capitalist economy. For this reason, the EPA endorses deterrence as a major mechanism for controlling polluting behavior. In practice, however, deterrence often fails to accomplish the mission of significant pollution reductions, perhaps because of the insignificant relationship of penalty size to the benefit of the behavior for polluters. Consequentially, the EPA also relies on compliance strategies without having to resort to the use of punishment or coercive means of social control.

Compliance Strategies

Compliance strategies involve procedures to obtain the cooperation of corporate actors. In terms of environmental law, this idea has been implemented by offering corporations the opportunity to become involved in a variety of voluntary compliance programs, including self auditing, where each business monitors its own polluting behavior and reports its violations to the EPA. Companies that do so are offered the opportunity to correct the infractions without penalty, or to receive a reduced penalty. There are other benefits that come along with self-policing as well, such as fewer EPA inspections in the future (Stretesky, 2006). In short, under voluntary compliance programs that focus on self-auditing and self-policing, penalties are suspended to gain the cooperation of businesses and to reduce violations and levels of pollution. Evidence suggests that this strategy has not been effective (Stretesky, 2006; Stretesky and Lynch, 2006).

Blended Strategies

Some environmental strategies blend several of the ideas described above. For example, in 1990, the federal *Clean Air Act* was amended to include the National Ambient Air Quality Standards (NAAQS). The NAAQS forced states to become more active in ensuring that levels of air pollution and air quality were brought within limits delineated within the *Clean Air Act*. States could meet CAA provisions using numerous alternatives as long as their plans were approved by the EPA, and targeted geographic areas that were currently in noncompliance with NAAQS standards for specific pollutants. If the state failed to submit a workable plan, or if the plan failed to achieve compliance by a specified date, then the state could be penalized by, for example, a reduction in federal funding, or by the imposition of offset requirements.

In order to determine whether a state's plan impacted air pollution levels, the EPA needs to monitor air quality. The EPA could directly monitor air quality with scientific equipment. While the EPA does have air monitoring stations across the U.S., these stations cannot determine the source of the pollutants. Consequently, to obtain a useful estimate of pollution levels for an individual manufacturer, the EPA requires pollution producers to monitor their emissions, and to submit pollution emission reports to the EPA. The EPA then sums up the pollution reports of all facilities within a noncontainment area (an area that has elevated levels of pollution and does not meet the standards defined in the CAA or NAAQS) to determine whether there has been a reduction in pollution emissions. If an area within a state (or larger region) continues to remain in noncompliance by a specified deadline, then a remediation program identified by the EPA can be imposed.

The EPA can also access law enforcement tools with broader powers and scope when violations become serious and persistent. Such tools are available, for example, when pollution violations fall under the purview of the *Comprehensive Environmental Response Compensation Liability Act* (CERCLA, also known as the Superfund Act), which deals with hazardous waste sites.

CERCLA enforcement tools: An example of compliance strategies

CERCLA (42 USC Chapter 103) or the *Superfund Act*, provides the EPA with broad enforcement powers that "force" the cleanup (usually referred to as remediation) of hazardous waste sites to protect public health. For instance, if a hazardous waste site presents an "imminent hazard," the EPA is authorized to take any steps necessary to protect public and environmental health, including civil injunctions and unilateral administrative orders. Civil injunctions require court action, while unilateral administrative orders may be pursued directly by the EPA without court intervention. An offender must satisfy a unilateral administrative order by a specified date under threat of penalty ($25,000 per day for each day in noncompliance), unless (1) the order is reviewable as stated in EPA regulations (Ferrey, 1997, p. 320), or (2) a noncompliance defense can be offered. Noncompliance may also result in the imposition of additional penalties including remediation costs, punitive damages, and noncompliance fines.

CERCLA also allows the EPA to employ civil procedures to sue defendants for (1) cleanup or other remediation expenses; and/or (2) to obtain restitution for damages and injuries. In most cases, however, the EPA will first attempt to gain the *voluntary compliance* of offenders through *informal negotiations and settlements*. In these proceedings, the EPA may threaten to use the civil or administrative procedures described above in an effort to "persuade" offenders to comply with a hazardous waste site cleanup request.

To this point, we have examined the theories behind environmental law and the types of responses and remedies environmental law offers. Below we review the contents of several major federal environmental laws.

MAJOR FEDERAL LEGISLATION

The sections that follow summarize major federal legislation employed by the EPA to regulate environmental pollution. Since it is beyond the scope of this book to analyze environmental law in detail, this chapter summarizes the most important environmental laws, and offers guidance to further investigation of these regulations. We restrict our discussion to the following: the *Clean Air Act*;

the *Clean Water Act*; the *Comprehensive Environmental Response Compensation and Liability Act*; and the *Resource Conservation and Recovery Act*. More extensive details may be found by consulting these laws directly (see also Ferrey, 1997; Findlay and Farber, 2000; O'Grady, 2006; and the U.S. Code uscode.house.gov/search/criteria.shtml;www.gpoaccess.gov/uscode/index html).

The Clean Air Act (CAA. 1963. Amended 1970, 1977, 1990; 42 USC Chapter 85)

Before passage of this Act in 1963, there were no national clean air standards. The *Clean Air Act* was designed to reduce air pollution levels by establishing national, uniform standards for ambient (outdoor) air quality. One of the main tools for accomplishing these tasks is technology-based standards for pollution emissions.

Statutes related to the *Clean Air Act* include:

- *National Ambient Air Quality Standards*
  (NAAQS, 1977, Amended 1990; 40 C.F.R. pt. 50). NAAQS gave the EPA authority to promulgate national air quality standards for seven "criteria" air pollutants: (1) sulfur dioxide (SO_2; contributes to acid rain), (2) lead (Pb; associated with brain dysfunctions and other central nervous system and behavioral disruptions), (3) carbon monoxide (CO; a constituent of smog), (4) nitrogen oxides (NO(x); associated with smog and global warming), (5) ozone (O_3; related to the formation of smog), (6) particle matter -10 (PM-10, or particles less than 10 microns in size), and (7) particle matter -2.5 (PM-2.5, particle matter less than 2.5 microns; respiratory irritation and illness). To reflect regional needs, criteria air pollutants standards may vary by air quality control regions (AQCRs). There are currently 250 different AQCRs in the United States. NAAQS regulates existing sources of air pollution using "reasonably available control technology" (RACT; *Clean Air Act* § 172), which is the lowest level of pollution emission attainable through the application of reasonable and cost effective technology.

- *New Source Performance Standards*
  (NSPS; *Clean Air Act* § 111). NSPS regulates *new* sources of air pollution (new facilities and points of pollution emissions), which are evaluated using the more stringent pollution standards called "best available control technology" (BACT) criteria. BACT rules require balancing the use of best available control technology against the cost of instituting new technologies and controls. In effect, if instituting a BACT standard would cause adverse economic impact, then the EPA can suspend the BACT requirement for a facility. BACT criteria apply uniformly across states, meaning that individual states cannot reduce the air pollution control standard below BACT. This prevents individual states form lowering air pollution criteria in an effort to

attract new businesses that do not employ BACT. NSPS issues are also addressed under two additional regulations: Prevention of Significant Deterioration and New Source Review.

- ***Prevention of Significant Deterioration***
  (PSD; CAA § 112). PSD requirements apply to areas that have already met NSPS air pollution standards (NSPS attainment areas) and are designed to prevent a decline in air quality in areas that have already obtained clean air status. Areas achieving clean air status are ranked (Class I, II, and III), with Class I areas facing the most severe restrictions on new sources of pollution. Once clean air status has been achieved, major new or modified stationary sources of pollution are required to apply for a permit from the EPA. Permit outcomes depend on the applicant's impact on air quality in the attainment area and the attainment area's class rating.

- ***New Source Review***
  (NSR; CAA § 111). NSR rules apply to NSPS noncontainment areas *(areas that have not achieved clean air status)*. Proposed major new or modified stationary sources of air pollution in those areas must apply for a preconstruction permit from EPA (CAA § 111(a)(4)) and met the following requirements: (1) the proposed site's new pollutants are offset by the closing of existing facilities; (2) the State has an approved State Implementation Plan (SIP) ; or (3) the site employs Lowest Achievable Control Technology (LACT) to minimize pollution emissions.

- ***National Emission Standards for Hazardous Air Pollution***
  (NESHAP; CAA Title III, 1990). NESHAP was created to control the emission of toxic air pollutants that may cause death, illness, or are carcinogenic (cancer causing) or mutagenic (cause genetic mutations). Under NESHAP, the EPA was directed to create rules protecting air quality and health that generate an "ample margin of safety" from exposure to toxic outdoor air pollutants that produce these outcomes.

- ***New Federal Motor Vehicle Emission Limitations***
  (NFMVEL; Title II, CAA, 1970, Amended 1990). NFMVEL allows the EPA to regulate three forms of motor vehicle tailpipe emissions on new vehicles: (1) hydrocarbons (HC), (2) carbon monoxide (CO), and (3) nitrogen oxides. NFMVEL also allows the EPA to establish deadlines for automakers to comply with regulations related to these emissions. Fines of up to $10,000 per noncomplying vehicle sold may be levied on a new vehicle manufacturer. Additional compliance mechanisms include emission control regulations, the vehicle fleet program, and CAFE (corporate average fuel economy).

- *Acid Rain Precursors and Ozone Protection Statutes*
  (Title VI, CAA, 1990). This legislation targets source emissions of pollutants (see NAAQS standards) specifically linked to acid rain especially at coal and oil powered electric generation stations. Title VI employs emission reduction standards and includes an allowance trading provision similar to those described earlier under flexible market incentives. The ozone protection provisions specifically address the release and phase out of hydrochlorofluorocarbons (HCFCs) and chlorofluorocarbons (CFCs).

- *State Implementation Plan*
  (SIP). To achieve air pollution reductions defined by NAAQS, each state must submit a SIP to the EPA that details how it will enforce NAAQS rules and meet air pollution attainment goals. Each state is required to provide scientific models of air pollution outputs for each AQCR within its boundaries, and specify plans for monitoring and maintaining air quality in each AQCR.

The *Federal Water Pollution Control Act* (FWPCA, 1972) and the *Clean Water Act* (CWA, 1977; 33 USC §§ 1251-1387)

Originally passed as the Federal Water Pollution Control Act, the *Clean Water Act* (CWA) sought to prevent pollution discharges into waterways over which the federal government has constitutional authority (i.e., navigable waterways) by the year 1985. In addition, the CWA was designed to establish fishable and swimmable waterways that protected marine animals and wildlife by 1983. This Act also specifies states' duties in achieving these goals (§ 101(b)). The CWA employs a permit system and the designation of water quality standards to achieve these goals. Facilities discharging pollution to waterways must obtain a permit from the EPA. The FWPCA specifically sets limits for point source water pollutants that include Publicly Owned Treatment Work (POTW, i.e., municipal sewage treatment plants) and industrial sources of water pollution (§ 301). Three point source pollutant categories are regulated: (1) toxic (§ 307), (2) conventional (§ 304), and (3) nontoxic, nonconventional.
Statutes related to these acts include:

- *National Pollutant Discharge Elimination System*
  (NPDES; Title VI FWPCA). The NPDES regulates the amount and concentration of pollutants discharged to waterways, and allows certified dischargers to obtain a permit to discharge pollutants to waterways. Dischargers must monitor and report waterway discharges to federal and state authorities (40 C.F.R. § 122.41(j) and l(4)). Federal or state governments may amend NPDES permits to meet the standards of the FWPCA or CWA (40 C.F.R. §§ 122.41 (b) and 122.62(a)). This regulation also requires that states submit a State Implementation Plan (SIP) to meet clean water standards.

- ***Effluent Guidelines and Standards***
  (FWPCA; § 307(a)). Requires the EPA to establish a list of, and set limits for toxic pollutants discharged to waterways.

- ***Best Practicable Control Technology***
  (BPT; 33 U.S.C. § 1311(b)(1)). BPT defines the minimum pollution control standard for a given class of industrial pollutants. These controls must be cost effective and attainable under normal conditions. Individual dischargers that fail to meet BPT standards must cease operation.

- ***Best Conventional Pollution Control Technology***
  (BCT; 33 U.S.C. § 1314(a) (4) (1996)). More stringent than BPT, BCT sets standards for conventional pollutants balancing costs of control against benefits derived from a control measure.

- ***Best Available Control Technology Economically Practical***
  (BAT; 33 U.S.C. § 1317 (a) (2)). The most stringent water pollution control standards, BATs are set for a class of point source dischargers of toxic and nonconventional pollutants, and constitute the performance of best-performing facilities. BATs must consist of already available technology, and must also be feasible. BATs for toxins are health based, however, and do not require cost-benefit considerations (Ferrey, 1997, pp. 206–207).

- ***Pollution Permit and State Control of Permitting Processes***
  (402 CWA). Under § 402, the EPA is authorized to issue permits to individual polluters for point source emissions, and to authorize state plans for water permitting rules, regulations, and enforcement procedures. Any state wishing to control the CWA-permitting process must apply to the EPA and obtain authorization for its plan. Individual point source emission permits must meet BPT, BCT, and BAT requirements. Rules for point source emissions are established on an industry wide basis, though individual variances are allowable.

- ***New Pollution Sources—New Source Performance Standards (NSPS)***
  (NSPS; 306 CWA). NSPS rules apply to new plants or significantly modified facilities that are major sources of pollution and which came on line after implementation of the 1977 *Clean Water Act*. NSPS facilities must meet more stringent pollution control requirements than existing pollution sources, and are held to BAT standards unless the facility applies for and is granted a waiver on the grounds that implementing BAT would be economically or energy inefficient. The EPA may modify NSPS restrictions when water quality measures indicate a decline in water quality (§ 303 CWA).

- *Non-point Sources*
  (§ 319 CWA, 1987). Section 319 of the CWA targets non-point source pollution (e.g., storm water run-off) in waterways that have failed to meet water quality standards. Under 319, states with waterways that fail to meet specified water quality standards must submit a non-point source pollution control implementation plan to the EPA for approval.

- *Water Quality Standards*
  (§§ 302, 303, and 304 CWA). WQS apply to individual bodies of water that fail to comply with the water quality standards set forth in § 301 of the *Clean Water Act* according to the designated primary use of the body of water (§ 304 CWA). Under this circumstance, the EPA is required to place further limits on effluent discharges, NPDES permits, and water pretreatment programs and facilities discharging into the non-complying water body to protect the minimal conditions for the existing designated body of water's use. Under the WQS, the EPA may also override a state's body of water designation (§ 302 CWA). To maintain water quality, § 303 of the CWA established "total maximum daily loads" (TMDL) levels for both point source and non-point source pollutants, which can be met by altering permitted discharges from individual facilities. A state may not escape water quality standards under these sections of the CWA by altering the body of water use designation (§ 302 CWA). Cost is not a consideration when meeting WQS standards.

- *Publicly Owned Water Treatment Facilities*
  (POWTs; Title IV, 33 U.S.C. §§ 1381–1387 and 406 CWA). In an attempt to reduce waterway pollution, this section of the CWA established a loan program to facilitate building POWTs. Individual dischargers can avoid obtaining a NPDES permit if they discharge effluents to a POWT. To employ this option, however, the discharger must meet pretreatment requirements.

- *Fundamentally Different Factor*
  (FDF; 33 U.S.C., § 1311). An individual facility within an industry may petition the EPA for an exception to industry-specific pollution emission standards if it can demonstrate that it is fundamentally different from other facilities in its industry class.

- *The Safe Drinking Water Act*
  (SDWA; 42 U.S.C., §§ 300f–300j). The SDWA supplements the CWA in an effort to improve drinking water quality by creating health-based standards for public drinking water systems. A public drinking water system is a source that either supplies water for 25 people, or has 15 connections that operate on a regular basis. Water supplies must employ BAT. State water supply regulations may exceed the

requirements of the SDWA. States are responsible for monitoring drinking water quality and ensuring that it meets the standards specified under the SDWA.

- *Ocean Dumping Act*
  (ODA). The ODA was designed to ensure that the standards imposed in the CWA did not lead to ocean dumping of effluent pollutants, and allows the EPA to monitor and control ocean dumping through the use of a permit system.

The Superfund Act or the *Comprehensive Environmental Response, Compensation and Liability Act* (CERCLA 42 USC 103), and the *Superfund Reauthorization Act of 1986* (SARA)

CERCLA directs the EPA to determine who is responsible for creating a hazardous waste site to facilitate its cleanup or remediation. CERCLA established an information-gathering network, liability provisions, the Superfund trust account that pays for a portion of site remediation, and federal authority to respond to and cleanup hazardous waste sites. CERCLA's provisions apply to hazardous substance once released into the environment, and applies retroactively, that is to actions that have already occurred. CERCLA applies to all hazardous substances and chemicals listed under the *Resource Conservation and Recovery Act* (RCRA), (2) the *Clean Water Act* (CWA), (3) the *Clean Air Act* (CAA), and (4) the *Toxic Substances Control Act* (TSCA), and *specifically excludes* petroleum, nuclear waste, workplace releases, and federally permitted pesticide contamination, because each of these releases is governed by agencies other than the EPA (e.g., OSHA regulates workplace releases).

Statutes related to the *Superfund Act* include:

- *Hazardous Substance Release Notification*
  (42 U.S.C., § 9603). This CERCLA provision requires that the person in charge of a facility must immediately report a hazardous chemical release to the EPA's National Emergency Response Center, (42 U.S.C., § 9602(22)), and notify the EPA if they operate a hazardous waste treatment, storage, and disposal facility (TSDF; see 40 CFR 264-265, and RCRA § 3004).

- *Facility*
  (42 U.S.C., § 9601(9)). Under CERCLA, a facility is any site or area where a hazardous substance has been deposited, stored, placed, or disposed, excluding in-use consumer products and vessels.

- *EPA Response Formats*
  (42 U.S.C., Ch. 103, §§ 9640, 96405). CERCLA authorizes the EPA to undertake both short-term and long-term responses to known hazardous waste sites. Short-term responses include emergency responses. The EPA employs money from the Hazardous Substance Response Trust

Fund (the Superfund; 42 U.S.C., §§ 9611, 9612) to address short-term and emergency responses. Such remediation efforts are limited to $2 million. CERCLA also authorizes the President of the United States to take action in cases where there is an immediate threat to public health (42 USC § 9604(a)(4)).

CERCLA includes a mechanism for determining the seriousness of the threat posed by a hazardous waste site (the CERCLA Hazardous Ranking System, 40 CFR, §. 300, Subpart L, Appendix A). Sites that receive a high hazardous ranking score and which pose a persistent threats to public health that require long-term remediation are added to the National Priorities List (NPL) following procedures specified in the National Contingency Plan (42 U.S.C., § 9605). CERCLA allows the EPA to recover remediation costs it incurs from cleaning up hazardous waste site from potentially responsible parties (PRPs; 42 U.S.C., Ch.103, § 9607).

- **Superfund Reauthorization Act of 1986**
  (SARA; 42 U.S.C., § 9621). SARA strengthened the *Superfund Act* by enhancing state responsibilities, providing for voluntary settlements between PRPs and the government, and including additional mechanisms for replenishing the Superfund. Cleanup requirements where also strengthened to enhance public health.

- **Enforcement Tools**
  (42 U.S.C., §§ 9604, 9606, 9607). CERCLA provides the EPA with several mechanisms for rule enforcement. The least formal is the voluntary cleanup request (§ 9604), which may occur under threat of a formal sanctions (§§ 9606, 9607). EPA can respond to "imminent hazards" to public health using civil injunctions and judicially nonreviewable unilateral administrative orders (§ 9606). Fines up to $25,000/day for violations of injunctions and orders, and punitive damages to PRPs of up to three times the government's remediation costs are also incorporated into the statute.

- **Civil and Criminal Penalties**
  CERCLA rules include a variety of civil and criminal penalties that apply to violations of notifications requirements (§ 9603(a)(b)), destruction of records (§ 9603(d)(2)), financial responsibility (§ 9608), and orders and settlements (§ 9620; 9622). Individual criminal liability may be imposed (§ 9607(a)) without proximate cause or actual knowledge of the violation. Criminal penalties are pursued by the Department of Justice.

Resource Conservation and Recovery Act (RCRA), or Law Pertaining to the Management of Solid and Hazardous Wastes

RCRA created a "cradle to grave" tracking system for hazardous solid waste that allows the transportation, handling, storage, and disposal of hazardous waste to be regulated. RCRA encourages reductions in solid waste through recycling and improvement in manufacturing technology, alternatives to land disposal, safe land disposal when such disposal is required, and increased state responsibility for managing solid waste disposal. RCRA regulates hazardous solid waste defined in § 1003(27), and § 1004 (see also 40 C.F.R., § 261(D)).

Statutes related to RCRA include:

- ***Regulation of Waste Generators***
  Waste Generators are defined as any person or site that produces hazardous wastes. Record-keeping and hazardous waste labeling requirements used to promote "cradle to grave" hazardous waste tracking (RCRA § 3002), and a description of the manifest system for tracking hazardous waste (RCRA § 3003) are key features of regulating waste generators. The manifest contains information about the waste such as contents, place of origin, shipping container identifiers, dates of transfer and receipt, identification of intended handlers and final destination, and the identities of waste generators, handlers and shippers. The manifest is an official record that follows the hazardous waste from generators, to handlers and shippers, to storage and disposal.

- ***Regulation of Waste Handlers (RCRA §§ 3004, 3005, 3008)***
  RCRA established a permit system for handling of hazardous waste. Persons wishing to do business as owners/operators of a hazardous treatment, storage and disposal facility (TSDF) must receive a permit from the EPA. A TSDF must have an EPA identification number, analyze accepted wastes, inspect and monitor the facility, maintain emergency equipment, have an emergency release plan, train facility operators, and provide records of these endeavors to the EPA. Furthermore, TSDFs are required to notify the EPA of all hazardous wastes treated, shipped, stored, or disposed (§ 3010). Definitions of hazardous waste accidents, leaks, and cleanup procedures are defined under § 3004, while improper treatment, storage, and disposal is addressed by § 3008.

- ***Inspections, Sampling, and Information Gathering***
  (RCRA § 3007). Section 3007 authorizes any EPA agent to formally request information from a regulated hazardous waste facility. The EPA may not, however, require former owners or owners of inactive hazardous waste facilities to produce requested information (compliance with such a request is voluntary). Regulated facilities have

the right to requested that information collected by the EPA remain confidential. Section 3007 defines the conditions under which the EPA may sample and inspect active and inactive hazardous waste facilities *without a warrant*. When doing so, the EPA must provide a receipt for samples, make samples available to facility operators upon request, and provide sample test results. Inspections, unlike sampling, require a warrant demonstrating *probable cause*. Information gathered under 3007 may be used to compel a hazardous waste handler to engage in monitoring and testing (for terms see, RCRA § 3013). Remedies for noncompliance with an EPA request for information are addressed under RCRA § 3008.

- *Land Disposal*
RCRA bans the land disposal of hazardous waste unless an exception is granted by the EPA under RCRA § 3004(d)-(f).

- *Imminent Hazards (RCRA § 7003)*
Section 7003 allows the EPA to sue any person who has contributed or is contributing to *imminent and substantial endangerment* of the public health or environment through the unsafe disposal of hazardous waste. Case law defines the evidence needed for establishing these criteria (evidence of potential or suspected rather than actual harm evidence of exposure, or as including a minimal showing that hazardous chemicals are present at a particular location).

- *Public Participation (RCRA § 7004.*
Under this provision, any member of the public may petition EPA to amend or repeal, or provide public notice concerning any RCRA regulation. Section 7004 requires that EPA maintain guidelines for public participation in the development, implementation, and enforcement of any RCRA regulation (see also 40 CFR Part 124).

- *Underground Storage Tanks*
(RCRA, Subtitle I, §§ 9001-9010). The RCRA contains important regulations governing underground storage tanks (USTs). Subtitle I established an independent enforcement and remediation program for USTs.

- *Medical Waste (RCRA Subchapter X, § 6992)*
The RCRA medical solid waste provision, an experimental program, applies only to 10 states (New York, New Jersey, Connecticut, Illinois, Indiana, Michigan, Wisconsin, Pennsylvania, Ohio, and Minnesota), and established a separate mechanism for the tracking medical wastes.

- *Citizen Initiated Actions*
(42 USC 82, Subchapter VII, § 6972). Citizens may invoke RCRA provisions through civil suits against facilities/ handlers/owners, or

against the EPA for failure to enforce RCRA. These suits are required to demonstrate potential harm. Prior notice of intent to litigate is required. Such suits are banned where EPA provides evidence of planned enforcement actions, or ongoing actions.

- ***Criminal Enforcement Provision***
(RCRA § 3008). Violations of RCRA regulations may result in criminal actions that are pursued by the Department of Justice. Maximum criminal penalties are $50,000 per day, and/or 5 years in prison.

CONCLUSION: UNDERSTANDING LAWS

Laws are one mechanism for addressing societal concerns and protecting the general public from harm. Environmental laws became necessary because it was clear that the free market was neither capable of nor interested in protecting the public and environment from the kinds of industrial harms (e.g., pollution, loss of habitat, etc.) that emerged in the wake of economic growth.

Legislation serves the important role of recognizing public interest and determining whether an issue is significant and/or substantial enough to warrant the special protection law represents. The public recognition of environmental problems as social problems, and the legislative identification of these issues as "law-worthy" requires acknowledging the existence of persistent problems that cause damage to the social and/or natural worlds. For this to occur, the public must possess knowledge of the harms around them, and must desire action on those harms. In the absence of these conditions, the public must rely on the social benevolence of legislators who, in democratic theory, should act in the best interest of the public. But, in order for either of these outcomes to produce environmental laws, there must first be a basis for believing that the environment needs to be protected. The needed evidence of environmental harm or the health of the social and natural world is produced by scientists acting as academics, government agents, and sometimes through independent organizations or even corporations. Absent this kind of knowledge, particularly in the form of research, ill-defined legislation is quite possible.

Understanding environmental law can be burdensome, as can the effort to create effective environmental legislation. Environmental law is, by its very nature, interdisciplinary, requiring knowledge of ecosystems, toxic chemicals, legal systems and codes, government and public policy. Thus, understanding how and why environmental law works or is designed requires a wide range of knowledge. It also requires acknowledging the role competing interests play in shaping environmental legislation and recognizing that often, private and corporate interests play a more important role in shaping environmental legislation than does scientific knowledge or public interest. For example, as the review presented above illustrated, many environmental rules require balancing scientific evidence of harm and technological innovations for controlling pollution with the interests of corporations in producing profit. This is why many environmental laws note that the benefits of pollution control technologies must be balanced against the costs of that technology. Although it is widely recognized that effective legislation should be based on due consideration of numerous factors (e.g., legal and social concerns), one of the factors often overlooked is the negative impacts the interests of the private sector in profitable economic conditions have played in the persistence of harm to the environment.

Today, much of the burden of enforcing environmental laws has fallen upon the EPA and state level environmental protection agencies, although other federal and state regulatory agencies and law enforcement groups also play a role in identifying and enforcing environmental law. A more detained coverage of the enforcement role in the EPA's history and public concerns about environmental protection are the subject of the following chapter.

CHAPTER 6.

Enforcing Environmental Laws and Regulations

INTRODUCTION

No matter how extensive the number of environmental laws and regulations becomes, these laws are meaningless absent consistent monitoring and enforcement practices designed to enhance industry compliance. For example, some suggest that weak, under or un-enforced environmental legislation contributed to continued pollution with relative impunity, despite the notable number of laws passed during the 1970s (Brown, 1979, 1988; Goldman, 1991). Put simply, what is the purpose of laws if they are not properly enforced?

Decades ago, Nader, Brownstein, and Richard (1981) characterized environmental crime as a serious health and safety concern for millions of Americans. One could argue that environmental crime remains problematic. Millions of Americans continue to be exposed to environmental pollution, and serious public health problems associated with pollution remain today. For example, environmental pollution makes a significant contribution to the rates of many diseases, especially cancers, respiratory problems, and learning disabilities (Colborn, Dumanoski, and Myers, 1997; Wargo, 1998; Steingraber, 1998; Lappe, 1991; Lynch and Stretesky, 2001). To what extent could these problems be mitigated by more stringent enforcement of environmental laws and regulations? To be sure, meeting all legal standards set forth in environment rules would help alleviate these conditions. But, the law is not necessarily the best or only solution to this problem. In large, the problem is not only one related to enforcing law; it is also related to the emphasis placed on profit which privileges profit over environmental and public health. For the reasons reviewed above, Cable and Benson (1993, p. 465) suggest that "The impact and effectiveness of national environmental regulation is a matter of debate."

This chapter discusses environmental regulation enforcement and forces on: the history of EPA enforcement efforts; the public's role in shaping the enforcement of environmental crime; complex problems encountered when enforcing environmental laws; the extent of environmental crime; what happens when environmental harm becomes a crime; and the penalties associated with environ-mental crime.

ENVIRONMENTAL ENFORCEMENT EFFORTS

For much of American history, harms to the environment were unregulated. The earliest Act to regulate pollution was the 1899 *Rivers and Harbors Act* (also called the *Refuse Act*), recognized as the first identifiable attempt by Congress to criminalize polluting (Friedrichs, 2004). It was not until the 1970s that an extensive array of laws designed to protect the environment were legislated (Starr, 1991). Before the 1970s, environmental harms were primarily addressed through private civil suits brought by concerned parties (Friedrichs, 2004). Even in the 1970s, the *Refuse Act* was an important piece of legislation, as the government turned to this Act and its strict liability principle to prosecute environmental criminals (Cohen, 1992).

The environmental movement of the 1960s and early 1970s brought about increased societal concern for environmental issues, and less concern for industrial profitability at the expense of the reckless destruction of natural resources (e.g., Hedman, 1991). Public opinion on the environment, for example, paved the way for the creation of the EPA by President Nixon in 1970, and passage of the *Clean Air Act*.

Certainly, harms against the environment occurred before the 1970s, yet the government appeared disinterested in penalizing such practices. There was hope in the early 1970s that new laws and the creation of the EPA would change this situation. Despite these emerging conditions, there was little effort to prosecute environmental criminals, largely due to the interests in protecting economic development. For instance, while Nixon created the EPA, he was not interested in environmental conditions, and frustrated initial EPA efforts to regulate the environment (Davis, 2002, pp. 90-91, 95). And while the EPA adopted an enforcement orientation upon its inception, this strategy was not carried out effectively.

Early enforcement efforts at EPA were confined primarily to promulgating and enforcing regulatory rules, and it was not until the Carter administration that criminal enforcement was more fully pursued (Hedman, 1991). Before the Carter Administration, the EPA had issued guidelines for pursuing criminal sanctions under the *Clean Air Act* in June of 1976 (McMurry and Ramsey, 1986). Yet, these new rules were not vigorously enforced. Adding to this increased emphasis on enforcement, over 30 major pieces of environmental legislation were passed by the federal government during the 1970s. Civil sanctions, penalties, and injunctive relief generally constituted the government's primary approach to judicial enforcement of environmental regulations and statutes prior to 1981, and the filing criminal charges remained a low priority (McMurry and Ramsey, 1986).

The enforcement-oriented approach adopted by the EPA slowed following the oil embargo of the early 1970s, a time when society became increasingly concerned about economic security and oil and gasoline prices, and less concerned with environmental issues (Hyatt, 1998). However, as McMurry and Ramsey (1986) note, several factors generated increased emphasis on enforcement at the EPA in 1977. First, there was a change in EPA leadership which brought a more active administration to the agency. Second, statutory compliance deadlines activated by the *Clean Air Act* and the *Clean Water Act* enhanced the scope of these laws. Finally, the EPA budgeted more resources toward the enforcement of environmental crimes.

Faced with an increased focus on enforcement, the EPA implemented its Major Source Enforcement Effort (MSEE) in the later 1970s, a program designed to bring violators into compliance with the *Clean Air Act* and the *Clean Water Act* (McMurry and Ramsey, 1986). The MSEE program sought to share enforcement activities with the states, while using civil judicial enforcement actions to deter potential violators and bring about expeditious compliance (McMurry and Ramsey, 1986). Civil penalties served as punishments and helped eliminate the competitive advantage gained by those who disregarded environmental statutes (McMurry and Ramsey, 1986). The main objective of the program was rapid compliance from a large number of violators.

Early EPA investigators and inspectors were trained in the technical aspects of environmental regulation who sought to gain compliance through negotiation and cooperation. They were not criminal investigators trained to believe that environmental harms could be considered white collar crime (McMurry and Ramsey, 1986). Nevertheless, the message had been sent that filing criminal charges would become part of the EPA's enforcement repertoire.

Despite the assertion that federal regulators would strengthen criminal enforcement of environmental laws, only 25 federal criminal cases were referred to the Department of Justice for criminal prosecution during the 1970s (DiMento, 1993), reflecting the conservative practices of the Nixon and Ford administrations. The number of enforcement actions increased under the Carter and Reagan administrations, with the increase during the Reagan administration attributable to societal concern for environmental harms and extensive coverage of corrupt EPA practices (Friedrichs, 2004).

Cohen (1992) describes several significant changes that emerged with regard to the criminal enforcement of environmental crimes during the 1980s, including the EPA's development of its Office of Criminal Enforcement and the Department of Justice's newly formed Environmental Crimes Unit in the Lands Division. In addition, Congress redefined certain environmental offenses from misdemeanors to felonies (Starr, 1991). While some government officials claimed an enhanced commitment to addressing environmental crime cases (e.g., Thornburgh, 1991; Strock, 1991), others suggest that prosecutions of environmental crime cases leveled off, that sanctions were considerably lighter when compared with other crimes, and compliance with environmental statutes was poor (e.g., Adler and Lord, 1991). For instance, in their analysis of environmental crime enforcement against Fortune 500 companies, Adler and Lord (1991) discovered limited evidence of environmental crime enforcement: while nearly two-thirds had violated federal environmental laws between 1984 and 1990, only 6 percent were prosecuted. As further evidence, Adler and Lord added that it wasn't until 1984 that a large corporation was prosecuted under federal environmental laws. Friedrichs (2004, p. 275) best describes the situation regarding enforcement of environmental crimes in suggesting that:

> Despite some modest increases in prosecutions, fines, and prison sentences for individual corporate executives, there has been a systematic reluctance to imprison environmental offenders or to fine corporate environmental offenders more than a fraction (1 to 5 percent) of the statutory maximum for these offenses.

Today, the EPA's Office of Enforcement and Compliance Assurance (OECA) seeks to protect the environment and human health by ensuring compliance with environmental requirements. OECA's wide scope of activities includes monitoring and enforcing violations of air and water pollution, hazardous waste, toxic substances, and pesticides using the Office of Criminal Enforcement, Forensics and Training (OCEFT) to monitor violations of U.S. Criminal Code (Title 18) associated with environmental crimes. Criminal enforcement actions are reserved for those who knowingly disregard or are criminally negligent of environmental laws. In addition, the OCEFT Homeland Security Division addresses terrorist-related threats through providing criminal investigative support to other law enforcement agencies as they pertain to the environment.

STATE AND LOCAL LAW ENFORCEMENT EFFORTS

The effectiveness of the EPA in protecting the environment is related to the ability of the agency to work cooperatively with other groups, particularly state regulatory agencies, which often model themselves after the EPA (Epstein, 1998). State environmental regulatory agencies must adopt minimum federal environmental protection standards, although they may impose more stringent regulations than those offered under federal law (Hyatt, 1998; Edwards, 1996). As a result, much variation exists among the enforcement practices of the state regulatory bodies, which may be due to differing societal views on particular environmental issues, state fiscal policies, the influence of various interest groups across states (Hunter and Waterman, 1996), and the geographic distribution of certain industries and natural resources across the country. Even within states, cooperation among agencies is essential to environmental crime prosecution. For example, the state police focus on criminal investigation whereas the attorney general, who may be assisted by an environmental crime task force, oversees prosecution (Situ and Emmons, 2000). These two activities are related, and cooperation of these agencies is essential to effective environmental crime enforcement.

State environmental regulatory agencies play a significant role in protecting the environment when they take the following actions that contribute to the betterment of the environment (U.S. EPA, OECA, 2007):

- write rules
- set standards
- issue permits
- conduct monitoring
- provide information to the regulated community and the public
- assess environmental quality
- provide compliance assistance
- conduct inspections
- take enforcement actions

In doing so, state regulatory agencies contribute roughly 94 percent of the environmental quality data provided in the six major EPA national data systems, and have come to occupy an increasingly important role in the regulation of environmental crime (Epstein, 1998).

In recent years, state environmental agencies have expanded their enforcement efforts. This has occurred during a period where the George W. Bush administration has limited and cut the EPA's budget (Schaeffer, 2003) and issued, on average, fewer than half as many federal environmental citations as the Clinton administration (Borenstein, 2003). Between 2000 and 2003, EPA data demonstrate enhanced enforcement efforts on behalf of states. For instance, there was a 203 percent increase in field citations and a 178 percent increase in stipulated penalties. From 1995 through 2003, the number of penalties imposed by state regulatory agencies expanded by 49 percent, resulting in over $892 million in penalties assessments (U.S. EPA, OECA, 2007).

In addition to state agencies, local law enforcement agencies also play a role in environmental enforcement. Historically that role has been limited, but has expanded in recent years as local agencies become more aware of environmental crime. In their daily activities such as patrolling, local law enforcement officers are ideally situated to identify and react to emerging environmental harms. Unfortunately, training officers to identify and respond to environmental crimes has been neglected. With greater concern for homeland security, however, local law enforcement officers are becoming more cognizant of issues beyond street crime, and are being increasingly trained for and charged with identifying environmental crimes (see the environmental crime investigation chapter for further details).

Discussion Box 6.1. A Focus on the Effects of Lax Environmental Law Enforcement: The Great Lakes Effect

A number of environmentalists have noted that the Bush Administration has done a poor job enforcing environmental laws, and has done so by rolling back a number of environmental standards. The consequence of reducing environmental law enforcement efforts and rolling back legal pollution requirements and standards is that the environment becomes more polluted, which in turn has long-term negative consequences for human, animal and planetary health.

Indeed, not only has the George W. Bush Administration undermined U.S. environmental laws and regulations, it has done so while claiming that levels of environmental pollution have declined. Not so, says the EPA's Inspector General's Report from February, 2005. That report specifically noted that the Bush Administration proposal to alter the *Clean Air Act* and allow elevated levels of mercury emissions from power plants was a violation of the *Clean Air Act*, and failed to adequately assess the impact of this rule change on human health. Moreover, EPA Inspector General Nikki Tinsley disputed a report that U.S. air quality has shown steady improvement under the GW Bush Administration.

A recently released study shows, for example, that the level of several toxins—PCBs, methyl-mercury and dioxin—have all increased in the Great Lakes in recent years. Much of the increase in pollution is due to reductions in air pollution standards under the G.W. Bush Administration which have contributed to the escalation in mercury and dioxin levels in the Great Lakes. But, it should be noted that the situation with respect to the Great Lakes in unique because the waterway borders the U.S. and Canada, and consequently requires international cooperation to combat pollution.

At the local level, the challenge that remains is to convince police that environmental crimes are serious behaviors deserving their attention. This can be accomplished by modifying the initial and continued training officers receive to emphasize the personal and community safety problems posed by environmental harms.

The challenge of enforcing environmental crime at all levels of government undoubtedly hampers efforts to protect the public. Consider the challenges posed if similar obstacles applied to enforcing the penal code. For instance, what would happen if criminal legislation was as unclear, or vague, or if street criminals opposed "street crime laws" and used the same types of resources (expensive, top quality, influential attorneys and lobbyists) environmental criminals use to avoid detection and prosecution. Or, consider a society in which first-responders (e.g., police officers) disregarded the threats associated with street crime. Such situations seem chaotic and absurd at best.

THE ROLE OF THE PUBLIC

The general public plays a significant role in addressing environmental concerns. Public attitudes help shape societal action, and public action typically follows enhanced public concern for the environment. The actions can emanate from government and businesses in response to public pressure, or it can be the result of the public taking action, as evidenced by the influence of the environmental movement. To be sure, the public has become more willing to respond to environmental crimes. For example, the 2001 Environmental Council of the States report noted that environmentally related citizen complaints increased by 38 percent between 1995 and 1999 for the thirty-five states for which data are available.

Public Opinion

Public attitudes toward environmental crime shifted during the 1980s, and the public became more likely to view these crimes as similar to street crimes and less likely to perceive them as a cost of doing business (Humphreys, 1990). Carter (1998) suggests this change in public attitude is attributable, in part, to law enforcement agencies becoming increasingly aggressive in pursuing environmental crime offenders. Clifford (1998) echoes Carter's observation, adding that law enforcement agencies believe enforcement actions can improve public health. Clifford also noted that increased emphasis on environmental crime by law enforcement encouraged local prosecutors to develop and implement strategies and techniques to successfully prosecute environmental crime offenders.

Despite advances in environmental law, protection, and prosecution, surveys indicate that a majority of Americans (53 percent) believe that laws implemented to protect the environment have not gone far enough, and that preserving nature is more important than preserving economic growth (Lev, 1996). Gallup's annual environment poll sheds further light on public opinion of environmental concerns. A March 2007 poll indicated that 41 percent of Americans are worried "a great deal" about the "greenhouse effect" or global warming, an increase of 13 percent since March of 2004. These concerns are divided along political lines, with 85 percent of Democrats worried "a great deal" about global warming, compared to 46 percent of Republicans. Further, the survey found that most Americans are worried a great deal about pollution of drinking water, rivers, lakes, and reservoirs, contamination of soil and water by toxic waste, and maintenance of the nation's supply of fresh water for household needs (Saad, 2007). While some of the public's concern regarding these issues may be attributable to Al Gore's documentary *An Inconvenient Truth*, it remains that the public is aware of and concerned about environmental issues.

To be sure, the public has recently been inundated with homeland security concerns, which could both positively and negatively influence perceptions of environmental protection. For instance, the wars in Afghanistan and Iraq and concerns over additional attacks on U.S. soil undoubtedly shift public attention away from environmental destruction. Further, local law enforcement agencies face the additional burden of recognizing and reacting to terrorist threats, which could detract from the historically limited efforts they put forth to recognize environmental harms. However, public recognition of environmental protection could be enhanced as concern for homeland security involves recognizing terrorist attacks against sites that fall under jurisdiction of environmental protection agencies, thus leading to increased focus on these locations. Further, homeland security threats could increase local law enforcement's recognition of environmental harms as departments increase in size and officers become increasingly tasked with greater scrutiny of unusual activity. Greater local law enforcement awareness of environmental harms would draw public attention to the issue. Only time will tell how the situation plays out.

A typical response to public opinion on this matter is to question how much the public really knows about environmental law and pollution. While the public's knowledge on specific issues may be wanting, its overall opinion reflects some current trends in pollution, such as rising levels of pollution in recent years, and weakened enforcement of environment laws under the George W. Bush administration. One could argue that recent general neglect of the environment provided a strong impetus for public action.

Public Action

As noted, the actions of the public influence environmental well-being. The public's opinion and practices affect many arenas in both positive and negative manners. For instance, the popularity of SUVs led automakers to design ever larger, more environmentally harmful vehicles. As public concern for the environment (and higher gas prices) expanded, SUVs became less popular and more environmentally-friendly automobiles were introduced to the market. Consumer preferences certainly impact the environment. Along these lines, the public can play a role in other areas of environmental protection.

In addition to traditional forms of activism associated with the environmental movement, some areas have witnessed an extension of community-oriented policing ideas to involve citizens in environmental protection. O'Rourke and Macey (2003) studied proactive citizen groups that monitored air emissions near industrial facilities as part of a grassroots effort to respond to under-enforcement of environmental rules. The researchers note the benefits of such community policing efforts, including greater public awareness of environmental harm, enhanced public discourse on the matter, and overall more effective enforcement of polluting activities. The need for greater awareness of industry activity is evident throughout the environmental crime literature, and using responsible citizens to actively engage in regulation provides optimism for enhanced environmental protection.

OBSTACLES TO ENFORCING ENVIRONMENTAL REGULATIONS

As discussed in Chapter 4, the EPA is a useful starting point for any discussion of environmental enforcement efforts. As noted, the EPA is assisted in fighting environmental crime by state and local environmental regulatory agencies, law enforcement groups, and numerous environmental interest groups. Such a fragmented, decentralized approach to formally enforcing environmental crime arguably results in uncoordinated enforcement efforts that resemble a "jigsaw puzzle" approach (Hyatt, 1998, p. 117). The primary challenges to formal environmental law enforcement are limited resources to fight environmental crime, piecemeal or unclear legislation, a lack of coordinated responses among jurisdictions (including international concerns), balancing industry concerns for over-regulation, and the difficulties in assessing the extent of environmental crime.

A key problem is lack of resources, and many environmental regulatory agencies' public health protection goals are limited by budgetary constraints. The lack of adequate funding restricts an agency's ability to closely monitor industry practices. Environmental regulators, in turn, rely on self-monitoring by industries, which are encouraged to report their activities to regulators, a practice that contrasts with government approaches to traditional crime. Imagine for a moment a system of criminal law enforcement in which the police relied on criminals to voluntarily report when they have violated the law. One can only speculate that such an effort by police would be met with great suspicion. But do such policies work?

Stretesky (2006) recently examined the EPA's Self-Policing Policy, which waives or reduces penalties when regulated entities discover, disclose and amend environmental violations, to determine if inspections and enforcement actions were associated with industry practices of disclosing environmental regulations under the policy. He found no evidence that inspections and enforcement increases use of the policy. He did find, however, that larger entities were more likely than smaller ones to report infractions. His findings suggest that "regulatory agencies such as the EPA can do relatively little to increase the self-policing of environmental violations" (Stretesky, 2006, p. 672).

Another constraint facing environmental regulators includes broadly defined legislation that creates too much discretion for EPA officials. Mintz (1995) and Ross (1996) both argue that broadly drafted legislation grants vast discretion to EPA administrators in establishing rules consistent with regulatory statutes and in enforcing new and existing laws, and in taking actions to ensure industry compliance with federal environmental legislation.

The EPA has been criticized for failing to adopt and retain a comprehensive strategy consistent with environmental regulation and protection. In part, the absence of a comprehensive strategy is impacted by the fact that Congressional activities impact the EPA's mission and the regulations it enforces. In turn,

Congress also lacks a comprehensive environmental protection strategy (Hyatt, 1998). This is to be expected, as the membership of Congress changes on a regular basis. The result, however, is a piecemeal approach to environmental protection, where Congress passes separate laws as perceived needs or threats arise, or in a reactive rather than in a preventive manner.

Another complicating factor is that the EPA must balance business interests with its duties as an enforcement agency. EPA enforcement managers, often the target of critique, are tasked with the heavy burden of ensuring that environmental legislation is enforced and particular interests are recognized. In doing so, these individuals assume a wide array of duties ranging from (Mintz, 1995, p. 14):

> ...hiring, training, overseeing, evaluating, and retaining their staffs to preparing and justifying budget requests, relating to other managers at a peer level, responding to inquiries from investigative entities (such as the EPA Office of Inspector General and the GAO), and keeping abreast of the frequent changes in law, science, and policy that may have an impact on their enforcement work.

Regulating the environment is also difficult because public environmental concerns tend to be local in nature, while much environmental policy is national. For instance, within a local area, the public may be concerned with the effect of a specific hazardous waste site, high levels of specific pollutants, or the pollution of an identifiable body of water. National laws or policies may, however, be ill-equipped to respond to these kinds of local variations.

Another area that presents enforcement difficulties is in relation to international law and treaties. Free trade agreements and the shifting of industry to countries with limited environmental legislation have enhanced environmental concerns on an international basis (e.g., Seis, 1999). Environmental harm has no boundaries, and emerging countries dependent on expanding their industrial base may be hesitant to restrain the financial benefits of a growing economy. Unfortunately, it is extremely challenging to investigate and prosecute environmental crimes in developing countries, especially in a context where these crimes most often harm the world's poor (Schmidt, 2004). Commenting on the need for greater international networks to facilitate cooperation among law enforcement, prosecutorial, and nongovernmental agencies, Schmidt (2004) notes that networks would simplify working internationally, particularly with regard to the broad spectrum of cultures, different languages, and varied legal systems and governments, by creating standards that are understood by all. Unfortunately, industry interests provide large obstacles to environmental protection.

BALANCING INDUSTRY CONCERNS

The significance of criminal sanctions is noted in Szasz's (1986) suggestion that incarceration is one business cost that cannot be passed on to consumers. However, the criminalizing of environmental violations remains controversial (for discussion of related issues see, O'Hear, 2004). To be sure, business owners would rather pay a fine than go to prison, but then who wouldn't? Businesses are seen as having rights that are not associated with individuals, such as the right to pursue a legitimate business. But, where does the right of a business to pollute interfere with the public's right to a healthy environment? The problem for environmental regulators is balancing these two competing interests. Given these parameters, overcriminalization or criminal enforcement can be considered harmful to business practices and unnecessary for the protection of public health (Cohen, 1992, 1998). Some even suggest that business rights are violated in the U.S. when aggressive U.S. laws reduce the ability of American-based businesses to compete on the international marketplace (Tucker, 1982; Wiedenabum, 1986).

Determining the appropriate level of enforcement is a difficult, yet necessary condition for stable production and markets. The term "appropriate level," however, is highly subjective and is typically interpreted differently by regulators, society, and industry. The perils of under-enforcement are well documented in the environmental crime literature, although one must also consider the consequences involved with over-enforcement. To be sure, in some cases the costs associated with producing goods and services increase as businesses are required to meet increased regulation and enforcement. In other cases, however, sound environmental practices are also good businesses practices that reduce costs. As an example, consider Subaru's Lafayette, Indiana manufacturing plant built in 2004, which uses an extensive recycling program to produce no landfill waste. The plant is built on a tract of land designed in cooperation with the National Wildlife Federation, and acts as a nature preserve. The factory has received an award from the EPA under the "Waste Wise" program to recognize its achievements. In addition, the plant is cooperating with Interface, Inc., a manufacturer of environmentally friendly flooring and textiles, to provide a fleet of low emissions vehicles Interface requires to obtain a 100 percent Smartway certification from the EPA. The use of EPA rewards and certification can be used by these companies to market their products as environmentally friendly in an atmosphere where consumers are concerned with the environmental impacts of the products they purchase.

Despite the importance of criminal sanctions for controlling environment crime, there is also a concern that overcriminalization could also result in reducing the stigma attached to the label "criminal." Cohen (1998), for instance, notes that by criminalizing minor infractions runs the risk of criminal law risks becoming trivialized. For instance, if every harmful action is criminalized, the criminal law loses its unique ability to apply the moral stigma of being labeled a criminal. Absent that moral stigma, individuals may show much less respect for environmental laws and be less likely to care about truly egregious environmental violations. It could be argued, however, that Cohen's concern is exaggerated, since criminal cases constitute a tiny fraction of environmental enforcement actions. At the same time, one must consider Hyatt's (1998, p. 139) position that "Despite the small numbers, felony prosecutions of environmental crimes stand out as the major change in environmental enforcement over the past 20 years. Civil judgments carry little public stigma, but, in contrast, criminal sanctions can serve as effective deterrents." The problem is balancing these two observations. Proposed solutions to address the problem of over-criminalization and overdeterrence include greater cooperative efforts among involved parties, and greater reliance on sentencing guidelines. The latter, however, have apparently done little to address the issue. In his study of legal responses to environmental crime, Cohen (1992) found that the *Sentencing Reform Act of 1984*, which instituted sentencing guidelines at the federal level, did little to address the problem of overcriminalization and overdeterrence. Cohen (1992, p. 1106) argued that sentencing considerations should be based on harms caused by offenders and the offender's probability of getting caught: "...criminal sanctions for environmental crimes should be inversely related to the probability of detection."

Recognizing these issues, the EPA also employs negotiation rather than purely adversarial enforcement strategies to gain compliance with environmental regulations. Speaking to the integral role bargaining and negotiation play in EPA enforcement, Mintz (1995) notes that most of the time bargaining appeals to the goals and interests of both the agency and the enterprises subject to enforcement action. Kraft (2001) agrees, adding that negotiations are preferred when compliance with regulations is perceived as expensive, burdensome, and too rigid. Critics argue that environmental compliance policy could be made more effective by offering financial incentives for industry (Sexton, Marcus, Easter, and Burkhardt, 1999). One might wonder why law enforcement agencies need to offer incentives to comply with the law, and whether such a system should also be extended to ordinary crimes. While the EPA has used criminal and civil penalties, it tends to encourage compliance through cooperative strategies and agreements, and recently instituted an interactive compliance assistance web site for this purpose (Kraft, 2001).

HOW MUCH ENVIRONMENTAL CRIME EXISTS?

A growing body of research on environmental crime that dates back to the mid-1980s (Rebovich, 1998) has provided greater insight into the extent and nature of environmental crime and the effectiveness of environmental legislation. Certainly, much work remains to be done on these issues (Rebovich 1998, p.

351). Research on environmental crime and enforcement matters is encouraged by the EPA, which offers grants and other avenues of support for empirical evaluations. This research, however, has limited value unless it is employed by the government to reform environmental enforcement and regulations.

One of the problems remaining in this literature is measuring the extent of environmental crime. Although numerous data sources on environmental crime and pollution exist, none provides a single, comprehensive measure of this phenomenon. Similar to difficulties experienced when measuring traditional crime, attempts to measure environmental crime seem futile (Epstein, 1998). Such limitations in measurement do not, however, extend to data concerning government environmental crime enforcement efforts. Table 6-1 depicts select enforcement findings from 2002 to 2006.

Table 6.1. EPA Enforcement Actions FY 2002–2006

Action	2006	2005	2004	2003	2002
EPA Inspections/Evaluations	23,000	21,000	21,000	18,000	18,000
Civil Referrals to Department of Justice	286	259	268	259	252
Civil Judicial Case Conclusions	173	157	176	195	216
Criminal Sentences (years)	154	186	77	146	215
Fines/Restitution (millions)	$43	$100	$47	$71	$62

Sources: U.S. EPA FY 2006 OECA Accomplishments Report & U.S. Environmental Protection Agency, Office of Enforcement and Compliance Assistance, available online at:wwww.epa.gov/compliance/resources/reports/endofyear/eoy2006/sp-criminalcases.html.

As Table 6-1 indicates, the number of EPA inspections and evaluations has increased somewhat over the past few years, as has the number of civil referrals to the Department of Justice (see however, Borensten, 2003, for comparison of trends across presidential administrations). At the same time, the numbers of civil judicial case conclusions, criminal sentences, and fines were much lower in 2006 than in 2002. This may be the result of expanded use of informal compliance strategies such as self-policing. For example, in fiscal year 2006 the OECA obtained commitments from governments, industry, and other regulated groups to reduce pollution by nearly 900 million pounds. These entities will invest roughly $4.9 billion to reduce pollution and achieve compliance with environmental legislation. These data, much like data concerning traditional crime, are to be interpreted with caution, as one cannot tell from merely observing these numbers whether fluctuations from year to year or across time frames are attributable to enforcement practices, differences in measurement practices, or a decrease in deviant behavior.

WHEN ENVIRONMENTAL HARM BECOMES A CRIME

The EPA does not handle criminal case prosecutions, but must refer criminal cases to the Department of Justice for prosecution. Researchers have argued that investigators and prosecutors seeking criminal prosecution of environmental violators must compete for resources with those involved with imposing civil sanctions. When coupled with the loss of control of criminal cases through Department of Justice referrals, these circumstances may lead to a decreased likelihood of criminal prosecution. In addition, fiscal constraints limit the complexity and number of criminal cases that can be processed (McMurry and Ramsey, 1986). Adding to the difficulties faced in seeking criminal charges are overlapping and occasionally confusing statutory requirements, including criminal sanctions noted in environmental laws and general criminal statutes that pertain to environmental violators (McMurry and Ramsey, 1986).

As noted, the criminal prosecution of environmental offenders is a somewhat recent development, beginning in the late 1970s. Increased enforcement efforts at that time coincided with Department of Justice and EPA attempts to address issues pertaining to hazardous waste disposal, which in 1978 led the newly formed Hazardous Waste Task Force to identify 52 civil actions using nuisance portions of the *Resource Conservation and Recovery Act* (RCRA; McMurry and Ramsey, 1986). Even without budgeted resources, the government began to increase the number of criminal prosecutions (McMurry and Ramsey, 1986).

Department of Justice attorney Peter Beeson was named director of the EPA Office of Criminal Enforcement created in January 1981. The office was charged with actively pursuing criminal sanctions and generally enhancing the effectiveness of the enforcement program. It was not until October 1982 that criminal investigators were hired by the EPA; most had law enforcement experience yet no background with regard to environmental issues (McMurry and Ramsey, 1986).

The Department of Justice's Land and Natural Resources Division established a special unit within its Environmental Enforcement Division to investigate and enforce environmental crimes at about the same time (McMurry and Ramsey, 1986). The newly developed Environmental Crimes Unit received referrals from the EPA and oversaw prosecution of criminal environmental cases (McMurry and Ramsey, 1986). Criminal enforcement became an established part of EPA enforcement practices, particularly with regard to blatantly egregious or harmful violations (McMurry and Ramsey, 1986). Criminal enforcement had clearly become institutionalized at the EPA, which had and continues to have well-defined procedures and requirements regarding case selection and prosecution, although compliance and cooperation through civil enforcement remained the objectives for the EPA (McMurry and Ramsey, 1986). The EPA's enforcement efforts would soon take a different approach as congressional pressure and the EPA's recognition of the potential of seeking voluntary compliance generated greater activity and a criminal program much broader in scope (McMurry and Ramsey, 1986).

The mid-1980s brought about a change in federal prosecution practices regarding environmental offenses when the federal government increased efforts to prosecute environmental offenders criminally as opposed to civilly (e.g., Habicht, 1984; DiMento, 1990). Friedrichs (2004) cites the uncharacteristic increase in criminal prosecutions of environmental offenders during the 1980s, given the conservative Reagan administration's hands-off approach to private enterprise. Upon entering office, the Reagan administration discouraged enforcement efforts. However, a widely publicized scandal in 1983 involving corrupt EPA officials forced a change in the enforcement approach at EPA. The increased emphasis on enforcing environmental laws is recognized as a reaction to, in part, widespread coverage of the scandal and increased citizen concern regarding environmental protection.

Despite these enhanced enforcement efforts, some suggest that compliance with environmental statutes lagged and greater enforcement was needed (Adler and Lord, 1991; Hedman, 1991). Federal sentencing guidelines implemented in the late 1980s attempted to provide consistency in sentencing, and included enhanced penalties for environmental offenders (see Cohen, 1992, for a discussion of sentencing guidelines and environmental crimes). However, it appears that much work remains in properly sanctioning and deterring harms against the environment.

PENALTIES FOR ENVIRONMENTAL HARMS

One of the main objectives of the EPA is voluntary compliance with environmental regulations (Hyatt, 1998). As an example, the EPA introduced a self audit policy in 1995 which encouraged regulated entities to voluntarily discovery, correct and disclosure violations of federal environmental laws to EPA (U.S. EPA, 2000b). In return, the EPA can reduce civil penalty amounts associated with violations, and forego criminal prosecutions that would stem from violation disclosures. Another voluntary EPA program is the National Environmental Performance Track, which identifies groups of leading and lagging facilities (Coglianese and Nash, 2006). Leading facilities are relieved of some regulatory requirements to allow them to innovate compliance strategies. In addition, leaders are not regulated as closely, increasing the level of scrutiny that can be applied to other companies (U.S. EPA, 2006).

In many cases, except for those involving the most egregious violations of law, the EPA attempts to gain voluntary compliance through negotiated settlement. If such strategies fail, the EPA can still invoke adversarial processes of enforcement (Hyatt, 1998). Where voluntary compliance is not obtained, cases become the responsibility of the EPA's Office of Enforcement and

Compliance Assurance (OECA) , which organizes evidence of noncompliance, engages in civil enforcement proceedings, and assists the Department of Justice in criminal enforcement cases when necessary (Hyatt, 1998). While many infractions are routine and promptly resolved, criminal violations present greater difficulty for enforcement officials and require extensive resources, particularly in the form of time, causing delays in case settlements, or avoidance of prosecution (Landy et al., 1990).

In general, the OECA "...seeks to ensure full compliance with laws intended to protect human health and the environment. OECA staff work to identify and reduce noncompliance, maintain a strong enforcement presence, and increase the use of compliance assistance tools and incentives policies" (U.S. EPA, 1999, p. 7). In identifying its priorities, the EPA claims to provide a strong enforcement effort while attempting to deter regulated groups into seeking assistance, and using "incentive policies and providing fairness in the marketplace to ensure that noncomplying facilities do not gain an unfair competitive advantage over facilities that have dedicated resources to compliance" (U.S. EPA, 1999, p. 7).

In noncriminal cases, the EPA uses several sources of information gathering including:

- self-monitoring,

- record keeping and reporting by individual sources of pollution,

- inspections by government personnel, and

- the specific complaints of concerned citizens (Mintz, 1995).

Most EPA inspections are announced prior to a site visit with the intent to ensure that vital personnel will be present (Mintz, 1995). Kraft (2001) notes that visits and inspections to industrial facilities are infrequent, regardless of the public impression put forth by the EPA.

The EPA employs a three-pronged approach to confront environmental violators: administrative enforcement (also known as regulatory enforcement), civil enforcement, and criminal enforcement (Ross, 1996; Hyatt, 1998). The enforcement process generally begins with the EPA gathering information and, if warranted, notifying an alleged violator and requesting a stop to the alleged questionable behavior. Compliance on behalf of the accused results in no further action. When an offender fails to comply, informal negotiations between the EPA and the accused result, with the intent of reaching a settlement agreement. Failure to reach an informal agreement institutes a formal process initiated by issuance of a Notice of Violations. Once the informal negotiation fails, an Administrative Order is issued and an administrative hearing is scheduled before an administrative law judge. The court's decision can be appealed to the EPA administrator and to the federal court with the possibility of reaching the U.S. Supreme Court. Failure to reach agreement under administrative law may lead to

EPA officials taking more punitive steps, such as adding names to a list of companies ineligible for federal contracts, loans, and grants. After exhausting all efforts to reach an agreement and determining that such a resolution is unlikely, the case will then be turned over to the Department of Justice for civil or criminal processing.

In civil and criminal cases, the Department of Justice reviews the case to determine a course of action. To be sure, there is great discretion inherent in the decision to prosecute, and the separation of the two agencies (the EPA and the Department of Justice) can contribute to philosophical orientations and goals (e.g., Barker, 2002). Minor infractions or cases involving first-time offenders are generally addressed through the civil enforcement process, in which offenders are required to rectify the problem and may have to pay a fine. More serious cases or cases involving offenders with a long history of violations are primary targets of criminal enforcement actions (see Discussion Box 6.1). Offenders in these cases are prosecuted in criminal courts and may be fined and/or incarcerated (Hyatt, 1998, p. 128; Mintz, 1995, p. 11). Much like those prosecuting traditional crimes such as rape, robbery, and murder, prosecutors must consider a variety of issues in determining whether or not to proceed with each case. Among the considerations for those prosecuting environmental harms are (Hyatt, 1998, p. 130; Rebovich, 1996): the degree of harm to the environment; the degree of provable criminal intent; the offending company's prior record; the offending company's cooperation during the investigation and its willingness to pay to remedy the problem; media interest in the case; the possibility of organized crime connections; and the cost of the prosecution and the available investigative resources.

As suggested, the EPA anticipates and encourages voluntary compliance and formally sanctions upon failure to reach agreement. In discussing this informal approach to environmental regulation at both the state and federal levels, Kraft (2001, p. 137) argues that "Even where the laws appear to be coercive in nature and invite adversarial relations between government and industry, the reality is that the enforcement process is fundamentally one of self-compliance and negotiation." Kraft adds that, due to their visibility and symbolism, civil and criminal actions are sometimes used to signify the EPA's pro-enforcement efforts in attempts to encourage voluntary compliance.

Another way to address enforcement issues is to examine criminal penalties meted out to environmental defendants. A study of this nature was performed by Michael O'Hear (2004), who examined criminal sentences for environmental crimes for the years 1996 through 2001 under federal sentencing guidelines. During this period, 663 environmental defendants were sentenced, with 36 percent receiving prison sentences. In comparison, O'Hear notes that 81 percent of non-environmental criminals received prison sentences during the same time period. Nearly 60 percent of environmental offenders received sentences of less than one year, while only 2 percent received sentences in excess of six years.

Non-environmental criminals received much longer sentences. For example, more than 22 percent received sentences greater than six years, and only 24 percent received sentences less than one year (see O'Hear, 2004, Tables 2 and 3). This outcome, however, is consistent with the criminal histories of environmental and non-environmental criminals; 88.3 percent of environmental criminals received the lowest federal sentencing guideline criminal history score while only 54.5 percent of non-environmental criminals received the lowest history classification score. Cases classified with the lowest criminal history score provide judges with unlimited sentencing discretion, which also helps to explain the difference in the proportion of prison sentences across these groups of offenders. Indeed, downward departures from sentencing guidelines are much more likely for environmental criminals: 81.5 percent receive a sentence under guideline minimums compare to 60.7 percent for non-environmental offenders. (see Discussion Box 5.2, p. 103).

LOOKING AHEAD...

Recent developments in society and the federal government point to greater enforcement of environmental harms. Recent concerns for global warming have encouraged many to recognize the significance of protecting the environment. Several recent large-scale natural disasters (e.g., Hurricane Katrina, and the 2004 Indian Ocean earthquake which generated a series of large-scale tsunamis) and extreme weather patterns have led those with minor interests in the environment to give greater consideration to human impacts on the environment. To be sure, Former Vice President Al Gore's documentary *An Inconvenient Truth*, which earned two Oscars and numerous other awards, focusing primarily on global warming, undoubtedly influenced public perception of environmental harm. The general public's interest in environmental protection is significant in that politicians and policymakers generally appeal and respond to public wants. It is assumed that public servants will respond to society's concerns about environmental degradation.

Further, the terrorist attacks of September 11, 2001 led to significant restructuring of federal law enforcement. The restructuring was designed to promote cooperation among agencies and centralize many federal law enforcement responsibilities. Changes at the federal level also include an increased number of law enforcement agents (Reaves, 2006). Such recognition of the historical limitations of federal law enforcement will presumably impact environmental protection.

Discussion Box 6.3. Father-Son Receive Longest Environmental Crime Sentences

In December, 2004, Alexander and Raul Salvagno, owners of an asbestos abatement company, received the most severe sentences handed down in an environmental crime case. The case was complex, and involved violations of racketeering (RICO) and tax statues, which added to the severity of the sentence.

The Salvagnos operated an asbestos abatement company that conducted illegal operations on more than 1550 sites over a ten-year period. During this time period, they induced more than 500 employees, including asbestos workers and laboratory employees, to engage in illegal behaviors. The Salvagnos were charged with 18 violations of the *Clean Air Act*, the *Toxic Substances Control Act*, and the *RICO Act*. They were convicted on 14 counts.

The Salvagnos were charged with illegal asbestos removal procedures and operating an illegally owned laboratory, Analytic Laboratories of Albany, which was used to produce more than 75,000 fraudulent laboratory tests. The Salvagnos' fraudulent removal practices were discovered when a number of state facilities they had worked on were examined by state inspectors.

Before sentencing, the judge noted that the Salvagnos knowingly exposed workers and building occupants to asbestos, resulting in a substantial likelihood of serious injury or death. Alexander Salvagno was given a prison term of 25 years, ordered to forfeit $2,033,457.70 in illegally obtained assets, and to pay $23,039,607 in restitution to victims. His father, Raul Salvagno, was sentenced to 19.5 years in prison, $1,707,156.40 in forfeitures, and $22,875,575.46 in victim restitution. In this case, additional penalties were handed out to thirteen high-level supervisors who worked for the Salvagnos.

As we have seen, however, environmental protection requires efforts beyond those available at the federal level of government. Particularly, it will take enhanced efforts at the local level to ensure greater environmental crime enforcement. There's a demonstrated need for local level law enforcement to more effectively recognize and react to environmental harms. The general public also needs to play a role in environmental crime enforcement efforts. Many grassroots efforts demonstrate the importance of society not relying solely on regulators or law enforcement to confront environmental crime. The recent shift by many local law enforcement agencies toward a community policing philosophy, in which police departments have increasingly relied on the public's assistance in fighting street crime, needs to more effectively include recognition of environmental crime. In other words, citizens should be encouraged to be aware of traditional and non-traditional forms of crime. The complex nature of enforcing environmental crime requires a complex series of events and contributions from all in society.

CHAPTER 7.

An Overview of Environmental Crime Investigation

INTRODUCTION

This chapter examines some of the basic elements involved in environmental crime investigations. While environmental crime and street crime investigation techniques may be similar, environmental crime investigators (ECIs) must possess specialized knowledge of environmental regulations, the handling of hazardous and toxic substances, experimental sampling techniques and testing protocols, and be able to interpret scientific test results. It is unlikely that any single investigator will possess the broad range of knowledge necessary to undertake the typical environmental crime investigation. As a result, ECIs are often members of a team that consists of experts from different fields. To illustrate the complexities involved in environmental crime investigations, this chapter provides an overview of several important elements of environmental crime investigations. Specifically, in this chapter we examine (1) some basic similarities and differences between environmental crime and ordinary crime investigations; (2) the team approach to environmental crime investigations; (3) elementary aspects of environmental crime investigation procedures; (4) the collection and maintenance of environmental crime evidence; (5) environmental crime sampling techniques; (6) an introduction to the importance of laboratory guidelines; and (7) the uses of secondary data in environmental crime investigations.

Because this is the only chapter that examines the investigation of environmental crime, we provide a brief overview of the issues (for elaboration see Suggs and Yarborough, 2001; Suggs et al, 2002). Moreover, many issues related to environmental crime are beyond our areas of expertise. Because none of us are chemists, for instance, we provide only rudimentary coverage of environmental and analytic chemistry issues, and direct those interested to other sources where this information can be obtained (see Suggs and Yarborough, 2001).

SIMILARITIES AND DIFFERENCES BETWEEN ENVIRONMENTAL AND ORDINARY CRIME INVESTIGATIONS

Environmental crimes have distinct characteristics that require investigating them in unique ways. To be sure, many of the techniques that apply to investigations of ordinary crimes also apply to environmental crimes (on investigating white collar crimes, see Bazley, 2007). However, because of the nature of environmental crimes, care must be taken in the collection and preservation of chemical evidence that may be hazardous or toxic, or which has the potential to interact and react with other chemicals or substances. The reactive characteristics of some chemicals collected during the investigation of an environmental crime are a concern for several reasons. These chemicals can present dangers related to explosion, fire, or the production of toxic gases, meaning that they need to be collected and stored in ways that prevent these outcomes. In addition, because some of the chemical evidence may be reactive, it must be stored in approved containers that will not react with the chemical in ways that will change or destroy the evidence. In contrast, ordinary crime evidence such as hair or blood samples are not reactive in the same way, and can be stored and collected in a variety of containers.

Environmental crime evidence requires the utmost care with respect to adhering to proper scientific protocols for data collection and management. Like ordinary street crimes, samples must be subjected to standard protocols. However, in the case of environmental crimes, additional steps must be taken to ensure that samples are not contaminated. Moreover, the analysis of these samples may require the use of equipment and scientific techniques that are costly. Finally, the analysis of environmental crime samples may be undertaken at centralized locations, requiring the shipping and tracking of evidence from one site to another, and possibly from one lab to the next until the sample is completely analyzed.

Like any other type of evidence, chemical evidence is subjected to "chain of evidence" requirements. Where cases involve specific kinds of chemicals, or the samples were taken from a specific medium of exposure (e.g., soil, water), the evidence may be subject to statutorily imposed evidence requirements found in environmental law statutes. These requirements impact the way in which environmental crime investigations proceed, including the investigation and appropriate laboratory techniques. Because environmental crimes involve chemicals, investigating these crimes requires laboratory research and testing, and knowledge of scientific equipment and chemical testing protocols. The implications of this observation for a team investigative approach are emphasized throughout this chapter.

Environmental crime investigations often involve more than laboratory work. For example, it may be necessary to employ paperwork searches. For instance, ECIs may need to determine who is responsible for an abandoned chemical hazard by tracking the ownership of a piece of property where hazardous waste has been disposed illegally. Or, investigators may need to review a company's environmental audit records to determine if an environmental violation has occurred. These "paper" dimensions of an environmental crime investigation are essential, since a successful prosecution must establish the legal responsibility of the defendant.

Victims of many street crimes are relatively easy to identify and locate. Environmental crime investigation, however, may often require that ECIs use secondary data to illustrate the real and potential harms caused by an environmental crime. For instance, unlike many street crimes, individuals victimized by environmental crimes may not know that they have been victimized, or fail to identify the source of their injuries. ECI investigators may need to access data from a number of different federal and state agencies to collect information about the local populations and environmental conditions that can be used to describe the extent of damage an environmental crime has caused. In other cases, ECIs must be familiar with geographic information system data and analysis, or the use of EPA record systems and data. For instance, the EPA logs a variety of enforcement data (including inspection and enforcement histories) into their Online Tracking and Information System (OTIS). That database enables federal, state, local, and tribal investigators to access a wide range of data relating to enforcement and compliance at specific facilities. OTIS may be useful to ECIs who need to identify potential offenders, suspects, and for conducting pre-inspection reviews.

The Team Approach

Given the unique nature of toxic and environmental crimes, special investigation units consisting of personnel trained in appropriate environmental crime scene techniques are sometimes found in state or local agencies. At the federal level, the EPA maintains a staff of law enforcement officers, scientists, and attorneys who make up its Criminal Investigations Division (CID) located within the Office of Criminal Enforcement, Forensics and Training (OCEFT) . The EPA CID may also work with other federal agencies, or state and local authorities to examine environmental crimes.

According to the EPA, the typical environmental crime involves any or all of the following elements: (1) the illegal disposal of toxic waste (air, water or land discharges that violate the law, and/or the disposal of toxic waste in excess of permitted limits, and/or the illegal discharge of oil in U.S. waters); (2) falsification of data related to testing (laboratory fraud) or reporting of discharge amounts; (3) the misapplication of pesticides, and (4) the illegal importation of ozone depleting chemicals (U.S. EPA, 2001). These offenses are defined by the laws examined in Chapter 5. In some cases, federal laws also spell out the specific criteria for a violation. For example, the RCRA requires the use of specific laboratory tests when investigating environmental crimes.

It is useful to reiterate at this point that the investigation of environmental crime is complex, and requires the kind of interdisciplinary knowledge that few individuals possess. Consequentially, ECIs are undertaken by teams of investigators with different educational backgrounds and training, and through the use of laboratories that specialize in chemical analysis. Below, we review some basics of environmental crime investigations including investigative procedures and evidence collection methods.

ELEMENTARY ENVIRONMENTAL CRIME INVESTIGATION PROCEDURES

When arriving at the location of a reported or suspected environmental crime, the first step the investigator must undertake is an initial assessment concerning the threat to public safety the suspected hazard presents. Threats to public safety may be extremely obvious (e.g., abandoned, leaking barrels near a populated area or in a water source), or may be hidden from the naked eye. At each suspected environmental crime scene, the investigator needs to employ her/his senses of observation to protect the public, but also to ensure that s/he is not placing him/herself in danger. Immediate signs of danger include the presence of chemical odors. Not all noxious chemicals, however, have a distinct odor, and dangerous conditions may still exist in the absence of peculiar aromas. Visible signs of danger are also useful starting points in an initial site inspection. For instance, the existence of hazardous waste storage barrels that present visible evidence of physical strain or damage are important indicators of potential public health threats. Abandoned toxic waste storage barrels under stress or suffering from decomposition or damage will display evidence of physical damage, extensive rusting or corrosion, chemical crystallization on outer surfaces, swelling, and leaking. Barrels in stressed physical condition may also emit audible sounds including hissing and pinging.

In the absence of apparent visual, olfactory or audible signs of danger, the investigator *should not assume* that there is no immediate threat. Rather, the investigator should proceed with extreme caution, and treat the "chemical suspect" as if it were armed and dangerous. These precautions include wearing appropriate safety equipment such as chemical splash suits, goggles, gloves, and respirators (see Image 7.1 below) before inspecting the area further or proceeding with preliminary field tests. This is an important issue because law enforcement officers who respond to hazardous waste related crimes are in danger. For example, research on hazardous materials releases indicates that police officers were the second most likely occupation to be injured by hazardous materials releases (Zeitz et al., 2000). Researchers have also found that law enforcement officers are at a high risk of acute pesticide-related illness (Calvert et al., 1996). This elevated risk of injury due to chemical exposure has not gone unnoticed by the police. For example, in Boston the police department warns their officers about environmental hazards in their community, stating

> ...one of the most common incidents/offenses in this area is found in illegal auto body shops...[but] ... other hazards are ....especially dangerous to police themselves. Many university research facilities, hospitals, printing companies, and even film development shops contain toxics that can be lethal to the untrained emergency responder (Vermette, 2007).

Image 7.1. An example of properly attired investigators at a hazardous waste site.

Picture courtesy of the Center for Disease Control. Public access photo # 1530, CDC Public Health Image Library.

Scientific equipment is often required to identify the existence of invisible chemical threats. In some cases, however, simple chemical tests can be used to verify and discover chemical threats. For example, pH paper can be used to determine the presence of extreme acid or alkaline substances. More complicated, electronic methods include the use of radiation detectors, combustible gas indicators, and photoionization indicators that assess the presence of volatile organic compounds (VOCs)—chemicals that easily vaporize into the atmosphere and present an explosion or fire hazard. As noted, some VOCs present imminent dangers from explosions when exposed to a spark or flame. Others, however, present long-term pollution dangers associated with a potential to cause disease. (For a more complete discussion and guidance on initial approach to sites, and for details on field sampling and testing, testing equipment and equipment and test parameters, see the recommendations of the *Federal Remediation Technologies Roundtable* (FRTR) Screening Tools, www.frtr.gov/site; Drielak, 1998).

In the event that sufficient evidence of an immediate public threat exists, the area should be evacuated and secured. The investigator should immediately contact local emergency HAZMAT (hazardous material handler) teams, the state department of environmental protection (if s/he is from another agency) and the U.S. EPA. Finally, the owner should be notified of the contaminated site (if identifiable) in an effort to determine the types of chemicals that may be present on the site.

Potential environmental crimes may present themselves to investigators in different ways. The location and potential dangers found at large waste sites are likely to be known to investigators ahead of their arrival on the scene. This knowledge is likely to be the product of a long-term investigation rather than an accidental discovery, or this knowledge may be the result of previous periodic inspections of known hazardous waste producers or handlers or may be known from information present in the EPA's cradle-to-grave tracking system created by *Resource Conservation Recovery Act*. The accidental or routine discovery of hazardous chemicals that local or state police are more likely to encounter is a different matter. Such cases tend to involve the discovery of one or several hazardous waste barrels near a road side or in an abandoned building, lot, or wooded area. If these barrels have been dumped maliciously the offenders may have taken precautions to obscure identifiers on the barrels, including the removal of shipping labels and those describing the barrel's contents and origins. In such circumstances, the officer should secure the scene and contact HAZMAT or, if available, the special environmental crime investigative unit in the local or state police department, and the EPA.

Investigators trained in environmental crime procedures prepare the scene for chemical sampling using approved scientific methods (see discussion below and Innis, 2004) and equipment (e.g., the use of coliwasa tubes, see below) in a manner that fulfills legal requirements (for the purposes of maintaining the integrity of the data and the chain of evidence required for successful prosecution). For example, when drawing samples from 55-gallon drums, in-ground storage tanks, tanker-trucks, or other large containers, it is necessary to have a sampling device that reaches the bottom of the container, since chemicals may be mixed and of different weights and densities, creating chemical layers within the container. Under such conditions, investigators will often use a coliwasa tube (**Co**mposite **Li**quid **Wa**ste **Sa**mpler; see Image 7.2) to take samples that represent all the layers within a barrel or other large container (Innis, 2004).

Importantly, the coliwasa also contains a check valve or ball float at the bottom end to prevent sample leakage. Once collected, the sample from the coliwasa tube is transferred into a Whirl-Pak© bag.

Image 7.2. Workers use a coliwasa tube to obtain a sample from a 55-gallon drum.

U.S. EPA public access image gallery photograph, emergency response photographs, group 1.

The sample taken by investigators is used for one of two purposes. First, if local, state or federal authorities will pursue a criminal or civil case, then evidence must be well documented in order to be useful in the prosecution. After carefully sampling, documenting all evidence, and storing a small amount of material for further analysis, the bulk of the hazardous chemicals will be destroyed in accordance with law. Second, where there is insufficient evidence to justify a prosecution, the entire lot of hazardous materials should be disposed of in an appropriate manner. Thus, knowledge of the chemicals to be destroyed is essential.

The barrels in which illegal chemicals are stored can also be an important piece of evidence, and should not be destroyed (for detailed discussion see Drielak, 1998). In the U.S., containers certified for the transportation of hazardous waste are required to bear permanent identifying markings on a nonremovable component of the container (49 CFR 178.3A(1)(3)). For example, a 55-gallon steel drum may be impression-stamped. The stamping processes can be performed from the inside or outside of the container, causing a raised identification number to appear on the outside of the barrel. From the outside of the barrel, the identification number reads normally (left to right). From the inside of the barrel, the number reads in reverse. Thus, even if an offender has made an effort to remove the barrel tracking number, its inverse impression may be readable.

In accordance with EPA rules, the manufacturers of barrels and containers that can be used to store hazardous waste are required to identify and record the barrel identification number so that each container can be linked to a specific purchaser. The purchaser is required to maintain a tracking system for each barrel, noting its contents and the names of other parties to whom the barrel has been transferred. This information is also reported to the EPA when the barrels are used to store or transport hazardous waste under the cradle-to-grave hazardous waste tracking system, which requires that a manifest or record of the container's contents, owners, and transfers be recorded and transmitted to the EPA (40 CFR 262.21(f)(2)). Using the EPA manifest system and manufacturer records, storage barrels can be traced from one owner to the next.

Environmental criminals who dump waste illegally endeavor to hide their tracks by destroying barrel tracking numbers and paperwork. Often, the offenders will remove all identifying labels, use grinders to eradicate the barrel tracking number, and sometimes use sandblasters to remove all other outwardly traceable information. Fortunately for law enforcement, the stamped identification code is much more difficult to eradicate or disguise. Because the tracking number is stamped into the barrel or container itself, grinding the impression does not remove all traces of the number (Drielak, 1998).

ENVIRONMENTAL CRIME EVIDENCE: COLLECTION AND INVESTIGATIONS

It is useful to divide the collection of environmental crime related evidence into two broad types: (1) ecological and human toxicological evidence, and (2) environmental forensic evidence. *Ecological and human toxicology* involves the use of scientific techniques to assess the presence of toxic chemicals in the environment or in humans. Various techniques are used to make these assessments in water, air, or soil, to separate and test chemical mixtures, and to test for the presence of environmental toxics in human tissue, hair, bone, or teeth. Isolating and identifying toxins from samples, especially where numerous toxins may be present, can be a difficult and time consuming task, and requires specialized training and advanced degrees in fields such as chemistry, biology or toxicology. Often, the analytic-chemical techniques used include chromatography and spectrometry (see Image 7.3).

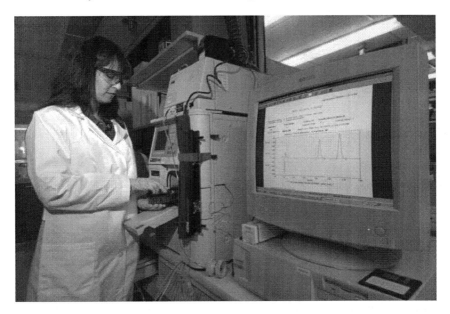

Image 7.3. CDC chemist Madhulika Chaudhary-Webb prepares a High Performance Liquid Chromatography for use.

Picture courtesy of the Center for Disease Control. Public access photo # 7300, CDC Public Health Image Library.

There are various types of chromatography—for example, gas, liquid, and solid (Northrop, 2002)—as well as two-dimensional gas chromatography, or GC x GC (Frysinger, Gaines and Reddy, 2002). Each is based on the idea that the unknown sample can be identified by assessing the amount of time it takes the sample to pass through a given medium (a known gas, liquid or solid). Spectrometry and mass spectrometry can also be used to identify chemicals. Spectrometry employs a measure of the light frequency emitted from an exposed sample to identify its chemical contents, while mass spectrometry employs a molecular ionization process to identify chemicals (see, Saferstein, 2002a).

In the investigation of environmental crime, toxicological risk assessments can also be employed. These are used to determine the health threats presented by specific chemicals. Risk assessments may become the basis for the abatement of hazards (e.g., whether a waste site should be listed as a Superfund Site), or as the basis for legislation designed to protect the public from exposure to a chemical. Toxicological risk assessments also have uses at other phases of an environmental crime abatement and prosecution. For example, the assessment can be used by a prosecutor to determine the seriousness of an offense, and can be used to justify the penalty the prosecutor will seek.

Environmental forensics involves the scientific collection of environmental crime evidence for use in a trial or other regulatory procedures used to assess blame and determine penalties. The collection of environmental forensic evidence is guided by statutory rules of evidence collection. Because numerous analysts and laboratories may be employed to assay the evidence, it is important to follow rigorous procedures with respect to tracking the evidence so as to maintain the chain of evidence. One of the difficulties encountered in an environmental crime investigation is that there may be different rules for collecting, analyzing and maintaining the chain of evidence for different types of chemical contamination or contaminated media (e.g., air, soil, water, tissue samples, etc.). Furthermore, it may be necessary to test numerous media for contamination within one investigation. Thus, in a single investigation, the investigation team may need to be familiar with and employ several different scientific approaches, chain of evidence requirements, and a number of different statutes that relate to different chemicals or contaminated mediums.

The investigation of environmental contamination in specific exposure media (e.g., air, water, soil) can also require specialized knowledge. For example, the effort to trace the source of a toxic chemical leak in soil requires knowledge of how chemicals with different properties travel in soil, or knowledge concerning the composition of soil and the geological characteristics of specific locations (Murray and Tedrow, 1998), or how chemical "plumes" develop and spread and can be mapped using chemometric methods (see Johnson and Ehrlich, 2002), or how geologically specific characteristics such as fractured formations (Theodoropoulou, Karoutsos, and Tsakiroglou, 2001) can impact the spread of a chemical spill. An oily chemical may, for instance, penetrate sand more easily than it does clay soils. In certain soil types, chemical dispersal may occur quickly, but may be limited to a smaller distance. In other cases, a chemical may move slowly through a certain type of soil, but may travel long distances. Moreover, the leaching of a chemical in a soil type may be impacted by the level of moisture in the soil, the presence of other geological factors, and the presence of groundwater (Atmadja and Bagtzoglou, 2001). A chemical spill or deposit on sandy solids sitting over an underground water source, for instance, is likely to travel much greater distances, especially if it penetrates the underground waterway, than a chemical spill or deposit on clay soil sitting over a rock base. Even the type of rock and its formation may impact the spread of chemical leaching in the environment. Dense, tightly packed stone will impede leaching, while porous, loosely packed stone will allow the spill to spread further. (For discussion of forensic geology see Murray and Tedrow, 1992; Murphy and Morrison, 2002; for scientific studies of leaching under various conditions, see articles in the *Vadose Zone Journal*, e.g., Javaux et al., 2006a, 2006b; Uwe, Jann and Kögel-Knabner, 2006; Poulsen at al, 2006; see also, Shackleford, 1989).

Why should we be concerned with soil types, chemical qualities, and leaching? In a criminal investigation, or a civil or administrative investigation seeking to determine potentially responsible parties (PRPs; the person or persons responsible for a chemical leak, spill, deposit, or release; e.g., 42 U.S.C. § 9605) for an environmental crime, the ability to trace the origin of the leak or spill is of the utmost importance for establishing criminal or civil liability for damages. Thus, knowledge of geography, chemicals, soils, and even waterways becomes necessary. The investigator may, for instance, know that a certain area is currently contaminated with a chemical. There may, however, be no immediate or apparent source for the chemical contamination. Likewise, the chemical contaminating the area may be commonly used in manufacturing. By recognizing the chemical, how it moves through water, air and soil, and knowing about local geography, the investigator stands a better chance of being able to trace the contamination to its source.

QUALITY ASSURANCE PLANS

In order to facilitate collection, maintenance and analysis of chemical evidence, the activities undertaken by environmental crime investigators (ECI) should be guided by a quality assurance plan (QAP). The QAP can serve as a basis for training ECIs, and later as a checklist for environmental investigations (Central Virginia Environmental Crime Task Force, 2005). The QAP should cover the following:

- maintenance of the chain of evidence
- collection of reliable samples
- the handling of samples and the use of control sample collection procedures
- preservation of non-chemical physical evidence
- appropriate testing and sampling methods and procedures

Specific elements contained in QAPs are examined below in more extensive detail.

The QAP outlines a diverse array of knowledge an ECI may need. Consider, for example, that an investigation involves legal issues (e.g., search and seizure, probable cause), the discovery, recording and tracking of evidence, and locating and interviewing witnesses and suspects (investigative skills), constructing appropriate sampling techniques (the use of research methods and statistical skills), knowledge of the correct testing equipment, the ability to calibrate the test equipment, and the ability to interpret the meaning of the test data for several different media (e.g., air, surface water, groundwater, soil). Much of the work involved in an environmental crime investigation involves the application of specialized knowledge. And more so than the investigation of ordinary crime, much environmental crime investigation involves the use of scientific knowledge and training. As additional evidence of the importance of this diverse body of knowledge in environmental crime cases, consider the standard operating procedure and quality assurance manual maintained by EPA's Region 4 office in Atlanta (U.S. EPA, 2001), which consists of nineteen sections spanning nearly 400 pages (excluding appendices and references). We review the topics covered in this manual, beginning with Section 2, since they provide a useful overview of the issues ECIs are likely to encounter.

Section 2 covers warrants, search and seizure, facility entry, types of investigation, investigative strategies, applicable sampling techniques, required record keeping, and report writing issues for each of the following investigative categories:

1. potable water supply investigations

2. civil enforcement investigations

3. criminal investigations

4. *Clean Water Act* compliance monitoring inspections

5. Superfund investigations

6. *Resource Conservation Recovery Act* investigations

7. Underground Storage Tank (UST) inspections

8. Underground Injection Control (UIC) investigations

9. Ambient air monitoring and evaluations

Section 3 examines sampling, field records, and document controls, including information on the chain of custody and related evidence control documents, procedures for obtaining receipts for samples, and the proper construction of field records. Section 4 examines safety protocols, while sampling designs and related quality assurance procedures are examined in Section 5, and include reviews of sampling techniques (e.g., simple, random, stratified, grid), and specific sampling issues related to sampling different media (e.g., soil, surface water, ground water, waste samples, air samples, and UTC and UIC samples). Section 6 describes the installation of monitoring wells. Sections 7 through 14 provide in-depth discussions of several issues reviewed in less detail earlier in the manual, including ground water sampling (Sec. 7), potable water sampling (Sec. 8), waste water sampling (Sec. 9), surface water sampling (Sec. 10), sediment sampling (Sec. 11), soil sampling (Sec. 12), soil sampling (Sec. 13), and ambient air monitoring (Sec. 14). Sections 15, 16 and 17 examine field measurements and equipment for different purposes, important chemical characteristics, and equipment calibration.

The wide range of issues that ECIs must confront makes it easy to see why a team approach is necessary. This brief summary of the content of this EPA publication is designed to illustrate the expansive knowledge ECIs must access and employ, and why team approaches for the investigation of environmental crimes are important. And more so than the investigation of ordinary crime, much environmental crime investigation involves the use of scientific knowledge and training. For these reasons, it becomes clear why a team approach is appropriate. Discussing team approach implications, Suggs et al (2002, p. 92) examine why cooperation among the ECI team is important:

> The investigator should maintain contact with laboratory personnel to discuss sampling activities, to determine if appropriate analytic techniques are available for use, and to ensure that resources are available to complete the analysis within applicable holding times (established time limits for sample analysis). Multiple laboratories may be needed. Laboratory personnel should be involved as early as possible in the [investigative] planning process. The analytic chemists(s) should be familiar with the types of samples being collected, the purpose of each sample in proving the case, and the appropriate analytic methods that could prove the allegations.

Discussion Box 7.1. "Finger-Printing" Oil

Chemicals can contain "chemical fingerprints" that may allow investigators to trace them to their origins (Wang, Fingas and Sigouin, 2002). This idea has been used for nearly thirty years by the Coast Guard to trace oil spills and determine potentially responsible parties for spills. Using a combination of gas spectrometry and mass spectrometry, the Coast Guard has created chemical fingerprints from oil samples acquired from refineries and other facilities where oil is stored. When an oil spill or leak is detected in a waterway, the Coast Guard can collect a sample, analyze it, and determine if it matches any of the known sites. They can use this information to prosecute the offender, correct the reason for the spill, and to collect cleanup or remediation expenses.

This technique can also be used to determine whether a spill was emitted by a particular vessel. In such a case, the oil fingerprint is not typically on file, but must be created from samples drawn from vessels. An investigation of this nature is more like an ordinary criminal investigation, as the authorities attempt to locate the offender using chemical and other evidence (see, Daley, 2006). Similar analysis can reveal the origins of a chemical spill that passed through the soil. This technique can be used to determine the origins of a leak if it has passed through soil with unique properties such as trace elements (see also, Suggs et al, 2002; Staniloae, Petrescu and Patroescu, 2001).

Popular television shows like *CSI* supply the impression that any one individual may have an expansive array of knowledge, and float effortlessly between tracking down suspects and witnesses, collecting evidence, and performing complicated laboratory tests (not to mention creating new equipment and scientific protocols as they proceed). To be sure, those involved in actual environmental crime investigations recognize that television shows present unrealistic characterizations of crime investigations, and glamorize these activities. In contrast to *CSI* and related television shows, much environmental crime investigation involves highly structured routines needed to satisfy legal and scientific requirements for evidence. (For an analysis of forensic science in detective fiction see, Gerber, 1997).

Laboratory Investigators

The work done in the ECI laboratory is equally important to the investigative field work. Indeed, the work of the lawyer or field investigator may be fruitless if laboratory work is deficient, unacceptable analytic methods are used, or the paperwork needed to maintain the chain of evidence is overlooked. Because the work of laboratory investigators is so important to the prosecution of environmental crime, the activity of the laboratory staff is guided by strict rules and procedures (e.g., the EPA quality assurance manual described above). Moreover, strict rules of procedure are also required by the nature of scientific investigations themselves, and scientists from numerous fields follow pains-taking procedures to guarantee the validity and reliability of the evidence and scientific tests they produce. Laboratory analysts should—and do—take great care to maintain laboratory notebooks for each case (including lab notes, data collecting and analysis techniques, data and data analysis printouts, equipment calibration information, for both the test and control samples in case; for examples of violations of these rules and procedures leading to criminal charges against laboratories, see, Suggs et al, 2002). This rigorous record is considered necessary to meet burden of proof requirements specified in law for the successful prosecution of environmental crimes.

As Suggs et al. (2002) note, laboratory personnel must take extreme care of the evidence and evidentiary record because the information they provide can be challenged during the regulatory process. For example, a successful evidence challenge during pre-trial would cause evidence to be inadmissible in court, and render a guilty verdict or administrative response less likely, especially where scientific information about the evidence is needed to establish that a certain level of environmental crime has been committed. For example, proving the legal elements of certain environmental crimes is contingent on providing evi-dence that the suspect emitted or disposed of an excessive concentration of specific chemicals in an illegal manner. Without valid sampling, testing and record keeping from laboratory personnel, such crimes cannot be prosecuted or proven.

Sampling Issues

When investigating an environmental crime, the ECI will often have to make decisions about sampling, including what and how to sample. These decisions are affected by what is being sampled—whether the samples come from air, water, soil, hazardous waste barrels, or some other environmental medium (Back, 2007). Before proceeding with the sample, the ECI must know what technologies apply to the sampling of different media. The ECI must also choose between complete or exhaustive sample and random sample techniques. For example, an ECI is assigned the duty of collecting samples from a site where unlabeled, hazardous waste barrels have been illegally stored. The barrels' contents must be identified before the case can proceed. If there are only a few barrels on site, the ECI has the option of drawing samples from all waste barrels, creating an exhaustive sample. In a case where the site is large and contains several hundred barrels, it may be difficult to draw samples from all barrels, and the ECI will have to rely on one of several different random sampling techniques to determine the contents of the barrels. Random sampling techniques are preferred when there are a large number of samples to be drawn.

In addition, when taking samples, the ECI must know that matching or replicate samples should be taken for at least 20 percent of samples. Matching or replicate samples involve additional samples taken from the same source. They are used to assess the reliability of the sample and chemical analysis, and help ensure the quality of the data and the validity of the conclusions reached from sample analysis. Chemical sampling issues are the subject of the EPA's SW-846, an on-line guide to sampling and test methods (www.epa.gov/epaoswer/hazwaste/test/main.htm; see also, Suggs et al., 2002 for extended discussion of relevant sampling issues and resources, including statistical models and guides).

Another quality assurance measure ECIs must employ is the use of "field blanks." A field blank contains a matching set of equipment and sampling instruments used to collect the samples (e.g., sample containers, test tubes, spatulas, beakers, etc.). The field blank equipment is carried along with the sample kit, and is employed to assess the possibility that the collected samples were contaminated from an outside source during collection, transportation, or analysis. (For further discussion see, Suggs et al, 2002; Central Virginia Environmental Crimes Task Force, 2005).

AN OVERVIEW OF OTHER LABORATORY GUIDELINES AND ISSUES

Laboratory analyses are an integral component of environmental crime investigations and environmental regulatory procedures, including efforts to promulgate environmental laws that protect public health and safety. In order to promote uniform analysis of environmental toxins and pollutants, the EPA maintains on-line laboratory and field guides for many (but not all) analytic and sampling procedures used in environmental and chemical analysis for various contaminated media (www.epa.gov/epahome/index/sources.htm). To emphasize the fact that the investigation of environmental crimes requires the ability to employ complex skills and knowledge to identify toxic hazards, we provide an example of on-line guides and procedures in Table 7.1 (an in-depth discussion of these laboratory and field guides is beyond the scope of this book; for extended discussion see, Saferstein, 2002a,b).

**Table 7.1. Examples of on-Line U.S. EPA Laboratory and Field
Guides for Analysis, Sampling and Evidence Collecting**

RCRA Waste Sampling Methods	(530/D-02-002)
RCRA Ground Water Monitoring	(530-R-93-001)
Test Methods for Evaluating Solid Waste	(530/SW-846)
Sampling Quality Assurance Guidelines	(540/G-90-004)
Chemical Analysis of Water Waste	(600/4-79-020)
Measuring Radioactivity in Drinking Water	(600/4-80-032)
Measuring PCBs in Transformer Fluid and Waste Oil	(600/4-80-045)
Handbook of Water Sampling and Sample Preservation	(600/4-82-029)
Measuring Acute Toxicity Effluents on Fresh and Marine Animals	(600/4-90-027F)
Methods for Determining Metals in Environmental Samples	(600/4-91-010)
Lead Based Paint Testing Technologies	(747/R-95-002A)
Clean Water Act Compliance Monitoring: Metals	(821/B-95-002)
EPA Methods for Analysis of Water	(821/C-99-004)

Source: www.epa.gov/epahome/index/sources.htm. The names of some of the documents listed in this table have been shortened for ease of presentation. Document numbers are shown in parentheses.

Suggs and Yarborough (2001) also provide an excellent discussion of a variety of sampling and testing issues pertinent to the investigation and regulation of environmental crimes. For example, they note that the EPA maintains resources for assessing RCRA wastes, which are comprised of land-based (see EPA test method SW-846; www.epa.gov/epaoswer/hazwaste/ test/main. htm), water-based (www.ntis.gov/search/product.asp? ABBR= PB99500209 &starDB=GRAHIST and www.epa.gov/tio/ tsp/ download/ gw_sampling_ guide.pdf) and air-based (40 CFR Parts 60, 61, and 63) wastes and chemicals. Additional protocols are available for Superfund Sites for air, water, soil, waste and biota (Suggs and Yarborough, 2001: 9; see also Table 7.2).

Suggs and Yarborough (2001, p. 9; emphasis added) note that "the library staff of Region 1 developed the EPA's most comprehensive list of sampling, measurement, and analytical test methods. The list is regularly updated and currently contains *about 1,600 methods*, with most of the listed sources accompanied by live web links to the actual method.". Suggs and Yarborough's discussion is also valuable because it illustrates important issues related to environmental chemistry, environmental organic chemistry, soil analysis, environmental forensics, inorganic mass spectrometry, x-ray spectrometry, air analysis, water analysis, organometallic compounds, and pesticide and hydrocarbon analysis (2001, pp. 9-12). The researchers also discuss sampling, sample extraction, and preservation of samples, and present a brief overview of specific techniques (pp. 13-26).

Table 7.2. Other Important U.S. EPA Referenced On-Line Analytic Methods Guides

Environmental Chemistry Methods (ECM)
www.epa.gov/oppbead1/methods/ecm12b.htm. The ECM contains information on testing for pesticides in soil and water samples. Methods are listed by chemical name. Only about 25 percent of submitted methods have been verified by the EPA. Methods for identifying chemicals, their metabolites and degradates are noted.

Ambient Monitoring Technology Information
www.epa.gov/ttn/amtic/criteria.html. Contains the "reference" and "equivalent" methods for identifying the criteria air pollutants under 40 CFR 53 (Ambient Air Monitoring Methods) and 40 CFR 58 (Ambient Air Quality Surveillance).

www.epa.gov/ttn/amtic. Provides access to the EPA's Ambient Air Monitoring Technology Information Center. Links to the Clean Air Scientific Advisory Committee (CASAC), National Air Monitoring Strategy, Air Quality Index (AQI) , various air monitoring programs and methods, among other links, can be accessed.

www.epa.gov/ttn/emc. Connects to the Emission Measurement Center, which provides specific details on technological methods for measurement of various air toxins.

Technical Guidance Documents
www.epa.gov/ttn/amtic/cpreldoc.html. Memorandum and technical guidance documents for air analysis and monitoring systems and stations.

National Environmental Methods Index
www.nemi.gov. A free, searchable on-line clearinghouse containing documents describing methods and procedures used to monitor air, water, soil and tissue samples. Also provides comparative information on costs of monitoring and sampling, as well as cross methods performance comparisons.

Water Science Methods for Clean Water Act and Safe Drinking Water Act
www.epa.gov/ost/methods. Links to laboratory analytic methods used by industries and municipalities to perform tests required under the *Clean Air Act* (CAA; 40 CFR CH.1, Parts 50-99) and the Safe Drinking Water Act (SDWA; 42 CFR CH 6, Subchapter XII).

Given the complex nature of environmental crime investigation, and the central role laboratories play in these investigations, laboratories assigned these tasks should be certified or accredited. This certification indicates that the laboratory recognizes and promotes appropriate scientific standards and procedures, especially those relevant to the examination of environmental and chemical substances and data. Further, certification acknowledges that the lab is adequately staffed and equipped, and that the staff has appropriate levels of training. (For further discussion of accreditation see, Hughes and Suggs, 2003).

SECONDARY DATA FOR INVESTIGATIONS

ECIs often need to access secondary data when they pursue a case. For instance, they may need information on an offender or company's prior record of environmental violations, or its reporting practices. These data may be obtained from EPA files, and through the use of other on-line data sources (see Burns and Lynch, 2004 for discussion). Researchers may need information about a contaminated area, including its geological or population characteristics. This information is available in the form of geographic information system (GIS) data maintained by different federal, state and local agencies. We examine the use of GIS data in the chapter on environmental justice.

ECIs may also need access to information concerning a suspected violating company, its financial state, and its association with other companies. A number of business guides and databases can serve as resource guides, including *Marketline, Investext Plus, Dun and Bradstreet, Million Dollar Database*, or *Moody's Investor Services*. Information provided on companies and industries by the Bureau of the Census and the Securities and Exchange Commission may also be relevant to an investigation.

ECIs may obtain prior criminal record data for environmental criminals from the Criminal Investigations Division, Office of Criminal Enforcement, Forensics and Training in the EPA. The EPA maintains these records in its *Criminal Investigative Index and Files* (OCEFT). The OCEFT allows EPA personnel to access compiled criminal records and other information on prior offenders drawn from violations of the *Comprehensive Environmental Response, Compensation and Liability Act* (42 U.S.C. 9603), the *Resource Conservation and Recovery Act* (42 U.S.C. 6928), the *Federal Water Pollution Control Act* (33 U.S.C. 1319, 1321), the *Toxic Substances Control Act* (15 U.S.C. 2614, 2615), the *Clean Air Act* (42 U.S.C. 7413), the *Federal Insecticide, Fungicide and Rodenticide Act* (7 U.S.C. 136j, 136l), the *Safe Drinking Water Act* (42 U.S.C. 300h-2, 300i-1), the *Noise Control Act* (42 U.S.C. 4912), the *Emergency Planning and Community Right-To-Know Act* (42 U.S.C. 11045); and the *Marine Protection, Research, and Sanctuaries Act* (33 U.S.C. 1415; see, www.epa.gov/privacy/notice/ epa-17.htm).

ECI investigators will also need access to a chemical database such as the *CAS* (Chemical Abstracts Service), the world's largest and most up-to-date chemical registry. All chemicals have a unique CAS registry number. These numbers are used by laboratories, other research guides, and the EPA to positively identify a chemical..

CONCLUSION

This chapter has provided an overview of some of the issues involved in the investigation of environmental crimes. As we have argued in earlier chapters, these crimes are an increasingly important concern, and threaten a broader section of the American public than the ordinary street crimes criminologists tend to study. Thus, it is necessary that criminologists and their students become more familiar with these crimes and how they are investigated and addressed. Moreover, given the extensive nature of environmental crimes and the limited resources devoted to detecting and investigating these offenses, local police departments must also become more familiar with the techniques of toxic crime investigation. These efforts, like the environmental crime investigation itself, must be based on interdisciplinary knowledge. To do so at the local and some-times the state level requires cooperation among agencies with access to different knowledge bases, research and technical capabilities.

Today, the challenges presented by environmental crime investigation are becoming more widely recognized. Specifically, as Steven C. Drielak (2006) of the EPA Homeland Security Program has argued, the global system of justice emerging in response to terrorism and the potential use of chemical weapons, has been reshaping law enforcement responsibilities and duties, thrusting upon them the need to become more familiar with environmental crime investigation and evidence collection. With respect to international environmental crimes that may, for instance, involve evidence concerning weapons of mass destruction, environmental crime investigation techniques will become increasingly impor-tant in international courts (Drielak, 2004). These concerns also increase the need for personnel trained in the overlap of environmental crime investigation and international law and court issues.

Useful On-Line Resources for ECI Investigations

- The Registry of Toxic Effects of Chemicals. Provides a summary of data on chemicals drawn from the broader scientific literature. Arranged alphabetically. www.cdc.gov/niosh/rtecs/ RTECSaccess.html

- Toxicological Chemical Profiles. Summary sheets and toxic chemical profiles available from the Agency for Toxic Substances and Disease Registry. www.atsdr.cdc.gov/toxpro2.html; and www.atsdr.cdc.gov/toxfaq. html

- *CERCLA* priority list of hazardous substances. www.atsdr.cdc.gov/cercla

- *CERCLA* minimum risk level list. www.atsdr.cdc.gov/mrls.html

- Ecological risk analysis. www.esd.ornl.gov/programs/ecorisk/ecorisk.html

- EPA Integrated Risk Information System (IRIS). A database of potential human health effects that may result from exposure to environmental hazards. Developed by EPA to provide information to those with health science background who lack extensive toxicological training. www.epa.gov/iris/

- Berkeley Carcinogenic Potency Project. An international data base with results from more than 6000 cancer studies of chronic, long term exposure of animals to nearly 1500 chemicals. potency.berkeley.edu/cpdb.html

- National Toxicology Program (NTP), U.S. Department of Health and Human Services. The NTP uses rigorous scientific methods to help identify toxic threats to human health. The NTP is comprised of research undertaken at the National Institute of Environmental Health Sciences (NIEHS), the National Institute for Occupational Safety and Health (NIOSH) and the National Center for Toxicological Research (NCTR). The NTP provides access to numerous study results, chemical fact sheets, and regulatory actions. ntp-server.niehs.nih.gov

- The United States National Library of Medicine provides public online access to a number of different databases including the International Toxicity Estimates for Risk (ITER); ChemIDplus, a database on more than 370,000 chemicals; TOXLINE, online access to the toxicological literature; the Chemical Carcinogenesis Research Information System (CCRIS), which contains information on the cancer-causing and genetic impacts of more than 8,000 chemicals; the Developmental and Reproductive Toxicology Database (DART), the Genetic Toxicology Data Base (GENTOX), which allows access to peer-reviewed genetic toxicological test results for more than 3,000 chemicals; the EPA's Integrated Risk Assessment System (IRIS); HSDB, the Hazardous Substances Database of peer-reviewed toxicological data for 5,000 chemicals; as well as access to the EPA Toxic Release Inventory.

- Envirofacts. A U.S. EPA information retrieval system that links its separate databases (e.g., TRI, Superfund, etc.,). It can be used to gather information on areas or specific companies, or to produce maps. www.epa.gov/enviro

CHAPTER 8.

Environmental Crime Data and its Uses

INTRODUCTION

For decades, corporate crime researchers lamented the difficulties associated with performing empirical studies of corporate crime due to a lack of data. This argument was extended to all types of corporate crime research, including the study of environmental crime. This position had some merit, and to be sure it used to be much more difficult to access corporate crime data because it was restricted in several ways. First, these data were treated as private and not open to public inspection. Second, there was and still is no central depository for corporate data similar to the Uniform Crime Report, a national dataset on street or ordinary crime maintained by the FBI. Researchers interested in street crimes can collect a variety of data simply by referring to the Uniform Crime Report. Collecting a national environmental crime data set, however, require collecting data from numerous agencies at the federal and state levels. This situation could be complicated if researchers wanted to examine case trial and outcome information since collecting this data required access to prosecutors and trial courts as well.

Beginning in the early 1990s, many federal agencies began to publish data that was accessible over the internet. Today, for example, the U.S. EPA and environmental agencies for almost every state maintain websites where environmental crime and prosecution data can be accessed. This improved level of open access has made it much easier for researchers to undertake a variety of studies of environmental crime and enforcement. Yet, despite enhanced data access, criminologists have devoted little attention to studying environmental crime, law, and justice.

To encourage such studies, this chapter examines some of the sources for environmental crime data, with the primary focus on federal data sources. Explanations of how to locate data, what data is available, and examples of how these data can be used are also provided. (Those who are interested in more detailed explanations of these data sources should see Burns and Lynch, 2004, chapters 7-12).

DATA SOURCES

Criminologists have largely neglected EPA data, limiting the study of the extent and effects and the forms of social control applied to toxic crimes (Lynch et al, 2004). As noted in an earlier chapter, environmental crimes may cause multiple deaths, injuries, and illnesses, and in this respect are often more serious than street crimes. These crimes can no longer be avoided by criminology, especially if its claim to be objective is to be taken seriously.

A number of different databases are available through the Internet from the EPA; however, users should be wary of potential obstacles. These databases are often updated and their web addresses changed, which sometimes makes these data difficult to locate. It is also important to point out that these data include complex coding, meaning that knowledge of database management and manipulation is needed to transform the data into analyzable formats. Easy access to EPA data is provided on the agency's homepage (www.epa.gov) using the "Quick Finder" section located near the top of the page. Clicking each link brings users to the "subtopics" page for each area, where an extensive number of additional links are located. Researchers interested in environmental crime may be interested in several of the following quick finder data access links:

- **Acid Rain.** Use the Quick Finder link labeled "Data and Maps" to access data on emissions, emission allowances, regulatory compliance data, air quality, data sets and reports, quick facts and trends, and facility information.

- **Air.** Under the Air link, users will find a series of subtopic links on air pollutants: air pollution, air quality, air pollution control, air pollution effects, air pollution laws (including enforcement, compliance, regulations, standards, legislation and permits), air pollution monitoring, atmospheric pollution (such as climate change and global warming), and indoor and mobile sources of pollution.

- **Cleanup.** Links to information on brownfields, cleanup technologies, the legal and enforcement aspects of cleanup, and Superfund data can be accessed using the quick finder cleanup link.

- **Enforcement.** Using this link, access to sublinks on civil enforcement, criminal enforcement, compliance programs, violation, voluntary compliance, reporting and settlements can be accessed.

- **Pesticides.** Pesticide regulations, enforcement, and health effects data are available using this link.

- **Superfund.** This link provides access to a host of data and laws related to the Superfund program.

- **TRI**. The TRI or Toxic Release Inventory contains data on toxic releases by businesses. Access to TRI data is available using the sublink, "The TRI Explorer" located under the heading "Search TRI Data."

- *Clean Air Act, Clean Water Act,* **and Hazardous Waste.** These Quick Finder links bring users to laws and regulations that apply to each of these areas.

MAJOR EPA DATABASES

The EPA also maintains and makes public several major databases. These databases contain information about compliance and assistance and many contain information that can be used to map out environmental crime. All databases are currently accessible through the EPA's website.

ECHO

ECHO stands for Enforcement and Compliance History Online. The ECHO system can be used to retrieve data on air, water and hazardous waste violations, formal and informal enforcement actions, the number of quarters in which facilities were in noncompliance over the past three years, and alleged current significant violations for individual facilities, by ZIP code, or for cities and counties by state. Air, water, and hazardous waste information can be searched simultaneously or individually.

An ECHO search produces online data tables. These tables contain hot links that allow further information to be collected on each reporting facility by clicking on the facility name. Facility information includes geographic location data (important when using GIS or Geographic Information Systems methods of analysis), details about inspections (who conducted the inspection, and the type of inspection), enforcement history and penalties, violation notices, and characteristics of the community in which the facility is located. ECHO data can also be downloaded as comma delimited files and imported into data analysis software. To illustrate the kinds of data ECHO generates, the data for air, water and hazardous waste for Nassau County, Long Island, New York are briefly described.

Nassau Air Pollution, Compliance, Inspections, Violations and Enforcement Actions

On the ECHO homepage, select the "Air Data" link. On the subsequent search page, use the subsection marked "geographic location." In that search box, first select the state, "New York." Doing so enables the county drop down menu. Select "Nassau County" from the county drop down menu. Then use the "search" button location at the top of this subsection. The search (run March, 2007) returned a summary table for 88 major facilities in Nassau County, New

York that includes the following information: (1) the name and location of each facility, (2) the facility or program ID number, (3) the number of full compliance inspections completed at the facility over the past three years, (4) the number of quarters the facility was in noncompliance over the past three years, (5) whether or not there are alleged current significant violations at each facility (no or yes), (6) the number of informal enforcement actions taken at each facility over the past three years, and (7) the number of formal enforcement actions taken at each facility over the past three years.

The same procedure can be followed to generate water and hazardous waste data for Nassau County. Employing these data, summary reports for air, water and hazardous waste regulations can be complied by the user.

Nassau Air data summary

Over the past three years, forty-two facilities (47.7 percent of all reporting facilities in Nassau) were inspected. Thirteen facilities had partial inspections. The remaining inspections were complete inspections, and seven facilities were inspected once, nine twice, 13 three times, and one was inspected four times. Twenty nine facilities (33 percent) were in alleged noncompliance for at least one quarter, with 21 facilities (72.4 percent) in alleged noncompliance for either 11 or 12 quarters, and three facilities in alleged noncompliance for seven or more quarters. Thus, nearly 83 percent of noncompliance facilities were in noncompliance for more than one-half of the recording period.

Only one facility was reported as having an alleged current significant violation. This facility (the Rockville Center Power Plant) also had the largest number of inspections (four), and was in alleged noncompliance for 12 quarters.

There were a total of 40 informal actions taken at 24 facilities. The majority of these facilities (13) had one informal enforcement action. Seven facilities had two informal enforcement actions, and four had either three or four informal enforcement actions. There were also a total of 22 formal enforcement actions taken at 19 facilities. Only two facilities had more than one formal enforcement action (one had two, and one had three). In 17 of the 22 cases in which there were formal enforcement actions, the facility also had at least one informal enforcement action.

Overall, five facilities had an entry in each data field (except alleged current significant violation). These data indicate, then, that only a handful of facilities in Nassau County were persistent and serious violators of air pollution standards. However, it should be kept in mind that a large percentage of facilities (88 percent) were in noncompliance with air pollution standards for more than one-half of the three year time period, and could be judged as persistent violators.

Nassau County Water Data

Only 13 facilities have water pollution permits that require them to report data to the EPA. Each facility was inspected at least once, and the average number of inspections was 6.4. These data indicate that water pollution-related inspections occurred more frequently than air pollution inspections. All thirteen facilities were in noncompliance for at least one quarter, and 8 of the 13 facilities were in noncompliance during more than one-half of the three-year period. None of the facilities had a current alleged significant violation, no facility had an informal enforcement action in the past three years, and only three facilities had formal enforcement actions. Two facilities had two formal enforcement actions apiece.

Nassau County Hazardous Waste Data

A much larger number of facilities—191—in Nassau County report hazardous waste data to the EPA. Of these, 30 were inspected. Most were inspected twice, but one facility was inspected once, one four times, one five times, and three received three inspections apiece, producing a total of 43 inspections. Relatively few facilities, 19, were reported to be in noncompliance, and of these facilities, only two were reported to be in noncompliance in seven quarters or for more than one half of the reporting period. Two facilities had alleged significant current violations, 17 facilities had an informal enforcement action (one facility had two, the remainder had one), and only three facilities had formal enforcement actions (one facility had two formal actions, the other two had one formal enforcement action apiece).

Envirofacts Warehouse

(www.epa.gov/enviro). Similar to ECHO, Envirofacts Warehouse provides access to several EPA databases on environmental hazards. Envirofacts is useful because it permits the retrieval of information from multiple databases in one location. Unlike ECHO which is limited to facilities with enforcement, compliance or inspection records, Envirofacts produces reports for all legally recognized facilities that produce pollution (e.g., facilities that have a pollution permit). For example, an ECHO search for air hazardous violators returned 88 facilities for Nassau County. Envirofacts records 540 facilities with air release reports. Combining these two data sets, it can be determined that 16.3 percent (88 of 540) of all facilities that report air pollution waste have some compliance issue. In addition, across all three searches (air, water, waste), ECHO identified 292 facilities with violations. In total, Envirofacts listed 4,311 reporting facilities in Nassau County. Since some of these facilities may have multiple violations across media types, it would be necessary to identify these facilities to accurately estimate the percent that were known to violate an environmental law.

The Envirofacts homepage links are divided into the following categories: "air," "waste," "water," "toxics," "radiation," "land," "compliance," "maps" and "other." The information that may be retrieved using some of these links is briefly described below.

Air report

These reports may be searched by ZIP code, city or county. Facility name and location information, along with information on number of exhaust stacks and points monitored within each facility are presented. Each facility can also be mapped. Facilities are also linked to a "facility detail report" accessed by clicking the "view facility report" link. Once on the facility detail report page, clicking on the facility name returns air hazard data from the AIRS/AFS database. The AIRS/AFS data indicate whether this is a major or minor facility, and whether emissions are within or above the threshold level, whether the facility has an approval emergency control plan, and whether the plant is in or out of compliance overall, at a specific emission point, or for a specific pollutant.

RCRA database information and toxic report details

If applicable, the RCRA information indicates materials produced at a facility. The toxic release reports include information about the chemicals transferred to other facilities and chemicals released to the air (the type of chemical, the amount released in pounds per year, and the release method).

Waste Report

These data may be retrieved by ZIP code, city or county. The waste report produces information from the RCRA (*Resource Conservation Recovery Act*) and CERCLIS (Comprehensive Environmental Response, Compensation and Liability Information System (CERCLIS)) databases. As an example, select "waste" from the main menu. On the next page, request information about CERCLIS sites which include hazardous waste handlers and generators by ZIP code, city or state (e.g., enter the county and state in which you live, and examine the results). In Nassau County, NY, for example, there are 43 listed CERCLIS sites. Next, use the column labeled "NPL Status" to determine if the listed site is on the National Priority List (whether it is considered a Superfund Site) and is designated for cleanup. Sites marked "Deleted from Final NPL" have undergone remediation and have already been cleaned up. The label "Currently on Final NPL," indicates sites designated for or in the process of being cleaned up. In Nassau County, three sites have been deleted from the NPL, and there are currently 16 Superfund sites. Further information on each site may be obtained by clicking on the case ID number. This information can be used to track the progress of site remediation. In addition, each site may be mapped using the link under the heading "Mapping Info." These maps display key features of an area where Superfund sites are located, such as the location of elementary schools, other toxic hazards, and the location of polluted ("impaired") waterways.

The RCRA data are much more extensive than Superfund data simply because there are a larger number of sites that fall under the purview of RCRA. For example, requesting a RCRA search for Nassau County returns 4,171 sites where hazardous wastes are produced stored or treated.

Toxic Release Inventory (TRI)

The Toxic Release Inventory contains data on toxic chemical releases and waste management by regulated facilities. These data are reported annually by regulated facilities. National and state data files are available for download (www.epa.gov/triexplorer). TRI data are included, but are not reported separately, in ECHO or Envirofacts.

The TRI Explorer can be used to generate hazardous waste release reports, waste transfer reports, and water quality reports. These reports may be generated by facility, geographic location, for specific chemical, years and industries. For general information, the "State Fact Sheet" link can be used. As an example, clicking on the "State Fact Sheet" link produces a map of the U.S. Clicking on any state produces a state specific map. Clicking on the state specific map activates the county summaries. Move the cursor over each county to obtain a summary of the total pounds of TRI releases produced in that county. With the cursor on a county, click to reveal a submenu that provides additional information about TRI releases, and an important link to the U.S. Census where population data for the county is readily available.

Accompanying the state map is a summary of TRI releases for the selected state detailing the pounds of toxic waste released, transferred and stored. An aggregated report for the entire U.S. can be produced using the "release report" link on the TRI Explorer homepage. Select this link, and then click "generate report." This report is organized by chemical agent. Proceed to the bottom right side of that table, which indicates that in 2004 more than 4.2 billion pounds of toxins were produced, disposed or released in the U.S., which, on average, is nearly 2,000 pounds of toxins per square mile of land in the U.S. Below the main table is a second table containing the total *grams* of dioxin related compounds (111,480.9248)—a highly toxic substance of special interest because it is a known human carcinogen with no safe exposure level (Mackie et al., 2003). In 2004, 111,480.9248 grams or 245.77 pounds of dioxin were released in the U.S.

Biennial Reporting System (BRS)

The BRS is a repository of information collected under the *Resource Conservation and Recovery Act* (RCRA) of 1976 as amended by the Hazardous and Solid Waste Amendments of 1984. The majority of BRS data is collected by states and/or EPA Regions using the Hazardous Waste Report, Instructions, and

Forms (commonly called the Biennial Report) produced by the EPA. The BRS database contains data reported by Large Quantity Generators (LQGs) and Treatment, Storage, and Disposal (TSD) sites. The BRS and TRI are similar; however, the TRI covers a broader range of toxic hazards because it is not limited to LQGs. Like TRI data, BRS data are also included within ECHO and Envirofacts reports, though these data are not reported independently.

OTHER EPA DATA SOURCES

In addition to the commonly used EPA data sources presented above, there are several other data sources that may be of use to criminologists. We briefly review several of these databases though many are integrated into ECHO.

Permit Compliance System (PCS) for Water Discharge Permits

The PCS allows access to water pollution permit information maintained under the National Pollution Discharge Elimination System (NPDES) . Searches may be performed by facility, geographically, by industry using the Standard Industrial Classification code (SIC) for an industry group, by chemical name, and by date of permit. The information produced by this search will sometimes be incomplete because individual states may have the authority to issue water pollution permits. In the basic table, the data includes facility information and the permit issue and expiration date. Specific information on permits and permit limits, violations, inspections, and other compliance measures for each facility may be acquired by clicking on the NPDES ID number in the first column of the table.

National Emissions Inventory (NEI)

NEI is a national database for point, non-point and mobile sources of air pollution. Similar information can be found in the Air Quality System (AQS) and AirData systems. These data are also employed on the AIRNOW (airnow.gov) website to produce daily maps of air quality in the U.S.

Integrated Risk Information System (IRIS)

Retrieves human health information associated with exposure to specific chemicals. Documents are searched by chemical name.

Emergency Response Notification System (ERNS)

Contains information on chemical accidents and spills. Data through 1990 is maintain by the EPA. More recent data is available from the National Response Center (NRC).

NON-EPA DATA SOURCES

There are a number of data resources maintained by a variety of state and federal agencies useful for examining environmental crime, law and justice issues. Some of these data sources are based upon EPA data but are presented in a more user friendly format. We review two major non-EPA sites: The Right-To-Know Network and Scorecard.

The Right-to-Know Network (RTK)

RTK simply presents EPA data in an easily accessible format, and fulfills the legal requirement of the public use and access language specified in the *Emergency Planning and Community Right-To-Know Act* or EPCRA enacted by Congress in 1986 under Title III of the *Superfund Amendments and Reauthorization Act*. Ralph Nader's U.S. Public Interest Research Group played a vital role in the implementation of EPCRA.

The RTK network is accessed via the web at www.rtk.net or www.rtknet.org. User can access data from several EPA programs, including

1. Toxic Release Inventory (TRI) ;
2. Biennial Reporting System (BRS);
3. Comprehensive Environmental Response, Compensation and Liability Information System (CERCLIS) ;
4. Civil Court Docket (DOCKET);
5. Emergency Response Notification System (ERNS);
6. *Resource Conservation and Recovery Act* Information System (RCRIS) ;
7. *Toxic Substances Control Act* Test Submissions (TSCATS);
8. Accidental Release Information Program (ARIP);
9. Facility Index System (FACILITY);
10. Permit Compliance System (PCS)
11. Risk Management Plan (RMP) Search.

While easy to use, there are currently no integrated data available from RTK that are equivalent to the EPA's ECHO database.

RTK currently produces its reports in "summary," "low," "medium," or "high" detail at the user's option. The "medium detail" option, in our opinion, has no specific use, and users should explore the data using the "summary" and "low detail" options, and request "high detail" searches when they find data of interest. The "low detail" option provides the basic data, while the "high detail" option adds, especially in certain data sets, extensive detail. "Summary" searches are useful for providing aggregate details for an area, and provide totals that users would otherwise need to calculate. Other search options provide additional information but do not include data totals for all facilities. For example, a user may be interested in the use of fines to address violations of a specific environmental regulation in the RCRIS database. Users can also run a "low detail" search to for a specific location to discover the number of reporting facilities penalized. In some databases, the "high detail" search option will also produce "free field" data that may include qualitative commentary on the facility or case (see for example, CERCLIS, RCRIS, and RMP data).

Data formats vary across RTK databases. Usually three print formats are available for both on-screen and E-mail requests: ASCII (American Standard Code for Information Interchange) text; comma delimited ASCII (Dbase readable); and tab delimited ASCII (Microsoft Excel readable). Unless users plan to import RTK data into statistical programs, the best and most readable option in many cases, is ASCII text.

Toxic Release Inventory (TRI) on RTK NET

The TRI contains data covering the release and transfer of toxic chemicals from manufacturing facilities. A facility is required to report a toxic release of chemicals to air, land, water, or underground to the EPA when the following conditions exist: (1) the facility has an Industrial Classification Code (SIC) number 20–39; (2) the facility employs 10 or more workers; (3) the facility manufacturers or processes more than 25,000 pounds of one of 350 chemicals listed in TRI regulations, or uses more than 10,000 pounds of the 350 listed chemicals in the manufacturing process in one year.

TRI data may be retrieved using either facility or geographic region (ZIP code, county, or state). Reports within a region are organized by facility. All RTK NET TRI data are reported by facility, regardless of how the search is produced. The area search allows users to identify all facilities in an area that report under TRI without having to know the names of these facilities. Facility searches are useful when the user knows the name of the facility they want to investigate, or to collect high detail data following a "low detail" search.

A "low" detail search produces basic facility information (name, address, parent company, contact information, Dun and Bradstreet Number, SIC classification, TRI ID), report submission information (number of submissions, toxins release by medium of release—air, water, stack, underground, land; total waste produced; off-site transfer amounts; and accidental releases or non-production related waste).

For example, users can produce a summary report for Nassau County, New York for the year 2004. This report shows the results for 24 facilities that reported TRI releases to the EPA. Among these facilities, Photocircuits Corp reported the largest quantity of waste with more than 1.2 million pounds, or more than one half of all reported TRI emissions for Nassau County in 2004. Further details about Photocircuits emissions may be obtained by clicking on the company name to produce a detailed report for that facility including forms or methods of release, and amounts of pollution stored, managed or recycled for each chemical released, stored or managed.

A summary report for Nassau County fills one page. The low detail report covers about 21 pages, while the high detail report is 125 pages in length. It may take several minutes to produce a high detailed report.

Biennial Reporting System (BRS) on RTK NET

The BRS is a waste tracking system that records the amount of waste produced, shipped, and received by waste manufacturers and handlers as required by the RCRA (*Resource Conservation and Recovery Act*). RTK provides five search formats for BRS data: (1) geographic area, (2) facility, (3) industry, (4) generated waste, and (5) received waste. All data, however, are displayed as facility-specific data. Thus, regardless of the kind of search requested, each output is similar to the extent that each is organized around the reports supplied by each facility (in a region, an industry, or by waste received or waste generated). BRS data are reported every other (odd) year.

Produce a BRS geographic area report for 2003 in summary format for Nassau County. The report should contain 95 facilities. Note that the BRS summary report does not present aggregate totals, and the user must add the columns of information to produce these totals. Note, too, that the BRS reports tons produced and tons managed as separate categories. In Nassau, the largest producer *and* manager of toxic waste is GDATP, Glen Cove.

As in the TRI report, further information about each facility can be easily obtained by clicking on the facility name. To obtain facility specific information for all facilities simultaneously, use the high detail search.

CERCLIS—Comprehensive Environmental Response Compensation and Liability Information System on RTK

CERCLIS contains data on hazardous waste sites produced by enforcing CERCLA, or the *Superfund Amendment and Reauthorization Act of 1986*. CERCLIS waste sites are the most serious waste sites. Some CERCLIS sites are also designated as NPL or Superfund sites, and designated for cleanup. CERCLIS searches are performed by area or site. No summary reports are available. For RTK CERCLIS data, high and low level outputs are equivalent. The low detail search for Nassau County includes 81 sites, and is 22 pages in length. The heading, "National Priority List (NPL) Status," indicates the site status. Unfortunately, this information is not complete in the RTK general CERCLIS search database. However, sites designated "No Further Remedial Action Planned" means the EPA has inspected the site, but has no plan to clean up that site. The phrase "Environmental Priority Initiative" means that the site has the potential for a hazardous waste release into the environment. To discover whether sites are on the NPL or have been removed, return to the CERCLIS search page and use the selection options under the search parameter, "NPL Status."

DOCKET on RTK

A DOCKET search is used to locate a facility, defendant or case. The facility and defendant searchers are self-explanatory. The "Case search" allows users to search for cases that violate a particular law, involve a specific violation or pollutant type, or by case number. DOCKET search records identify case outcomes including: (1) consent instrument with penalty; (2) consent instrument without penalty; (3) consent instrument with specified cost recovery; (4) dismissed by tribunal; and (5) specified cost recovery. These data are useful for examining case outcomes, and when linked with other data sets, such as Census data, can be used to conduct environmental justice research; or when linked with corporate financial records, can be used to analyze the relationship between corporate assets and case outcomes. DOCKET also lists the penalty amount and Superfund cost awarded, if any.

The Emergency Response Notification System (ERNS) on RTK

Data on reported unplanned releases of toxic pollutants into the environment are located using ERNS. ERNS records may be searched by: (1) area; (2) discharger; or (3) material discharged. Accidental chemical spills are sometimes reported by multiple parties (e.g., the facility; state or local authorities; members of the public) meaning a specific chemical release/spill may appear in the ERNS database more than once. Thus, it is important to cross-reference case information to remove multiple reports of the same incident from the data before analysis. Multiple reports, however, may be useful to researchers interested in identifying the characteristics of releases/spills reported by multiple parties. ERNS data indicate the location of the chemical accident, the medium of exposure (air, land, water, groundwater, facility, other), causes of the accident, whether operator error was involved, an event description, response actions, and whether persons were evacuated, and whether injuries or deaths occurred.

The operator error data is not very reliable. In our searches, we discovered that cases may be coded as operator error even when faulty equipment is involved. It is unclear whether this kind of error occurs because of reporting practices by responding facilities or agencies, or recording errors and common practices of EPA staff. In any event, one of the drawbacks of ERNS data is that there are no reliability checks of the data once the data have been recorded.

RCRIS—Resource Conservation and Recovery Information on RTK

RCRIS data compiles information that generators, transporters, treaters, storers, and disposers of hazardous waste must report under the *Resource Conservation and Recovery Act* (RCRA) , and is used by the EPA: (1) to track handler permits and compliance with Federal and State regulations, (2) to track required cleanup actions, (3) for program management and assessment purposes, (4) as a hazardous waste land-disposal inventory, (5) for assessing and implementing facility management and planning guidelines and plans, (6) for environmental program assessment, and (7) to support implementation of the RCRA. It should be noted that RCRIS data are restricted to land-based disposal of hazardous waste.

RTK NET RCRIS searches may be performed by (1) geographic area, (2) facility, or (3) industry. In RCRIS data, facilities are referred to as "handlers." The information returned indicates the number of "current" violations, or whether the facility has ever been fined (this is determined by referring to the "all penalties" category). To obtain specific information about violations including dates and number of prior violations and assessed penalties, click on the facility name. Because information on each facility is extensive (e.g., in a large area with many facilities, the text report may be longer than 200-300 pages), it is recommended that you use the "summary" report option and obtain information on facilities with current or previous violations by clicking on the facility name.

TSCATS—*Toxic Substances Control Act* Test Submissions

TSCATS allows users to search EPA data using chemical names and regional delimiters to search for hazardous waste emissions that qualify as toxic substances under the *Toxic Substances Control Act*. The TSCATS chemical search allows users to vary a number of different parameters to construct customized searches. The information produced by TSCATS allows users to identify reports that have been produced on specific chemicals so that they may refer to, or request these reports to aid their research efforts. TSCATS does not provide the reports. Given current Web-based technology and the Web's role in providing information access, future improvements to TSCATS should include an online library where these reports may be directly accessed.

ARIP—Accidental Release Information Program—On RTK

ARIP data describe chemical accidents that have been both reported to and confirmed by the EPA. RTK NET's ARIP does not contain all reports made to the EPA under the Accidental Chemical Release (ACR) program maintained through the Emergency Response Notification System (ERNS), which may limit its usefulness for some types of research (see for example, Lynch, Stretesky, and Hammond's 2000 study which employs ERNS data on accidental chemical releases). RTK NET's ARIP may be searched by geographic area, facility, or chemical. Search options include low and high detail reports. The low detail reports yield basic facility and event information, and include data on evacuations, deaths, and injuries, if any, as well as costs. Cost estimates, however, should be used with caution. All ACR incidents involve some costs simply because a facility loses chemicals with value into the environment (not to mention the loss of productivity that accompanies responding to an ACR). Yet, there are also public costs, such as the costs of responding to the incident (e.g., by police, fire or other emergency personnel). ARIP cost estimates, however, exclude the latter costs.

FINDS on RTK

The FINDS database is an easy-to-use facility locator, and includes three search options: (1) geographic area; (2) facility; and (3) industry. For research purposes, the FINDS system is useful for generating a list of facilities in an area that can then be matched against other EPA databases to determine facility reporting patterns, and to ensure that a complete data set has been extracted for an area or industry. The "low detail" FINDS search option returns a list of the names, addresses, and ID numbers for all facilities regulated by the EPA for the requested search. "High detail" FINDS searches return all the information contained in the "low detail" search option, plus a list of aliases for each facility, each facility's SIC code, and a list of regulations that each facility must meet.

PCS—Water Permit Compliance System on RTK

The EPA's Permit Compliance System (PCS) data is designed to track surface water permits issued under the National Pollutant Discharge Elimination System (NPDES) as governed by the *Clean Water Act*. PCS data are entered directly into the system by individual states or EPA regions. As a result, the PCS suffers from some data quality/reliability issues. For example, it is known that PCS data are inconsistent across states because each state or EPA region may have to meet different reporting requirements concerning the data that must be entered into PCS. Data may also be subject to variations in regional enforcement programs.

PCS data are aggregated from Discharge Monitoring Reports (DMR) completed by individual facilities. Individual facilities report their effluent discharges on the DMR to EPA regional offices or state regulators. The EPA aggregates these reports into Quarterly Noncompliance Reports (QNCR). For the purposes of the PCS, the EPA classifies water emitters as "major," "minor," and "no rating points."

PCS searches are performed by "geographic area," "facility," or record of "noncompliance." A geographic search for Nassau County produces 173 facilities with water pollution permits.

A low detail report produces the following information:

1. **Outfalls**. The number of points at which a facility releases effluents.

2. **Parameter limits**. The limits placed on a permit.

3. **Inspections**. The number of times a facility has been inspected under a given permit.

4. **Enforcement actions**. The number of enforcement actions against a facility under a given permit.

5. **Quarters in noncompliance**. Data for the past three years for minor facilities, and for the past five years for major facilities.

6. **DMR effluent violations, or DMR nonreporting violations**. The number of times a facility either reports effluent limits above permit parameter limits, and/or the number of times a facility failed to file a DMR report.

7. **Compliance schedule violations**. The number of times a facility failed to comply with imposed pollution limit schedules.

8. **EPA Permitted Facility**. Is the permit under which this facility operates issued directly by the U.S. EPA? yes, no.

9. **Permit reissues**. Number of times the permit for this facility was reissued.

10. **Year of Issue**. Year in which the permit for this facility was first issued.

11. **Year Closed**. Year in which this facility ceased operation (if applicable).

Care should be exercised when using the DMR data. It is generally unclear whether these represent DMR effluent reports, or the failure to file a required DMR effluent report, or both. For example, a number of facilities in Nassau show DMR effluent or non-receipt reports in excess of 100. Some of the permits were issued in the 1970s, so it is impossible to tell whether these involve non-reports (since there are 80 or more reporting quarters during this time period), or actual reports of DMR effluent emissions.

High detail reports may be quite lengthy. In our previous work (Burns and Lynch, 2004), we discovered that a high detail PCS for the city of Tampa, Florida exceeded 1,000 pages in length. The difference between high and low detail involves the additional information presented for each facility related to inspections, enforcement actions, non-compliance events, DMR reports and measures, monitoring events and reports, and outfalls (discharge pipes) found in the "high detail" report. Each is reported by date, with information concerning the outcome, reason for an event, chemical measures, and so on.

Risk Management Plan (RMP) Search on RTK

Facilities employing or storing hazardous chemicals that have the potential to damage the surrounding physical, human, or animal environment are required to maintain a RMP (40 CFR Part 68.155; OSHA, 1910.119). Risk management plans describe a facility's interpretation of the potential hazards at a facility, the potential risk to the community, and the plan of action the facility employs to prevent and respond to potential environmental hazardous releases. The quality of these plans varies from one facility to the next.

A RMP search allows users to locate risk management plans for facilities using one of three types of searches: geographic area, facility, or full text. A RMP search returns information to the user by E-mail. All reports are facility-specific regardless of how the information is generated (all search options ultimately require the user to access an RMP by facility). A RMP describes (1) general plant equipment; (2) plan goals; (3) on-site regulated substances (names of chemicals and amounts); (4) worst case scenario results summary; (5) alternative release scenarios; and (6) accidental release prevention programs and chemical-specific prevention plans. RMP are supposed to describe worst case scenarios, the potential extent of damage, and potential human harm. Many, however, are deficient in this regard. These plans help governments organize disaster response.

The Scorecard Network

The most user-friendly environmental data searches are performed using the *Scorecard* Web site (www.scorecard.org). *Scorecard* is maintained by Environmental Defense, a nonprofit organization with over 300,000 members nationwide. In addition to environmental violations and pollution levels, *Scorecard* can be used to access health related information on the effects of exposure to chemicals and health data. While a useful starting point for research, *Scorecard* is arranged for easy access and presentation of information, and does not permit the download of data in formats researchers would prefer.

The home page is designed around the main navigation menu, (Toxins, Air, Water, Agriculture, Environmental Justice, Health Hazards). Under each heading, several subheadings allow users to retrieve information on specific pollution issues. Clicking on subheadings under Toxins, Air, Water and Agriculture directs users to the pollution locator for each pollution type. Here, a map of the pollutant along with two pollution locator options is presented: one for ZIP codes and one for larger areas ("pollution locator"). As an example, click on the "Lead" link under "Toxins," and then on "Pollution Locator" above the map on the proceeding page. Use the "Search for a Geographic Area" option, and select "New York" for state. Then click the "go to county list" button, locate "Nassau County" and click on the "lead hazards" option. From here you can map lead hazards, obtain a summary of lead hazards and a comparison to other areas, and determine if the selected area is a "hot spot" for this pollutant. Links within each section can be followed to gather further information on an area. For instance, under the heading "Lead Hazard Indicators and Comparative Rankings," click on the link "counties." This will display a list of lead pollution in all New York counties, where Nassau ranks ninth in terms of the number of households with lead hazards. A drop-down menu at the top of this list allows users to select other measures of lead hazards for comparison purposes, such as the percentage of children under 5 who live in poverty exposed to lead in each county. It is also possible to change the state being examined from this page. This feature, available in each sub-pollution heading, makes it easy to compare pollution levels in different locations.

Though much of the data in Scorecard can be collected using the EPA or RTK websites, Scorecard has several unique features not found on those sites. These include information on animal waste, a growing problem (e.g., one pig excretes four times the level of waste as a human, and these wastes must be managed and processed to maintain environmental quality), and environmental justice. Scorecard also provides easy access to health and environmental regulations using the "Regulations" link under the "Heath Hazards" section.

How Toxic are conditions in Nassau County? To illustrate the uses of Scorecard, return to the homepage, select "toxic chemical releases", enter "New York" in the geographic search, locate Nassau County, and click on "Toxic Chemical Releases." Then proceed to the major chemical release link. Here, six aggregated measures for Nassau County are presented comparing the level for each pollutant to those for all other U.S. counties. Nassau ranks in the 50th percentile range (50-60 percent; meaning 50 percent of counties are cleaner) for total environmental releases, the 40th percentile for both cancer and non cancer related releases, the 60th percentile for carcinogenic air releases, the 70th percentile for developmental toxicants, and the 60th percentile for reproductive toxicants. Nassau, which has numerous industries, ranks about mid-way with respect to all other counties for the level of toxic releases. This information does not mean, however, that these conditions are healthy since the measure is comparative. What you can learn from these data is how clean or dirty an area is *relative* to other locations. But, even the cleanest locations pose dangers to health if they contain environmental toxins.

Proceeding down this page, the user can obtain information on pollution amounts by type of release. In Nassau, for example, there were more than 5.3 million pounds of production-related toxins in 2002. This figure is highlighted, which means you can click on it to discover the amount of each chemical pollutant produced. You may also click on the name of each chemical compound to find the total U.S. releases, the chemical ranking score, hazards associated with exposure, regulatory information, and, among other information, how each state, county or ZIP code ranks with respect to release of an individual chemical.

CONCLUSION

This chapter has reviewed a variety of environmental pollution data sources. As should be evident, much of the data needed to study environmental law violations is now available on the web through the EPA, or through other sources such as RTK-NET and Scorecard. Consequently, criminologists can no longer lament about the lack of environmental data. Rather, criminologists must begin to extend their studies to environmental crime, its extent, causes and consequences, the making of environmental laws, and the enforcement of environmental regulations, and build a literature equivalent to the one it has amassed on ordinary crime.

CHAPTER 9

Environmental Justice

INTRODUCTION

The study of environmental justice encompasses a wide array of issues that can be examined from multiple perspectives. For instance, some researchers observed environmental justice from a social movement approach (e.g., Bullard, 1990; McGurty, 2000; Pellow, 2000). This chapter discusses environmental justice from a criminological perspective. To do so, we examine the concept of environmental justice and several other key terms employed in the environmental justice studies (EJS) literature used to describe the association between environmental hazards and social disadvantage. The neglect of environmental justice issues by criminologists is reviewed, and reasons why criminologists should be concerned with environmental justice are offered. Relevant criminological issues are also demonstrated through a review of one of the most important cases in the early history of the environmental justice movement. Finally, some relevant empirical research illustrating environmental justice findings, recent developments, and methodological issues faced by environmental justice researchers are examined.

WHAT IS ENVIRONMENTAL JUSTICE?

Several key terms (equity, equality, justice, and racism) are used in the environmental justice literature to characterize the relationship between race, ethnicity, social class and environmental hazards. These terms tend to be poorly defined and consequently are often used interchangeably (Liu, 2000; Pellow, 2002; Rhodes, 2003). The four most often used terms, identified using a Web of Science's Science Citation Index (SCI) search, are described below. The SCI identifies over two thousand studies that comprise the EJS literature since 1990. Figure 9.1 illustrates the number of times major EJS terms were used in those articles. It was not until 1990 that these four common EJS terms were more widely employed in the SCI literature: (1) environmental racism, (2) environmental justice and injustice, (3) environmental equity and inequity, and (4) environmental equality and inequality.

Figure 9.1. Trends in Environmental Justice Studies Terms, 1990-2006

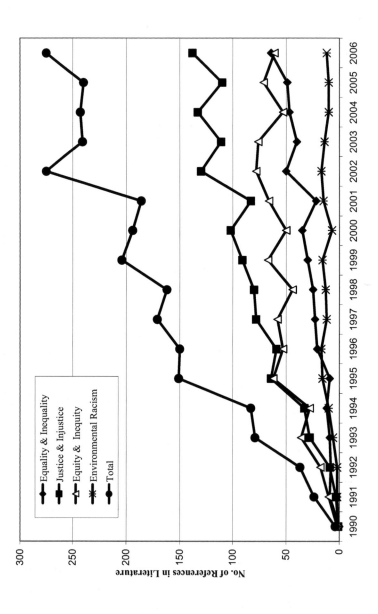

Environmental Racism

The origins of EJS studies are associated with the United Church of Christ's (UCC, 1986) study *Toxic Waste and Race,* and Robert Bullard's (1990) book *Dumping in Dixie: Race, Class and Environmental Quality.* These works focused on the association between community race and class characteristics and the distribution of environmental hazards, while using the term "environmental racism" to refer to both *direct* and *indirect* forms of racism evident in these spatial relationships. As an example of this global definition, Bullard (1996, p. 497) identified environmental racism as "any policy, practice, or directive (whether intended or unintended) that differentially affects or disadvantages individuals, groups, or communities because of race or color." In the broader literature on racism, Feagin (1977) distinguished direct from indirect racism, noting that *direct racism* involves a conscious intent to harm another individual or group based on racial characteristics (Feagin 1977, p.184), while institutional practices and policies that produce *indirect racism* occur "with no intent to harm" (Feagin 1977, p.186).

Early EJS studies interpreted the association between race and hazardous wastes as a direct indicator of racism. In this view, while intentional racism could produce environmental inequalities, institutional racism was the primary cause of environmental racism (Stretesky and Hogan, 1998). For instance, environmental hazards such as Superfund sites are often closer to minority communities. How can this spatial relationship be explained? To be sure, intentional racism can limit housing choices and produce this effect on a limited scale. The broader pattern of discrimination in the location of hazardous waste sites, however, is more likely a function of institutionalized racism which, unlike intentional or direct racism, is more likely to influence the association between community racial characteristics and hazardous waste siting decisions (Stretesky and Hogan 1998; Stretesky and Lynch, 2002).

Since the mid-1990s, a number of studies have examined direct racism as a cause of environmental injustice. Been (1994), for instance, argued that environmental racism exists only when the association between race and hazardous waste was the result of malicious intent. One way to address this question is to examine whether hazardous waste facilities are placed in minority neighborhoods, which would be environmental injustice caused by direct racism (See, Anderton, Anderson and Oakes, 1994), or whether the placement of a hazardous waste site produces a change in the racial composition of neighborhoods, which would be institutional racism.

Environmental Justice

The phrases *"environmental justice"* and *"environmental injustice,"* which comprise approximately 43 percent of all EJS SCI citations, are considered broader than the term environmental racism. More specifically, environmental justice and injustice focuses on race, ethnic, gender and class differences in exposure to environmental hazards, while environmental racism applies only to racial differences. Page and Sellers (1970) were the first to employ the term "environmental justice" in their study of workplace health, which concluded with a call for a "Workers Bill of Health Rights" that applied principles of environmental justice to the workplace. This idea has been expanded to include studies of the disproportionate exposure to hazardous materials as a result of the community variations in race, ethnicity, or class (Bullard and Wright, 1986), and is an important dimension of the EPA's (2006) definition of environmental justice.

Pellow (2000) argued that environmental justice and injustice are, in essence, opposites, and environmental justice is the struggle against environmental injustice. Rhodes (2003, p. 19) provides a concise yet broad definition of environmental justice as the equitable treatment of diverse races and classes with respect to the "development, implementation, and enforcement of environmental laws, regulations, and policies."

Environmental Equity

The terms environmental *equity* and *inequity* appear in approximately 28 percent of all citations to the EJS literature. Prior to the 1990s, these terms were used primarily within the environmental economics literature to discuss how economic markets and incentives impacted environmental conditions (Dickason, 1975; see also Rhodes, 2003). In the 1990s, however, these terms were redefined to focus on outcome equity. Equity studies make no assumptions about the causes of inequity in exposure, and treat equity as an empirical outcome. According to Liu (2000, p. 12) equity studies "leaves it open for an analyst to determine the relationship between environmental risk distribution and population distribution" (Liu, 2000, p. 13).

Environmental Equality

The term equality and inequality are traditionally the least likely terms to be used in the EJS literature, comprising about 17 percent of all citations to articles in this literature. Recently, however, the term has been employed more frequently (Figure 9.1). The increased number of citations to equality and inequality can likely be traced to Pellow's (2002) use of the term "environmental inequality formation" in his C. Wright Mills Award winning work entitled *Garbage Wars: The Struggle for Environmental Justice in Chicago*. Pellow (2000, p. 582) argues that "environmental inequality focuses on broader dimensions of environmental quality and social Hierarchies … [and] … addresses… structural questions that focus on social inequality and environmental burdens." In effect, environmental equality focuses on whether or not unequal outcomes exist before addressing the causes of environmental inequality. According to Pellow, the causes of environmental inequality are found in (1) socio-historical processes rather than discrete outcomes, (2) the role of multiple stakeholder groups as opposed to perpetrator-victim scenarios, and (3) the distribution of environmental hazards over their entire life-cycle.

A Choice of Terms

There is considerable debate about which term ought to be used in the EJS literature, and it is unlikely that researchers or activists will ever agree on the use of one term since, despite their overlap, each term emphasizes a different set of assumptions. Much EJS research examines the spatial association between race, ethnicity, class and environmental hazards, and addresses the question "do the socially disadvantaged reside closer to environmental hazards than socially advantaged?" However, definitions of "socially disadvantaged" and the assumptions researchers make about the causes of disadvantage (direct, indirect, institutional) vary from one study to the next. Furthermore, because there is no agreed-upon definition of disadvantage, debates in the EJS literature are likely to revolve around whether the existing distribution of environmental hazards is "fair" or "unfair." Debates about fairness are beyond the focus of this chapter and we adopt the relatively simple position that any unequal distribution of environmental hazards is unfair. Rather, our purpose is to describe the current state of the ESJ literature and the role that EJS can play in criminology and criminal justice.

THE RELATIONSHIP BETWEEN EJS AND CRIMINOLOGY

Many social science disciplines (e.g., political science, history, sociology, psychology) have contributed to EJS research. Criminology is not well represented among them (Simon, 2000) despite an interest in crimes of the powerful (Clinard and Yeager, 1980; Frank and Lynch, 1992; Pearce and Tombs, 1998; Simpson, 2002), and criminological research on environmental crime and justice remains underdeveloped. This is especially true when examining the extent of harm created by, and the extensive legal and social control efforts targeted toward, these offenses (Friedrichs, 1996). Indeed, there are few articles examining environmental crime in the criminological literature. In a recent study Lynch, McGurrin and Fenwick (2004) discovered that while only a small percentage of articles published in mainstream criminology journals (e.g., *Criminology, Justice Quarterly, Journal of Criminal Justice, British Journal of Criminology*) dealt with issues that impinge upon corporate crime (around 4 percent), even fewer examined toxic waste and environmental harm. For example, *Criminology*—the major journal in the discipline—had only two articles on corporate crime over a recent five-year period and no articles on environmental crime (Lynch, McGurrin and Fenwick, 2004). Environmental crime issues are absent from criminology and criminal justice textbooks as well. For instance, consider that among the top-selling criminology and criminal justice textbooks, approximately 1 in 22 pages was devoted to corporate and white collar crime, and that approximately 1 in 1,568 was related to environmental crime (Lynch, McGurrin and Fenwick, 2004). Clearly, criminology has been slow to embrace issues of environmental crime and justice (Zilney, McGurrin and Zahran, 2006).

Four established criminological research traditions can be used to justify the study of environmental justice. These traditions include research examining (1) the definition of crime, (2) the role of the state in controlling crime and doing justice (state responsibilities), (3) the study of crime victims, and (4) the sociological and environmental basis of the biological causes of crime. These traditions are examined briefly below.

The Definition of Crime

Criminologists have long been concerned with the process involved in the creation of laws and the definition of crime, and have focused on the way that power relations in society impact these processes (Box, 1989; Lynch and Michalowski, 2006; Quinney, 1970; Spitzer, 1975). Quinney (1970), for example, popularized the idea that crime is a social construction that reflects class inequality. Consistent with this argument, numerous studies examine the ability of corporations to shape the law. This emphasis could easily be extended to the study of corporate influences on environmental law and regulations that impact the definition of environmental justice. For instance, it is well documented that the chemical industry has consistently and forcefully opposed and shaped environmental regulations affecting the production of dangerous chemicals such as PCBs, lead, and asbestos (Ehrlich and Ehrlich, 1996; Fagan and Lavelle, 1996). This same situation exists in a number of industries, opening the possibility for numerous criminological studies of the process of law making and corporate influence. Some criminologists, however, object to studies of regulatory and civil laws that define corporate crimes or equity conditions such as environmental justice because these laws and rules are qualitatively different than criminal law. Yet the difference between criminal and regulatory law is artificial because it is a social construction that represents a political process where powerful social actors influence the decision-making processing using their financial resources (Burns and Lynch, 2004; Clifford, 1998). To be sure, in some cases the same act may be defined as a criminal, civil or administrative action depending on how the agency in charge of the investigation decides to proceed (Stretesky, 2006; Simpson, 2002). The study of environmental justice fits a number of the concerns outlined above.

State Responsibilities

Criminologists regularly study the role of the state in the criminal justice process. An important issue in the criminal justice process is the role played by discretion. The same types of research can be undertaken with respect to environmental justice. For instance, "how do victim or offender characteristics impact discretion in environmental justice cases?" "Are minority communities more or less likely to be protected by law?" "Are corporations that violate environmental laws in minority communities more or less likely to receive severe penalties?" "Are larger or smaller corporations more likely to be the targets of environmental justice suits?" To be sure, researchers have begun to answer some of these questions. O'Hear (2004), for instance, studied sentences handed out to "green collar" (environmental) and non-green collar defendants in federal courts between 1996 and 2001. He found that green collar offenders received shorter prison sentences than non-green collar offenders, and that they were also more likely to have their sentences adjusted downward. While O'Hear's study did not focus on race and class issues commonly found in environmental justice research and criminal justice research on sentencing biases (Lynch and Patterson, 1991; Mann, 1993; Miller, 1996; Tonry, 1995), such an extension could easily be accommodated.

Victimology

Environmental justice research is well suited for the study of victimization, a central concern within criminology (Kennedy and Sacco, 1998). For example, numerous databases describe the location of hazardous waste sites and other environmental offenses in ways that allow the use of community demographic characteristics to describe environmental victimization. The EJS literature has examined these issues in relation to abandoned toxic waste sites, the siting of Treatment Storage and Disposal Facilities (TSDFs), toxic waste emissions reported in the Toxic Release Inventory (TRI) , the distribution of agricultural waste and chemical accidents. In addition to identifying the characteristics of those more likely to be the victims of environmental crimes, an important aspect of both victimology and environmental justice research is the creation of policies that remedy victimization, or aid victims.

Environmental Justice and the Causes of Crime

Criminologists should also be concerned with issues of environmental justice because of the implications of that research for the potential association between exposure to pollutants and criminal behavior. The role of biology in crime has interested criminologists for some time, and remains a modern area of interest (e.g., Fishbein, 1990; Booth and Osgood, 1993). Environment-biology-crime connections have typically been the focus of studies conducted by medical researchers. Some of these studies demonstrated that environmental exposure to heavy metals such as lead, cadmium, and mercury influence criminal behavior (Denno 1990). Needleman (1990), for instance, noted that as much as twenty percent of crime is likely to be associated with environmental lead exposure. In a later study, Needleman, Reiss, Tobin, Biesecker, and Greenhouse (1996) found a significant relationship between bone-lead levels and both reported and observed delinquency and behavioral problems of adolescents. In a study of prison inmates, Pihl and Ervin (1990) found significantly higher levels of lead in violent inmates compared to those who committed property crime. These individual-level associations have also been discovered at higher levels of aggregation. Using time series data, Nevin (2000) found a relationship between lead and violent crime rates in the United States between the years of 1941 and 1998. Stretesky and Lynch (2001) found that counties with higher air lead levels also had higher homicide rates, even when controlling for racial composition, poverty, and several other forms of air pollution (see also Stretesky and Lynch, 2004). Criminologically, this research is interesting because it has the potential to explain higher crime rates in poor and minority communities in new ways and specifically in relation to minority and class environmental hazard exposure patterns found by environmental justice researchers (Bullard and Wright, 1993; Kraft and Scheberle, 1995; Stretesky, 2003).

The next section examines an important environmental crime that occurred in Warren County, North Carolina. This case is important because it illustrates the points made above by connecting criminological interests and environmental justice issues.

ENVIRONMENTAL CRIME IN WARREN COUNTY, NC

Warren County, North Carolina, is the birthplace of the environmental justice movement (Bullard, 1990; McGurty, 2000)—the location of the first major environmental justice protests occurred there in response to the siting of an environmental hazard. What many people do not know is that the environmental hazards in Warren County were the result of corporate crime.

The Warren County protests were a response to *criminal violations* of the *Toxic Substance Control Act* by Ward Transformer and Transformer Sales that began in the late 1970s. At the time of the offense, Ward Transformer, located in Raleigh, North Carolina, was one of the largest transformer companies in the U.S. Ward was in the business of purchasing, rebuilding, and selling electrical voltage transformers (*NY Times*, 1982). The oil contained in the used transformers that Ward purchased contained high concentrations of polychlorinated biphenyls (PCBs), a thick liquid used in electric fluids, heat transfer fluids, and hydraulic fluids. Their commercial utility was based on their chemical stability, including low flammability and electrical insulating properties (Erickson, 2001). PCBs were also used as additives in pesticides, paints, and adhesives. PCBs were widely used in the electronics industry until the U.S. Congress prohibited their manufacturing, processing, and distribution in 1976 in §6(e) of the *Toxic Substances Control Act* (U.S. EPA, 2006). Research suggests that PCBs have a variety of adverse health effects for the human immune system, reproductive system, nervous system, and endocrine system (e.g., see DeRoos et al., 2005; Steenland et al., 2006).

Over the years Ward built up an enormous stockpile of PCB-laced oil that needed to be disposed. Ward's president, Robert "Buck" Ward, asked several legitimate businesses to give him cost estimates for the PCB disposal. Ward believed those estimates were too high and contacted his friend, Robert Burns, to make a deal: Burns would dispose of the PCBs to erase the $50,000 debt he owed Ward. Burns and his two sons, Randall and Timothy, owned and operated a New York-based company called Transformer Sales, which agreed to dispose of the PCBs (*NY Times*, 1982). Instead of disposing of the PCBs legally, they were dumped along the roadside.

To carry out the roadside dumping, a "special" truck was produced by Burns with the help of Ward and his employees. The companies purchased a Ryder box van, installed a 750-gallon tank to store the PCB waste, and attached a hose to the tank that was concealed under the truck and directed at the side of the road. The hose could be turned on and off from the passenger's seat (*NY Times*, 1982). Randall and Timothy Burns completed more than forty trips with the truck, disposing of 31,000 gallons of PCB wastes along 243 miles of deserted North Carolina roadways.

These illegal disposal activities were eventually discovered by the authorities. The Burns were arrested, tried, and sentenced to prison. Robert Ward was also fined $200,000 to aid in the cleanup of the PCBs. The company later paid nearly $3.5 million to help offset the cleanup costs. This is only the beginning of the story, however, rather than its end.

In order to clean up the PCBs, North Carolina officials dug up the PCB-contaminated soil and disposed of it in on a 142-acre tract of land it had purchased in Afton, a predominantly (84 percent) African American community (Bullard, 2007) with an elevated poverty rate (20 percent of residents lived below the poverty level). Residents protested the placement of the hazardous waste site, and argued that the site's placement not only appeared biased (the waste deposited in Afton came from 14 other counties, General Assembly of North Carolina, 1983), but would threaten the health of residents when PCBs leached from the site. The residents were reassured that the use of "dry tomb" waste methods would prevent PCB leakage into the surrounding buffer zone (more than 100 acres) and the local water supply. Despite these assurances, residents organized a protest against the site, making this the first environmental justice protest in America. Residents lined the roadways to the site and lay down in the road to prevent trucks carrying the PCB-laden waste from entering the site. In all, more than 500 protestors were arrested.

The Afton protests became the catalyst for the environmental justice movement. Bullard (1990), for example, observed that the Warren County protests against the siting of the PCB landfill signified the first time African Americans mobilized a national broad-based group to oppose what they recognized as environmental racism. Moreover, the Warren County protests also led legislators to push for the first EJ study to be carried out by the U.S. General

Accounting office in 1983 (USGAO, 1983). Since the GAO study, dozens of empirical examinations of the distribution of environmental hazards have been conducted. These studies are reviewed below. Before examining this research, let us take a moment to review what has happened in Warren County twenty-five years later.

Ten years after the Warren County PCB landfill was opened, there were signs that its hasty construction was beginning to fail. By 1993, there was evidence of PCBs in the groundwater (Bullard, 2004) and that the "dry" disposal methods were failing to inhibit PCB leaching (Ballance, 1995). In 1994, test well samples indicated that contaminants including PCBs and dioxins had migrated off site (Balance, 1995). Later that year, a working group was formed to examine the best way to detoxify the landfill. Site remediation began in 1998, and was completed in 2004 at a cost of $17.1 million (North Carolina Department of Environmental and Natural Resources, 2004). While the site has been cleaned, the surrounding area has already suffered damage. In addition, the local population has been victimized by the site for 25 years with no remedy for damage to their health (Bullard, 2007, 2004).

EVIDENCE OF ENVIRONMENTAL INJUSTICE

A considerable number of studies fall under the scope of EJS. These studies are diverse in topic and focus and emphasize the production and consumption of dangerous chemicals as well as their geographic distribution. Also included in EJS literature are studies such as the one conducted by Del Olmo (1998) on class- and race-linked harms to individuals associated with the use of herbicides in the war on drugs. Given this tremendous diversity in studies, it is impossible to review all of the EJS literature in a single chapter. To make this review manageable, this chapter is restricted to an examination of the spatial distribution of environmental hazards across diverse races and classes. In general, studies that examine the spatial distribution of environmental hazards can be separated into studies of (1) hazardous waste sites, (2) treatment, disposal and storage facilities, and (3) studies of air pollution. In addition, we review several new directions in EJS and touch on some methodological issues that surround the study of environmental justice related issues.

Hazardous Waste Sites

Several researchers have examined the geographic association between race, ethnicity, economic indicators, and areas that contain hazardous substances in the form of active, inactive, uncontrolled, or abandoned disposal sites. Data on the location of many of these waste sites are recorded and made available to the public through various. EPA and commercial databases reviewed in an earlier chapter (e.g., the EPA's Biennial Reporting System [BRS], or Comprehensive

Environmental Response, Compensation and Liability Information System [CERCLIS]).

As previously noted, the environmental justice protest in Warren County was the watershed event that marked the beginning of the environmental justice movement in the United States. Shortly after the Warren County protests the USGAO (1983) released a study of the distribution of offsite landfills in EPA's Region 4 (Alabama, Florida, Georgia, Kentucky, Mississippi, North Carolina, South Carolina, and Tennessee). The GAO discovered that of the four off-site hazardous waste sites located in Region 4, three were located in communities that were predominately African American. Moreover, approximately one-quarter of the residents living near these waste sites were considered poor, and most of those poor were also African American (USGAO, 1983). The GAO report is important because it is often cited as the first study of environmental justice in the United States. However, in 1983 Robert Bullard also published a study of the geographic distribution of hazardous waste sites in Houston, Texas. The data used in Bullard's study were obtained from Houston's Solid Waste Management Division and Houston's Air Quality Board. Bullard discovered that nearly every one of Houston's garbage incinerators, mini-incinerators, and municipal landfills were located in predominately African American communities and near predominately African American schools. More recent research has confirmed Bullard's findings. For instance, Lynch and Stretesky (2002) studied the proximity of 84 public grade schools to hazardous waste sites in the Hillsborough County (Florida) School District between 1987 and 1999. Controlling for the percentage of students eligible for free lunch (a poverty measure), they found that grade schools nearer to environmental hazards (i.e., Superfund sites or disposal facilities) became disproportionately African American and Hispanic over time while grade schools situated farther from environmental hazards became disproportionately White. In California, Pastor, Sadd, and Morello-Frosch (2002) also found that minority district schools are more likely to be located in census tracts containing potentially hazardous facilities.

In 1987 the first national-level environmental justice study was published by the United Church of Christ (UCC). The study found that CERCLIS sites were most often located in ZIP codes where the population was dispropor-tionately African American and poor. Using multivariate discriminate analysis, the UCC determined that race was more strongly related to the location of CERCLIS sites than income. Kreig's (1995) study of Superfund sites in the greater Boston area replicated the UCC's results. However, he found that race was more strongly related to the location of Superfund sites in older industrial areas. Kreig hypothesized that new industrial growth attracted many workers from inner-city areas where old industrial jobs were declining. Those individuals who were able to take advantage of more technical and high-paying jobs were also able to make the move with industry. Since many poor African Americans were unable to move or were unqualified for these jobs, they remained in the older industrial areas where jobs were scarce and income relatively low. Industries that fled these older industrial areas also left their waste behind. As Kreig explains, urbanization may be the cause of hazardous waste, but structural inequalities account for variation in organization, which would impact the relationship between race and hazardous waste within any given area. Stretesky and Hogan (1998) examined the geographical correlates of Superfund sites across Florida between 1970 and 1990. They discovered that African Americans and Hispanics were more likely to reside near Superfund sites, and that the association between race, ethnicity and proximity to Superfund sites was increasing over time. This study showed little evidence of income inequality.

Other studies examining the relationship between race, economic indicators, and Superfund sites have not been so definitive. For example, Zimmerman's (1993) conclusions concerning the existence of environmental injustice were dependent on the type of statistic used, with weighted averages producing results indicating the presence of environmental injustice while unweighted averages did not. Hird (1994) also used census data to examine the residential, political, and economic characteristics of areas surrounding NPL sites. Hird suggests that Superfund sites are more likely to be found in counties that are more affluent, while NPL sites are more likely to be located in counties with higher percentages of non-Whites. Recently, Anderton et al. (1997) examined the spatial distribution of CERCLIS and NPL sites across 1990 census tracts. Their results varied by type of site and by the method of analysis. Specifically, the researchers discovered that the percentage of African Americans and Hispanics are significantly lower in tracts containing CERCLIS sites when compared to tracts containing no sites. These comparisons were roughly the same for NPL and non-NPL CERCLIS tracts. Their multivariate analysis of CERCLIS sites provided results that varied by type of site. When variables such as population density, percentage of industrial employment, and average value of owner-occupied housing were controlled, an increase in the percentage of African Americans, Hispanics, or families below the poverty line in any given tract decreased the incidence of NPL sites in that tract. These multivariate results were markedly different for non-NPL CERCLIS sites, as both the percentage of African Americans and Hispanics increased the incidence of those sites in that tract. Anderton et al. (1997, p. 17) note, however, "none of these effects is so large to be considered strong evidence of substantive inequality."

Treatment, Storage, and Disposal Facilities

Environmental justice researchers have also studied the demographics of Treatment, Storage, and Disposal Facilities (TSDFs). This line of research is, perhaps, the most controversial of all research in the EJS literature because it focuses on the issue of facility siting. For instance, Been (1994) reanalyzed the studies conducted by the USGAO (1983) and Robert Bullard (1983) and found that a majority of the facilities in each study were clearly sited in areas that could be classified as disproportionately African American. However, Been (1994) also found that areas around these sites became disproportionately African American over time. Other researchers have also found evidence that TSDF siting can be traced to intentional discrimination (Hamilton, 1995; Hurly, 1997; Pastore, Sadd, and Hipp, 2001).

There are studies, however, that find little evidence of environmental injustice (e.g., Mitchell, Thomas, and Cutter, 1999). For instance, Oakes, Anderton, and Anderson (1996) looked at the siting of hazardous waste facilities in the 1960s, 1970s, and 1980s. When they examined the demographics of census tracts at the time of siting they found that tracts with facilities did not have greater minority percentages or poverty rates when compared to tracts without sites (see also Been and Gupta 1997; Mitchell et al. 1990).

Recent research by Saha and Mohai (2005) suggest that contradictory studies of discriminatory siting can be explained. The researchers published the results of their study on facility siting in Michigan and argue that previous researchers have not considered their findings in the proper historical context. Saha and Mohai suggest that previous studies make more sense in light of the NIMBY or "not in my backyard" movement. They point out that the location of hazardous waste-producing facilities in the 1950s and 1960s was viewed as a tradeoff for economic growth. They found that in Michigan facilities were often placed in predominantly White, middle-class neighborhoods, and argued that little thought was given to the potential health effects associated with various environmental hazards. However, during the 1970s a greater public awareness about environmental hazards emerged and helped to fuel the NIMBY movement (Szasz 1994; Taylor 2000). For instance, Love Canal became a top news story in 1978 and made "toxic" and "hazardous waste" household words. People were no longer comfortable allowing hazardous wastes to be placed in their backyards. Saha and Mohai contend that as more attention was focused on toxic waste and environmental hazards, NIMBY protests by White middle-class grassroots activists made the siting of hazardous waste processing facilities in Michigan difficult. Some researchers such as Szasz (1994) showed that surveys of hazardous waste facility operators during the mid-1970s indicated that less than 50 percent of them believed that public opposition was a problem during the facility siting stage. However, by 1979 nearly all of the operators reported public opposition as a serious barrier to facility siting (Szasz, 1994). Thus, the siting of hazardous waste facilities followed a path of least political resistance—which often meant locating a facility in socially disadvantaged neighborhoods (Saha and Mohai, 2005).

Air Pollution

Many early EJ studies conducted in the 1970s focused on air pollution. For instance, Freeman (1973) used monitoring station data to examine the relationship between particulates and sulfates in the air and the percentage of minority residents across census tract areas in three cities (Kansas City, Missouri; St. Louis; and Washington, D.C.). He found that minorities in each city were exposed to higher levels of EPA-regulated air particulates (see also Asch and Seneca, 1978; Burch, 1976; Kruvant, 1975). Gelobter (1987) also used air monitoring data to examine the distribution of air quality over time and space. He found that between 1970 and 1986 there was an overall improvement in air quality but that minority communities consistently experienced elevated levels of air pollution when compared with White communities. More recently, Wernette and Nieves (1992) discovered that African Americans were over-represented in areas designated by the Environmental Protection Agency as non-attainment areas (that is, areas out of compliance with national ambient air quality standards).

Environmental equity studies that rely solely on air monitoring data are geographically limited. Even in large urban areas, air-monitoring stations are relatively spread out and may not produce sufficient data for analysis. This data limitation has been addressed through the use of self-reported data on chemical releases contained in the Toxics Release Inventory (TRI) . Approximately 25,000 facilities submit TRI reports to the EPA during each reporting period. Many of these reports disclose chemical releases to the air, and the TRI has been widely used to study environmental equity (Allen, 2001; Aurora and Cason, 1999; Perlin, Sexton, and Wong, 1999; Tiefenbacher and Hagelman, 1999). One of the first environmental equity studies to use TRI data was carried out by Bowen, Salling, Haynes, and Cyran (1995) The researchers examined reported toxic air releases across Ohio counties and across census tracts in Cuyahoga County. They determined that reported releases were not associated with the racial composition of the counties or census tracts (see also Cutter and Solecki, 1996).

Daniels and Friedman (1999) investigated the distribution of TRI air releases across counties and found evidence of racial bias even when they controlled for a variety of economic factors (e.g., urban/rural differences, manufacturing processes, and urbanization processes) (see also Perlin, Setzer, Creason, and Sexton, 1995). Other localized TRI studies have replicated Daniels and Friedman's results. In Downey's (1998) TRI data study of air, water, and land chemical releases across Michigan ZIP codes, racial composition was among the strongest predictors of the quantity of toxins released into the environment.

TRI data recently have been used to examine specific air pollutants rather than air pollution in general. Hird and Reese (1998) used TRI data to examine the distribution of 29 environmental hazards across all U.S. counties. The researchers focused on the distribution of carbon monoxide, lead, nitrogen dioxide, ozone, and sulfur dioxide. They discovered an association between county racial composition and each specific hazard examined.

Several studies have looked at the distribution of estimated air pollution. These estimates are based on air monitoring data, known pollution point sources, and meteorological conditions. Brajer and Hall (1992) developed a statistical model to estimate distributions of ozone across subpopulations in southern California (see also Korc, 1996). The results suggest that exposure to particles was above average in young people and African Americans. Liu (1996) sought to determine whether estimated ozone plumes and accompanying industry were more likely to be present in African American residential areas in New York and Philadelphia. Lui found that the wealthy and Whites were most likely to live in the source locations. Moreover, demographic patterns were relatively stable, as county census data failed to confirm that the racial composition of downwind plum areas was changing over time. Lui suggested that people are not as worried about air pollution as they are about other types of environmental hazards. Unlike toxic waste facilities, which often draw a great deal of public attention, air pollution is likely to be tolerated and viewed as being fairly distributed, largely dispersed, and a chronic rather than acute problem.

Morello-Frosh et al. (2001) examined estimates of pollutants based on a variety of actual data and real-world conditions and a variety of sources to estimate cancer potency values in 2,560 census tracts in the South Coast Air Basin (which includes Los Angeles, Orange, Ventura, San Bernardino, and Riverside counties). The researchers discovered that, even after controlling for population density, home ownership levels, and income, there was nearly a one in three likelihood that a person of color in Southern California was living in a high cancer risk neighborhood, compared to about a one in seven chance for Anglo residents.

NEW DIRECTIONS IN EJS

Besides the more traditional studies that focus on the distribution of hazardous waste, the siting of TSDF facilities, and air pollution, recent examinations of environmental justice have expanded to include other indicators of environmental justice. For example, recent EJS researchers have examined issues related to environmental enforcement, chemicals and crime, chemical accidents, and rural inequality.

Enforcement

One new direction in EJS studies (and highly relevant to criminology) focuses on environmental enforcement. For instance, Lavelle and Coyle (1992) used bivariate statistics to examine the U.S. EPA's Civil Enforcement Docket database. The researchers investigated whether potential race and class biases existed in the distribution of monetary penalties for violations of the *Clean Air Act*, *Clean Water Act*, and the *Resource Conservation and Recovery Act*. Lavelle and Coyle (1992) discovered that the average fine for violating federal environmental laws was higher in White ($153,067) ZIP codes when compared to minority ZIP codes ($105,028). Their findings suggest that Whites may receive higher levels of environmental protection via regulatory enforcement than minority communities, leading the researchers to conclude that there is a racial divide in the enforcement of environmental laws.

Rinquist (1998) and Atlas (2001) both reanalyzed the Civil Enforcement Docket database in an effort to replicate Lavelle and Coyle's findings using multivariate results. Rinquist's reanalysis did not find evidence of environmental injustice in the enforcement of environmental laws while Atlas found that violations in minority census-tract areas actually receive higher fines than those in White areas ($133,808 vs. $113,791). These findings suggest that there is no injustice in the enforcement of environmental laws. However, the results of the most recent research in this area suggest that the findings of Atlas and Rinquist may not be generalizable across all industries. For instance, Lynch, Stretesky, and Burns (2004a,b) examined fines against petroleum refineries according to the demographics of the neighborhood in which the offending companies are located. They found evidence of an inverse association between ethnicity and fines. These variations are apparent even after controlling for seriousness of the crime, previous enforcement and compliance history, and other case characteristics. Thus, it appears that refineries situated in Hispanic and low income ZIP codes tend to receive smaller penalties than refineries located in non-Hispanic and more affluent ZIP codes.

Behavior and Crime

Recent efforts have also been made to integrate environmental justice-related concerns into common explanations of crime. For example, in 2004 Stretesky and Lynch examined the relationship between relative deprivation and crime with the idea that environmental lead levels would either account for some of the association between those two variables or help specify the relationship between deprivation and crime. While lead did not mediate the relationship between race and crime as the researchers predicted, they did find evidence that lead moderated that relationship. That is, the association between lead and crime was strongest among those counties where relative deprivation was high and weakest among those counties where relative deprivation was low. They point out that this relationship is consistent with the literature on lead exposure and the EJS literature. The study by Stretesky and Lynch (2004) raises an important question that criminologists must eventually address. Specifically, is the well-studied and often-documented relationship between race, poverty, and crime really a function of disproportionate exposure to environmental hazards? Since lead is but one of many documented neurotoxins that have the ability to alter behavior, criminologists have a considerable amount of work to do before that question can be adequately answered (see also Stretesky and Lynch, 2001).

Chemical Accidents

Several researchers have recently applied the concept of environmental justice to the distribution of chemical accidents. Stretesky and Lynch (1999) examined the distribution of chemical accidents in Hillsborough County, Florida, and found that chemical accidents were more likely to occur near census tracts that were African American and poor than in tracts that were largely White and more affluent. In a follow-up study focusing on chemical accidents across the entire United States, Derizenski, Lacy and Stretesky (2003) found that chemical accidents were more likely to occur in census block groups that were disproportionately low-income. Elliott, Wang, Lowe and Kleindorfer (2004) conducted the most recent study of chemical accidents in the United States. The researchers studied all chemical accidents that occurred in the U.S. between 1994 and 2000 and discovered that larger and more chemical-intensive facilities tend to be located in counties with larger African American populations and that these were the facilities likely to have accidents. Unlike the research by Derizenski, Lacy, and Stretesky (2003), Elliott et al. (2004) also found that after adjusting for location of risk, the odds of chemical accidents increased for counties where residents were disproportionately African American.

Rural Inequality

Researchers working in the area of EJS have focused much of their work on urban pollution hazards. Less attention has been devoted to agricultural hazards, although that is beginning to change. This is especially true in the case of confined animal feeding operations (or CAFOs). Evidence suggests that large-scale hog operations decrease quality of life in the communities where they are located (Weida, 2001). This occurs because the environmental and social costs of operating CAFOs are externalized to the surrounding community. Particulates emanating from hog operations, for instance, may be responsible for a variety of adverse health effects among residents living near these facilities (Cole et al., 2000). Moreover, CAFOs pose a substantial risk to land and water, increasing the risk of nitrate poisoning in well water (see Cole et al., 2000). Finally, there is always a chance that large lagoons constructed to hold waste will leak or burst and cause large amounts of nitrates and ammonia to enter aquifers.

One of the first CAFO studies in the EJS literature was conducted by Edwards and Ladd (2000), who examined counties in North Carolina. They found that the decline in small hog farm production has had a negative impact on low-income, rural and African American counties. They argue that these unequal outcomes reflect institutional and structural patterns of economic development in rural communities. Wing et al. (2000) also found that large-scale hog operations were more likely to be located in disproportionately poor and non-White census block groups. In fact, there were nearly 19 times as many large hog operations in high poverty census block groups (highest poverty quintile) compared to low poverty block groups, and seven times as many large hog operations in high non-White census blocks (highest quintile of percent non-White) as compared to those blocks largely inhabited by Whites. Wing et al. (2000, p. 225) argue that the "[d]isproportionate impact of intensive hog production on people of color and on the poor may impede improvements in economic and environmental conditions that are needed to address public health in areas that have high disease rates and low access to medical care." Stretesky, Johnston, and Arney's (2003) study of environmental equity in large scale hog operations across the major hog producing states in the U.S. found considerable evidence of siting inequality, but only in states where large-scale operations were expanding quickly (e.g., Iowa, North Carolina, and Minnesota).

Methodological Issues

There are numerous methodological issues surrounding the study of environmental hazards (Downey, 2005). Rather than focus on the methodo-logical promises and pitfalls of each study we outline several important methodological issues below in the hope that they aid in the interpretation and design of EJS research. We focus specifically on units of analysis, control variables, and causal order.

Units of analysis may be problematic in the study of environmental justice because of a tendency toward aggregation bias. For example, Anderton et al. (1994) found that race and ethnicity were statistically related to the location of Treatment, Storage, and Disposal facilities (TSDFs) across the United States at the aggregated census tract level. However, this relationship was not replicated at the census tract level of analysis. These results led Anderton et al. (1994, p. 135) to conclude that "the appearance of equity in the location of TSDFs depends heavily on how areas of potential impact or interest are defined." Using TRI data, Bowen et al. (1995) produced similar findings when studying the quantity of toxins released into the environment by chemical manufacturers in Ohio. At the county level Bowen et al. found that there was a positive association between the percentage of African Americans in an area and the quantity of chemicals released. At the census tract level, however, the association failed to materialize. Similar trends have been found in recent environmental enforcement studies. For example, Lynch, Stretesky, and Burns (2004a) found that racial, ethnic, and income characteristics of census tracts surrounding oil refineries are not related to penalty amounts. However, refineries situated within the boundaries of Hispanic and low-income ZIP codes tend to receive smaller penalties than refineries located in non-Hispanic and more affluent ZIP codes.

Other researchers have argued that the association between environmental hazards and race may not exist without the appropriate control variables. For instance, Jay Gould (1986) was the first researcher to point out that it may be urbanization and not race, ethnicity, or median family income that influences the distribution of hazardous waste. Gould (1986) argues that it is important to identify ways of isolating the different impacts of toxic waste and urbanization, primarily because urban areas have greater industrial activity than rural areas. Anderton (1997) more clearly spelled out this concern by pointing out that any racial, ethnic, or economic demographic comparisons between urban and non-urban areas are likely to produce results that are confounded by the geographic nature and average size of nonmetropolitan census tracts. To solve this problem Anderton calls for controlled comparisons, such as those used in multivariate analyses (Anderton 1997, p. 513). It seems important, then, to control for urban/rural differences to ensure a variety of indicators that get at the fundamental underlying differences between those areas. For example, a measure of population density is a function of both area size and population and therefore would take into account census variations across urban and rural tracts.

Another criticism of EJS is that a large number of studies fail to control for property values in multivariate analysis. The argument is that undesirable land uses create low property values that cause Whites to move away from the hazard and the poor (who are largely African American and Hispanic) to move nearby the hazard. Indeed, empirical evidence suggests that even the rumor of potential hazardous waste facilities serves to reduce the residential property values of that area (Ketkar, 1992). In addition, several researchers have reported that the value of residential housing is considerably lower in areas containing hazardous waste facilities when compared to areas containing no waste facilities (see Pollock and Vittas, 1995). Vicki Been (1994) also argues that the reason that the poor and minorities are situated near hazardous waste is because market forces drive the poor, regardless of race or ethnicity, to these locations where cheaper housing is available. Many researchers argue however, that the fact that housing values are significant indicators of environmental hazards only serve to suggest that minorities and the poor face unfair constraints on their housing choices and therefore suffer from indirect discrimination because of their race or social class (Stretesky and Hogan, 1998).

A third methodological issue that is often discussed in the environmental justice literature relates to causal order. As previously discussed some researchers argue that for environmental discrimination to exist, hazardous waste must be placed in areas that are predominately poor and minority (Clark et al., 1995). Such a contention, however, assumes that discrimination exists only as a product of individuals and their choices. In contrast, many EJS researchers argue for a broader interpretation of the meaning of discrimination—one that considers how it is produced and reproduced within social institutions (see Blauner, 1972). Such an interpretation is important as it directly relates to the issue of causal order. For instance, as we have previously pointed out, discrimination in housing and employment may constrain housing choices and shape demographic patterns around undesirable land uses after their initial siting.

CONCLUSION

The main purpose of this chapter was to describe the EJS literature. That literature is quite large and continually expanding. As noted, however, there is serious debate as to what terms should be used to describe EJS studies, what should be studied, and how those studies should be carried out. Despite these conflicts it is clear that criminologists have not contributed much to that debate. This is true even though the field of criminology and criminal justice overlap considerably with the EJS literature. Thus, we have set out to describe environmental justice from a criminology and criminal justice perspective. We argue that environmental justice must be taken seriously by criminologists. Specifically, we demonstrate how crime has been part of the environmental justice movement from its very beginning. Moreover, much of the research in the area of environmental justice is closely related to important issues that are central to criminology and criminal justice and overlap considerably with the EJS literature. Still, there is much to be done. As environmental data become more accessible the challenge for criminologists will be to begin to address, in more detail, some of the issues we identified as important.

CHAPTER 10.

Environmental Crime: Challenges and Expectations

INTRODUCTION

Distinguished researcher and professor Todd Clear (2001, p. 3) has argued that "Too much of contemporary public policy legislation is based upon mistaken ideas about the causes and prevention of crime, and far too much of the public debate on crime policy rests on fallacious images of criminality and criminal justice." Clear's statement reflects the concern of many who believe criminological research is ignored by policymakers. We believe that this is especially true in the case of environmental crime. If the average criminologist (i.e., those who study street crimes) laments the lack of impact their research has on crime policy, the environmental crime researcher stands on the edge of the abyss ready to jump, having had virtually no impact on public policy whatsoever.

Environmental criminologists face a substantial challenge if they seek to have their work influence public policy. First, they must change perceptions about crime among the general public, the news media, and other criminologists. Second, they must alter funding priorities so that the government directs research monies toward the study of environmental crimes. And third, they must question and educate policymakers about the undue influence corporations currently have in shaping laws about what will and will not be considered environmental crime.

Environmental crime issues are continually overshadowed by the drama of conventional crime. Highlighted by the media in daily news reports, street crimes are also the focus of many television crime shows. Real-life docudramas such as "COPS" feature high-speed police chases and raids, while weekly series such as *NYPD Blue*, *CSI: Crime Scene Investigation*, and *Law and Order* cater to the stereotypical image of crime as a street crime of violence (Dowler, Fleming and Muzzati, 2006; Holbrook and Hill, 2005; Eschholz, Mallard and Flynn, 2004). In contrast, environmental crimes rarely appear in weekly television series. When these issues are addressed in entertainment media, the presentation is likely to be a full length movie such as *Erin Brockovich* or *A Civil Action*, which focus on the heroic and extraordinary activities of the main character rather than on the nature and extent of the crimes involved, or the widespread and ordinary nature of environmental victimization. Indeed, crime movies are dominated by the unreal action-thriller that sensationalizes crimes and the hunt for the criminal (e.g., *2 Fast 2 Furious*, and the *Lethal Weapon* movie series), or which features the rarest of criminal events (mass murder, serial killers, massive bank robberies; e.g., *The Italian Job*, *The Silence of the Lambs*, and *Natural Born Killers*).

The effort to change the perception of environmental crime among policy-makers, the public, and criminologists is one example of a priority related to the advancement of environmental protection. In the remainder of this chapter, we examine several challenges related to (1) future research; (2) community justice, (3) local efforts to address environmental crime; (4) future directions for EPA reform; (5) the blending of ecological issues within the context of sustainable development; and, (6) a new conservation agenda.

RESEARCHING ENVIRONMENTAL CRIME

Despite the fact that the literature on environmental harms and responses to them has grown exponentially in the past few decades, much work remains. Researchers such as David Simon (2000) highlight the need for testing crimino-logical theories including differential association or Merton's theory of anomie as explanations for environmental crime, noting that environmental crime offers a laboratory for testing and revising these theories of organizational practices. Recent research has also drawn on rational choice theories to examine corporate self-policing (Stretesky, 2006).

Rebovich (1998; 2002) has proposed that the study of environmental crime and criminals follow the same path as conventional criminology. This includes studies about whether get tough legislation (longer prison sentences, three-strikes legislation, etc), could be used to control environmental crimes. In addition, criminologists should focus research effort on: (1) identifying the characteristics of environmental criminals and the correlates of these behaviors; (2) identifying the characteristics of corporations and corporate sectors likely to violate environmental laws (e.g., size, number of employees, receipts, profits, industrial sector, type of industry, locations); (3) examinations of prosecutorial decisions to charge suspects accused of environmental crimes; (4) the effective-ness of environmental crime case prosecutions, penalties, intermediate sanctions, and other efforts to enhance compliance; and (5) the use of recidivism measures as indicators of crime control response effectiveness. Special interest should also be paid to enforcing international environmental laws and treaties.

As noted in an earlier chapter, studies of the types noted above cannot be undertaken without data. The establishment of centralized databases on environ-mental crimes and criminals that record offense types, offender characteristics, the number of events, prosecution, and sentencing outcomes similar to those for ordinary crime would do much to enhance environmental crime research. While the EPA has taken steps to improve data collection and dissemination, much work remains to be done (Mintz, 1995, p. 119-130) to a system which concentrates on "bean counting" rather than the quality or usefulness of the data it manages and collects (Mintz, 1995, p. 199). Mintz notes the unreliability of environmental indicators as a primary measure of the effectiveness of EPA enforcement efforts, adding that no particular enforcement measure provides a fair, accurate, and balanced picture of the efficiency and effectiveness of EPA enforcement programs or efforts. In addition, while the EPA and state environmental regulatory agencies should continue collecting data they already focus on, they also need to expand data collection efforts. Efforts have been made in this area, although much work remains. Expanding data collection and dissemination, however, are not top priorities at the EPA, which continually faces the challenge of budgetary limitations (Mintz, 1995).

Rosenbaum (2003, p. 180) points out that scientific research on environmental toxins and public health issues established the conditions necessary for collecting and maintaining the kinds of data needed for evaluating the effectiveness of environmental public health policies. Moreover, improved data sources have allowed researchers to develop more useful and elaborate statistical models to answer questions that tie public health and environmental pollution and policy matters together. This is the type of situation researchers hope will emerge with respect to environmental crime data.

COMMUNITY JUSTICE: INVOLVING THE PUBLIC AND TRANSFORMING FORMAL RESPONSES TO ENVIRONMENTAL CRIME

Over the past two decades, community justice has become increasingly ingrained in traditional criminal justice practices. Suited for locations where public safety is problematic and criminal justice practices notably active, community justice provides an avenue for reconsidering how traditional criminal justice approaches to social control can be revised and enhanced to improve the quality of life in high-crime areas (Clear and Cadora, 2003). Clear and Cadora identify two assumptions inherent within the idea of community justice: (1) differences among jurisdictions and communities require tailored responses to address the differences, and (2) informal systems of social controls (e.g., families, neighbors, friends) rather than formal systems of social control (e.g., the criminal justice system) form the most significant foundation for public safety. Though it applies to community justice systems that address traditional crimes, Clear and Cadora's view of community justice could also be applied to environmental crime. Indeed, there is a wide range of traditional community justice practices, ranging from community-policing efforts to teen courts, probation and parole efforts, and numerous volunteer and mentorship opportunities, which could also be applied with some modification to environmental crime. Since the 1960s, efforts to address environmental harms have often been promoted at the grass-roots or community level, indicating that community justice approaches may be a useful environmental crime control response.

Environmental justice researchers have addressed the benefits of grass-roots, community justice movements. Bullard and Wright (1993. p. 836), for example, describe a community justice process where the public becomes an equal partner in redressing environmental harms and as participants in environmental harm and crime research. To build these kinds of active community justice processes, researchers and lawmakers alike are required to move beyond the traditional view of members of the affected communities as "subjects" and "victims," and to view them as active agents capable of "making history" and participating in constructing venues for changing the life course of their communities. Consistent with their "holistic methodology for documenting, remediating, and preventing environmental health problems," Bullard and Wright (1993. pp. 836-37) suggested the following points of entry for community justice:

- Ensure public participation in research projects and emphasize input from the population under study.

- Encourage both regional and national congressional discussion of individuals, groups and communities affected or at risk of facing environmental harms.

- Develop and maintain a "Division or 'Bureau of Environmental Statistics'" under the direction of the EPA that collects and collates environment and health-related information on at-risk groups.

- Conduct follow-up research evaluations of earlier research on at-risk groups and communities, with particular consideration to the inconclusiveness of many government-sponsored studies regarding the dangers associated with physical proximity to hazardous waste.

The EPA has made some progress on community justice. For instance, the agency's Office of Research and Development, the "scientific and research arm of the EPA," is designed to identify, understand, and solve environmental problems, integrate the work of the office's scientific partners (e.g., academia, other agencies, and nations), and "provide leadership in addressing emerging environmental issues and in advancing the science and technology of risk assessment and risk management" (www.epa.gov/ord/htm/ aboutord.htm). However, community justice concerns are nowhere more evident than in the EPA's environmental justice programs, which include the National Environmental Justice Advisory Council, Environmental Justice Grants Programs, Environmental Justice Community Intern Program, and the Federal Interagency Working Group on Environmental Justice (www.epa.gov/compliance/environmentaljustice). Despite the good intentions behind these efforts, the EPA has failed to meet its own environmental justice mission as noted in several reports filed by the EPA Office of Inspector General (Anash et al, 2006; Carroll and Weber, 2004).

Historically, local environmental protection has been provided first by the federal government, and later by states. But, as Edwards (1998, p. 50) notes, public support for environmental protection has moved from the national level to the local level. They add that, tired of facing the effects of environmental harms, local community members have increasingly demanded action from the government. In effect, *because environmental crimes are local problems*, the most effective way to police these crimes is to decentralize the enforcement of environmental laws. There are both benefits and pitfalls to such an approach. The costs of enforcing environmental laws could, under such a model, become prohibitive to local populations, which would face the choice of allowing high levels of pollution, or perhaps outlawing industrial production altogether (Epstein, 1998). Epstein notes, however, that local communities already fund local police who could also be charged with enforcing environmental regulations. Adding these duties to those of local police makes sense (because police have intimate knowledge of the communities they serve), and would help dissolve the stereotype concerning the difference between the impact and seriousness of environmental and street crime on society. It should be noted, however, that doing so would require dramatic changes in the training of law enforcement officers, and would not come without increased costs to local communities. The use of community justice programs could help offset some of these additional expenditures, and allow local communities to become more involved in the fight against environmental crime.

REFORMING THE EPA

For many, one of the keys to redressing environmental crimes is reforming the EPA and its ability to enforce environmental laws and protect public health. A good overview of these issues is provided by Rosenbaum (2003, pp. 194-197), who openly admits that his suggestions have been proposed by the major independent commissions that have examined the EPA and suggested reform policies since 1990. Among other things, Rosenbaum calls for an EPA-Congressional charter that would clearly define the agency's mission, and provide relief for the EPA from unreasonable regulatory deadlines, administrative rules, and program objectives put forth in Congressional environmental legislation. Rosenbaum also calls for the EPA to substantially increase its environmental monitoring, data collection, and data interpretation (see also Bullard and Wright, 1993), and notes that the creation of the Office of Environmental Information constitutes a significant step in this direction. He further argues that the EPA should offer incentives and resources to states with the intent of improving the quality of environmental information collected at the state level.

One of the persistent problems at the EPA is establishing an organizational culture that is more considerate of innovative, alternative approaches to prosecuting environmental crimes and less dependent on command-and-control regulation (Rosenbaum, 2003). In anticipating how the EPA can prepare for reform efforts, Rosenbaum notes that Congress may be the most influential agency shaping EPA reform, an argument supported by Mintz (1995), who states that EPA's top officials should attempt to establish an amicable relationship with interested leaders on Capitol Hill, given the EPA's often turbulent relationships with Congress. These calls for enhanced regulatory reform efforts are reflective of calls for improvement within the EPA by numerous researchers. For example, a growing environmental concern is ocean health. Coastal waters in the U.S. have experienced a decline in fish populations and water quality in recent years. The EPA can impact ocean water quality through administering the *Clean Water* and *Safe Drinking Water* Acts, and in appropriate regions through the operation of estuary protection, ocean dumping, and regional waterway regulations. Some, however, charge that the EPA has not done all that it can to protect the integrity of ocean waters. In his testimony before the *U.S. Commission on Ocean Policy*, environmental law expert and director of The Ocean Conservancy, Tim Eichenberg (2002) noted that cruise ships, which generate the same types and quantities of waste as small cities, are exempt from several EPA ocean dumping regulations related to the discharge of sewage, gray water, and ballast. Eichenberg also noted that even when such regulations apply, the cruise ship industry often disregards environmental regulations, a fact evident in the nearly $60 million in environmental fines they paid between 1998 and 2002. Eichenberg (2006) has also pointed out that there are EPA regulatory issues related to aquaculture or ocean fish farming. Now, whether these policies and issues discussed above are considered by the EPA, they are issues of importance that shape the national response to environmental harms and regulatory strategy.

SUSTAINABLE DEVELOPMENT

Perhaps one of the most promising and pressing issues concerning environmental regulation and protection is sustainable development (Vig and Kraft, 2003. p. 391). Paehlke (2003. p. 57) defines sustainable development as "the capacity to continuously produce the necessities of a quality human existence within the bounds of a natural world of undiminished quality." As a policy, sustainable development involves the use of long-range planning, as opposed to immediate reactions, that blends three concerns: (1) human health, (2) ecosystem health and (3) ecosystem resources, sustainability and carrying capacity (Paehlke, 2003, p. 58). Sustainable development programs recognize that the world's ecosystem is incapable of supporting unbridled human growth, which is accompanied by excessive waste, over-consumption of natural resources, and high levels of pollution. Thus, in order to sustain development, humans must consciously plan out wise use of environmental resources, control levels of pollution, and, in some cases, control population growth as well. This is true because the earth has a limited carrying capacity—the number of people it can support.

To be successful, Vig and Kraft (2003) argue that sustainable development requires, at minimum, coordination among government agencies with the intent to prevent departments from working toward conflicting purposes, and that concerns for sustainability should supersede environmental policy given that public policy and private activities ultimately must be cognizant of environmental sustainability. They add that sustainable development has many meanings and deserves greater discussion and research than has occurred to this point, and that concrete indicators are required for the purpose of measuring progress toward sustainability in various areas. The advancement of sustainability requires a more interdisciplinary approach to ecological issues than we have seen in the past. At the very least, such an interdisciplinary approach results in the need for interaction and cooperation from a variety of fields and resources.

One of the critics of sustainable development is ecological economist and former Senior Economist for the World Bank, Herman Daly (1991, 1996, 1999). Daly argues that current environmental conditions necessitate a move beyond sustainable development to zero-growth or steady state economics. In his view, the most substantial threats to human societies are their belief in endless economic development and progress, and an unbridled appetite for the consumption of goods and the accumulation of wealth. In contrast, zero growth and steady state economic views stress that the natural world contains a fixed supply of resources. These fixed resources present a natural limit to the economic and population growth of human societies that humans have ignored. In the contemporary period, finite natural resource issues have been described in the end-of-oil literature (Campbell, 2003, Deffeyes, 2001; Goodstein, 2004; Heinberg, 2003). The capacity of the world to absorb human pollution is described in the global warming literature (Lovelock, 2006) and in studies on environmental pollution and toxic hazards (Colborn, Dumanoski and Meyers, 1997). Population growth, the impact of declining oil supplies on the price of fertilizer, and the effect of the world's changing environment on the limits of the world food supply have also received scholarly attention (Brown, 2005; Corson, 1995). These areas of research tend to support Daly's view that there are limits to growth, and a need exists to reorganize and reinvent human societies, goals and values to prevent serious future crises. A number of policies relevant to these issues are described by Corson (1995), who emphasizes, among other issues, the need to reeducate populations to promote consumptive and lifestyle values conducive to environmental preservation.

CONSERVATION FOR THE FUTURE

The roots of environmental protection are found in the early writings of conservationists who sought to keep the environment in harmony. The conservation movement faces many challenges in today's changing society, many of which are documented in this book. Steven Sanderson (2002) highlights a series of issues relating to the construction of a new conservation agenda that will survive in today's society including (1) moving conservation from the corridors of government to the field; (2) providing wildlife health surveillance and tracking the state of wildlife to protect against disease and extinction; (3) conducting scientific sustainability audits too assess the state of conservation efforts; (4) protecting cultural and ecological sites of global importance, which have relied on inadequate funding from national agencies for protection; (5) endowing conservation rather than governments; (6) creating global conserva-tion alliances to work more trustfully and effectively; and (7) creating a conservation code of conduct to promote corporate conservation ethics. Much like other groups with an interest in environmental protection, conservationists have had to adjust to changing times and interests to protect their turf.

In the preceding sections of this chapter, we have discussed but a few of the many challenges facing environmental protection in the future. While there remains promise for better protecting the environment (for instance, through greater actions taken at the local level, including active involvement among groups historically absent from activism), there remain numerous issues worthy of proactive efforts to prevent future problems. Further, there remain several promising alternatives and responses to better protect the environment.

EVOLVING AND FUTURE ISSUES

A look to the future of environmental issues would be incomplete absent a look at evolving and future issues as they pertain to environmental protection. Vig and Kraft (2003, p. 392-397) note that various environmental issues remain unresolved despite three decades of progress, and that along with sustainable development, the most important of these problems are (1) energy consumption and climate change; (2) biodiversity and endangered species; (3) clean water and wetland health; (4) the storage and treatment of hazardous and nuclear waste; (5) suburban sprawl, sustainable development, and mass transportation; (6) environ-mental justice; and (7) international treaties and leadership.

Vig and Kraft (2003) argue that there is hope for the environment in the future, despite these and related problems. They note that professionals from several fields (e.g., economists, business leaders, government officials, and environmental professionals) believe that more cost-conscious and efficient approaches are needed to properly address the growing environmental agenda (Vig and Kraft, 2003).

To demonstrate that all is not lost, Vig and Kraft (2003, pp. 399-403) identify several areas in which policy initiatives are receiving significant attention: (1) pollution prevention; (2) risk assessment; (3) environmental taxes, incentives, and markets; (4) collaborative planning; (5) environmental research and technology development; and (6) sustainability indicators. Their work in this area of identifying problems and noting proposed and current solutions is to be commended. Addressing these and related environmental concerns takes efforts on behalf of all: researchers, policymakers, industry, regulators, consumers, activists, and anyone with a concern for humanity. Simply identifying problems is not enough. Responding to current concerns and preventing future problems is the solution. All are encouraged to participate.

THE FUTURE OF ENVIRONMENTAL CRIME: OUR THOUGHTS

In light of the predictions, issues and recommendations that we have just reviewed, we offer our look into the future. Our projections, along with many others previously mentioned in this work, are non-exhaustive. Indeed, while many predictions can be found in previous accounts of projected issues facing environmental crime, we highlight what we believe to be the most significant developments and issues affecting the future of environmental protection.

Increased Environmental Crime Research

Empirical research on environmental crime dates back to the mid-1980s, a brief history by any account, and Rebovich (1998, p. 351) suggests that research in this area remains in its infancy. Reasons to expand data collection and analysis of environmental crime data include (1) to assess and improve effective regulation of the environment; (2) to demonstrate that environmental policy and regulations produce the expected results; (3) to achieve results in a timely and cost-effective manner; (4) that the results promote public health; and (5) that these policies are unbiased in their applications and with respect to the ideals and practices of environmental justice. An extensive array of research is required to make these kinds of assessments. The EPA could encourage independent researchers to examine these questions by maintaining an open, diverse and high-quality array of data that can be accessed with or without the need to obtain an EPA grant.

Public health and the exposure of the public to environmental toxins are serious issues. As we illustrated in the introduction to this book, exposure to environmental toxins causes much more extensive harm than street crime. Yet, street crime receives much more attention and interest. Based on the level of harm and growing awareness of these harms and improvements in the availability of environmental data, we expect environmental crime research to continue to expand. In addition, we expect increased interest in these issues as related environmental conditions (e.g., global warming) receive expanded attention, as funding opportunities (e.g., EPA grants) to study these behaviors grow, as data becomes more widely and more easily accessible via the Internet, as the inclusion of environmental law, crime, regulation and health issues become more widely integrated into collegiate curriculums, and as the literature on public health harms becomes more widely integrated into the criminological literature.

One of the obstacles to increased research in this area has been the government practice of removing "sensitive" material from public access. In light of recent events such as the September 11th, 2001 terrorist attacks and the war with Iraq, and with the corresponding concern for homeland security, public agencies throughout the nation have removed documents from public access. Certainly, much information remains freely available; however, many data restrictions are projected to continue in light of our concern for homeland security. While this seems to contradict our suggestion that data are becoming and have become more widely available for studying environmental crime, and that research in this area will continue to grow, only certain "sensitive" information has been removed and there remains available to the public a wealth of untapped information that would provide little, if any support to terrorist activities. Researchers should keep in mind the utility of the *Freedom of Information Act* if they are unable to locate information they need.

Potentially Enhanced Regulatory Efforts

Recent concern for homeland security may result in enhanced regulation of industry. One of the most promising results of recent events is the effort to better organize federal law enforcement activities which may increase the efficiency and effectiveness of environmental regulation. It is believed that government agents will become more involved in social control efforts, not necessarily out of concern for ecological destruction, but as a security issue. Efforts toward this move are evident in the EPA's recent cooperative efforts with the Department of Homeland Security. Any intrusion into industry for the purposes of national security could have the secondary effect of exposing harms to the environment, or could possibly deter violators who recognize their vulnerability to exposure given the government's greater involvement in their practices. Not all areas of industry will be affected by security concerns; however, an overall increase in formal social control efforts could result in enhanced environmental regulation.

The Continued Influence of Politics

Environmental activism is undoubtedly important to the advancement of environmental protection and the abatement of environmental hazards. Environmental groups have recently been described as "generally larger, stronger, better funded, and more knowledgeable than ever before. Membership has grown in recent years; there are now more than eight million dues-paying members of the major national organizations" and many more in the state and local groups (Meyer, 2005, p. 69)—a quadrupling of environmental group membership since 1980. Despite this higher level of support, environmental crime enforcement efforts will likely continue to be influenced by the party affiliation of those controlling the presidency and Congress.

Following an established pattern, Republicans will continue to promote less regulation than Democrats, although public opinion has been, and will be, a wild card in this trend. Few presidents (or politicians at any level) have been able to ignore public concern for the environment, though some have tried. Should society become increasingly concerned about environmental issues, the party affiliation of the president (or the Congressional majority) will have limited impact on environmental regulation. It is unfortunate, but it may take another significant environmental disaster (e.g., the damage caused by the Exxon *Valdez*, additional natural disasters impacted by ozone changes) before we see any substantial increase in public concern for the environment.

An Increased Focus on Global Environmentalism

The rise of globalism in many fields of study and society in general means that environmental regulation on a global basis will no longer be merely a topic of discussion, but instead a long overdue reality. The need to look beyond national boundaries is becoming popular in many countries, and global environmentalism is becoming one of the primary areas of concern. Evidence of movement in this direction is found in the recent protests of the World Trade Organization (Vogel, 2003), the recent "World Summit on Sustainable Development" (Taylor, 2002), the Kyoto Protocol, and the overall move toward global trade and commerce. In 1994, the Interpol Sub-Group on Wildlife Crime (later renamed the Interpol Wildlife Working Group) was created to meet regularly and exchange enforcement ideas on how Interpol could help maintain and support an international network of contacts with expertise in the enforcement in wildlife crime.

There exist many other examples of countries collaborating in efforts to address the international nature of environmental harm, although much work remains in this area, as finding common ground among countries regarding any issue can be problematic. In light of the earlier decision by President Bush to withdraw the U.S. from the Kyoto Protocol on climate change (Vig, 2003), the U.S., in particular, as a world leader in production and manufactured goods must consider its role in global environmentalism.

Increased Interdisciplinary Study of Environmental Issues

In addition to the need for environmental issues to be addressed in international terms, there is also a need for different fields of study to break down the traditional walls hampering interdisciplinary research and collaborate toward more effective research efforts. Elkington (1998) argues that environmental sustainability involves three sets of environmental values: resource sustainability, ecosystem health, and human health. Given the varied nature of the fields involved with these values, studying and researching these areas requires input from several perspectives, and is necessary to assess the impact of efforts surrounding sustainable development. One would be hard-pressed to find researchers who maintain expertise in each of these particular areas, thus cooperative research efforts are needed among the humanities and sciences.

The complex nature of environmental crime dictates the incorporation of knowledge from a variety of disciplines. For instance, criminologists and criminal justice researchers, by nature of their training, are generally unaware of the meaning behind many environmental indicators, while most environmental researchers are unfamiliar with criminal behavior and legal studies. Thus, the potential for interdisciplinary work is great.

Greater Societal Consideration of Sustainable Development

It is anticipated that the concept of sustainable development will grow in popularity and cross-discipline studies will provide insight regarding the effectiveness of this innovative approach. That insight is anticipated to provide a solid framework for directed efforts toward sustainability. The idea of being able to meet consumer needs while eliminating harms to the environment is attractive to all. For instance, consumers would continue to meet their needs and lead healthier lives, and industry leaders would face less pressure from government regulators, consumers and activists and still profit. There remain several questions regarding sustainable development, not the least of which concerns the operationalization of the concept. How do we meet everyone's needs while maintaining the environment? Continued research in this area is imperative.

Enhanced Involvement of Local Criminal Justice Agencies

Grassroots efforts are expected to influence environmental issues. With that movement will come greater emphasis on environmental issues as they pertain to local criminal justice agencies. Much environmental regulation has been offered by state, and particularly, federal agencies. Several recent events, including the terrorist attacks of September 11, 2001, have taught us that the federal government is ill-prepared to protect everyone. While large in structure, the federal government is highly specialized and provides a scarce physical appearance throughout the country. Society has learned that protection is effectively provided at the local level, as evidenced in traditional law enforcement efforts. Imagine what our traditional crime rates would be if we relied on the federal government to enforce street crime laws.

In response, societal concern for environmental issues will drive local criminal justice agencies to become more involved. Particularly, our police agencies and courts will play a more active role. Earlier in this work we discussed the need for continued involvement by local law enforcement agencies. As those most directly involved with the public, they are well-suited to assist with environmental protection despite such duties typically falling outside their agenda.

Our courts will also become more involved with confronting environmental harms. Rebovich (2002) suggests that much is expected of tomorrow's environmental prosecutor—the ability to emphasize law enforcement duties that not only uphold the letter of the law, but which also protect public health. These diverse goals will likely result in the environmental prosecutor feeling pressure to appeal to a variety of groups and interests. As the environmental prosecutor's role evolves, research must be redirected to provide information to address these often competing goals (Rebovich, 2002). Rebovich (1998, p. 352) also suggests that additional research attention be directed toward the ways in which enforcement efforts might impede the successful apprehension and prosecution of offenders.

The future may also bring further specialization in law enforcement at the local level. The nature of environmental crime is distinct from traditional crime, and sometimes requires special skills to confront. It is possible that local police departments will add specialized training and environmental harm units to fight environmental crimes. This specialization could extend to the courts where prosecutors trained in environmental law would handle such cases. To be sure, this type of specialization is already occurring, yet in piecemeal fashion and in isolated cases. An enhanced, systematic alteration in the regulation of the environment at the local level may provide the most fruitful criminal justice approach to environmental protection.

IN THE END...

Examining the future is an interesting, yet inexact pursuit. One can observe projections based on current quantitative trends, or one can observe qualitative factors to offer suggestions regarding what the future holds. A combination of both approaches may be most suitable. Regardless, the uncertainty of what to expect remains. We can provide projections that offer probabilities regarding what's next; however, the course of this country's environmental policy can change in one day.

The United States takes pride in being a diverse, multicultural society, the Land of Opportunities. Finding agreement and setting a course of action that appeals to all in a diverse country in which all are seeking to personally cash in on their opportunities is, at the very least, difficult to do. Future courses of action with regard to the environment involve input from a variety of interests, including individuals concerned about environmental degradation, profits, health and well-being, political reputation, and many other competing interests. The overriding challenge is to find a course of action that suits all interests, or at least a course that seems most important to all. While political reputations, profits and the like are important to some, we can all agree that protecting our environment should take precedent. Unfortunately, not all see things this way.

F. Scott Fitzgerald wrote that "Optimism is the content of small men in high places." No doubt our look at the future is, in places, optimistic and simplistic. We leave the hard-core forecasting to futurist researchers who give due consideration to all relevant variables, including political, social, and economic factors. Nevertheless, we do believe there is much hope with regard to environmental protection. Recent harms to the environment and political disregard of environmental issues have generated public concern. Whether this concern evolves into action remains to be seen.

References

Adler, J. (2006, July 17). Going green. *Newsweek,* 43-49, 50-52.

Adler, R., and Lord, C. (1991). Environmental crimes: Raising the stakes. *The George Washington Law Review, 59,* 781-861.

Allen, D. (2001). Social class, race, and toxic releases in American counties, 1995. *Social Science Journal, 38*(1), 13 -25.

Allen, M., and Milbank, D. (2003). Utah Gov. named as chief of EPA; nominee wants power moved out of Washington. *The Washington Post,* p. A1.

Anash, L., Barnes-Weaver, E., Carroll, D., Harris, J., Ramakrishnan, K., and Weber, S. (2006). *EPA needs to conduct environmental justice reviews of its programs, policies and activities.* Retrieved. from http://www.epa.gov/oigearth/reports/2006/20060918-2006-P-00034.pdf.

Anderson, A., Anderton, D., and Oakes, J. (1994). Evaluating TSDF siting over the past two decades. *Waste Age, 25*(7), 83-100.

Anderton, D., Oakes, J., and Egan, K. (1997). Environmental equity in superfund: Demographics of the discovery and prioritization of abandoned toxic sites. *Evaluation Research, 21*(1), 3-26.

Anderton, D. L., Anderson, A. B., Rossi, P. H., Oakes, J. M., Fraser, M. R., Weber, E. W., et al. (1994). Hazardous waste facilities: 'Environmental equity' issues in metropolitan areas. *Evaluation Review, 18,* 123-140.

Arora, S., and Cason, T. N. (1999). Do community characteristics influence environmental outcomes? Evidence from the Toxics Release Inventory. *Southern Economic Journal, 65*(4), 691-716.

Asch, P., and Seneca, J. J. (1978). Some evidence on distribution of air quality. *Land Economics, 54*(3), 278-297.

Athanasiou, T. (2002). *Divided planet: The ecology of rich and poor.* Athens, Georgia: University of Georgia Press.

Atlas, M. (2001). Rush to judgment: An empirical analysis of environmental equity in U.S. Environmental Protection Agency enforcement actions. *Law and Society Review, 35*(3), 633-682.

Atmadja, J., and Bagtzoglou, A. C. (2001). State of the art report on mathematical methods for groundwater pollution source identification. *Environmental Forensics, 2*(3), 205-214.

Back, P.-E. (2007). A model for estimating the value of sampling programs and the optimal number of samples for contaminated soil. *Environmental Geology, 52,* 573-585.

Balbus, I. (1977). Commodity form and legal form: An essay on the relative autonomy of the law. *Law and Society Review, 11*(3), 571-588.

Barkdull, J. (1998). Nixon and the marine environment. *Presidential Studies Quarterly, 28*(3), 587-605.

Barker, D. A. (2002). Environmental Crimes, prosecutorial discretion, and the civil/criminal line. *Virginia Law Review, 88*(6), 1387-1431.

Barnett, H. C. (1993). Crimes against the environment: superfund enforcement at last. *The Annals, 525*, 119 -133.

Bazley, T. D. (2007). *Investigating white-collar crime.* Upper Saddle River, NJ: Prentice Hall.

Bearer, C. (1995). How are children different than adults? *Environmental Health Perspectives, 103*(S6), 7-12.

Been, V. (1994). Locally undesirable land uses in minority neighborhoods: Disproportionate siting or market dynamics? *Yale Law Journal, 103*(6), 1383-1411.

Been, V., and Gupta, F. (1997). Coming to the nuisance or going to the Barrios? A longitudinal analysis of environmental justice claims. *Ecology Law Quarterly, 24*(1), 1-56.

Beirne, P. (1995). The use and abuse of animals in criminology: A brief history and current review. *Social Justice, 22*(1), 5-31.

Beirne, P. (1999). For a nonspeciesist criminology: Animal abuse as an object of study. *Criminology, 37*(1), 117-147.

Beirne, P. (2002). Criminology and animal studies: A sociological view. *Society and Animals, 10*(4), 381-386.

Beirne, P., and South, N. (Eds.). (2007). *Issues in green criminology: Confronting harms against environments, other animals and humanity.* Devon, UK: Willan Publishing.

Bellamy, J. F. (2000). *Marx's ecology: Materialism and nature.* New York, NY: Guilford.

Bellini, J. (1986). *High tech holocaust* London: David and Charles.

Benton, T. (Ed.). (1996). *The greening of Marxism.* New York, NY: Guilford.

Blauner, R. (1972). *Racial oppression in America.* New York, NY: Harper and Row.

Boer, T., Pastor, M., Sadd, J. L., and Snyder, L. D. (1997). Is there environmental racism? The demographics of hazardous waste in Los Angeles County. *Social Science Quarterly, 78*, 793-810.

Bookchin, M. (1965). *Crisis in our cities.* Englewood Cliffs, NJ: Prentice Hall.

Bookchin, M. (1971). *Post-scarcity economics.* Berkeley, CA: Ramparts Press.

Bookchin, M. (1987). *Philosophy of social ecology.* New York, NY: Black Rose Press.

Bookchin, M. (1988). *Toward an ecological society.* Montreal, Canada: Black Rose.

Bookchin, M. (1992). *Urbanization without cities.* Montreal, Canada: Black Rose Press.

Bookchin, M. (2005). *The ecology of freedom: The emergence and dissolution of hierarchy.* Oakland, CA: AK Press.

Booth, A., and Osgood, D. W. (1993). The influence of testosterone on deviance in adulthood: Assessing and explaining the relationship. *Criminology, 31*(2), 93-117.

Borenstein, S. (2003, December 9). Pollution citations plummet under Bush. *The Philadelphia Inquirer.* Pp. A1, A14.

Bowen, W., Salling, M., Haynes, K., and Cryan, E. (1995). Toward environmental justice: Spatial equity in Ohio and Cleveland. *Annals of the Association of American Geographers, 85,* 641-663.

Box, S. (1989). *Power, crime, and mystification.* London: Routledge.

Boyce, J. (2002). *The political economy of the environment.* Cheltenham, UK: Edward Elgar Publishing.

Brajer, V., and Hall, J. (1992). Recent evidence on the distribution of air-pollution effects. *Contemporary policy issues, 10*(1), 63-71.

Brender, J. D., Zhan, B. F., Suarez, L., Langlois, P., Gilani, Z., Delima, I., et al. (2006). Linking environmental hazards and birth defects data. *Journal of Occupational and Environmental Health, 12*(3), 126-133.

Brown, L. (2003). *Eco-economy: building an economy for the earth.* New York, NY: W.W. Norton.

Brown, L. (2005). *Outgrowing the earth: The food security challenge in an age of falling water tables and rising temperatures.* New York, NY: W.W. Norton.

Brown, L. (2006). *Plan B, 2.0: Rescuing a planet under stress and a civilization in trouble.* New York, NY: W.W. Norton.

Brown, L. (2006). *State of the world, 2006.* New York, NY: W.W. Norton.

Brown, M. H. (1980). *Laying waste: The poisoning of America by toxic chemicals.* New York, NY: Pantheon.

Brown, M. H. (1988). *The toxic cloud: The poisoning of America's air.* New York, NY: Harper and Row.

Brown, P., and Mikkelsen, E. J. (1990). *No safe place: Toxic waste, leukemia, and community action.* Berkeley, CA: University of California Press.

Bullard, R. (1983). Solid waste sites and the Black Houston community. *Sociological Inquiry, 53,* 273-288.

Bullard, R. (1990, 1994). *Dumping in Dixie: Race, class and environmental quality.* Boulder, CO: Westview.

Bullard, R. (1996). Environmental justice: It's more than waste facility siting. *Social Science Quarterly, 77,* 493-499.

Bullard, R., and Wright, B. (1987). Environmentalism and the politics of equity: Emergent trends in the Black community. *Mid-American Review of Sociology, 12*(1), 21-38.

Bullard, R., and Wright, B. (1993). Environmental justice for all: Community perspectives on health and research needs. *Toxicology and Industrial Health, 9*(5), 821-841.

Bullard, R. D., and Wright, B. H. (1992). The quest for environmental equity: Mobilizing the African-American community for change. In R. E. Dunlap and A. G. Mertig (Eds.), *American environmentalism: The U.S. environmental movement, 1970-1990* (pp. 39-49). New York, NY: Taylor and Francis.

Burch, R. (1976). The Peregrine falcon and the urban poor: Some sociological interrelations. In P. Richardson and J. Covey (Eds.), *Human ecology: An environmental approach* (pp. 308-315). Belmont, CA: Duxbury.

Burns, R. G., and Lynch, M. J. (2004). *Environmental crime: A sourcebook.* New York: LFB Scholarly Publishing.

Cable, S., and Benson, M. (1993). Acting locally: Environmental injustice and the emergence of grass-roots environmental organizations. *Social Problems, 40*(4), 464-477.

Cable, S., and Cable, C. (1995). *Environmental problems, grassroots solutions: The politics of grassroots environmental conflict.* New York, NY: St. Martin's Press.

Calvert, G. M., Barnet, M., Mehler, L. N., Becker, A., Das, R., Beckman, J., et al. (2006). Acute pesticide-related illness among emergency responders, 1993–2002. *American Journal of Industrial Medicine, 49*(5), 383-393.

Campbell, C. J. (2003). *The coming oil crisis*: Petroconsultants and Multi-Science Publishing Co. Ltd.

Cannon, L. (2000). *President Reagan: The role of a lifetime.* New York, NY: Public Affairs.

Carolinians angry over PCB landfill. (1982, August 11). *The New York Times,* p. 17.

Carroll, D. J., and Weber, S. J. (2004). *EPA needs to consistently implement the intent of the Executive Order on Environmental Justice.* Retrieved July 1, 2007. from http://www.epa.gov/oig/reports/2004/20040301-2004-P-00007.pdf.

Carson, R. (1962). *Silent spring.* Boston, MA: Houghton Mifflin.

Carson, R. T., Jeon, Y., and McCubbin, D. R. (1997). The relationship between air pollution emissions and income: U.S. data. *Environment and Development Economics, 2*, 433-450.

Carter, T. (1998). Policing the environment. In M. Clifford (Ed.), *Environmental crime: Enforcement, policy, and social responsibility* (pp. 169-203). Gaithersburg, MD: Aspen.

Central_Virginia_Environmental_Crimes_Task_Force. (2005). Resource Guide for the Investigation of Environmental Crimes (pp. 52): Central Virginia Environmental Crimes Task Force.

Chambliss, W., and Seidman, R. (1982). *Law, order, and power.* Reading, MA: Addison-Wesley.

Chew, S. C. (2001). *World ecological degradation: Accumulation, urbanization and deforestation, 3000 B.C. to 2000 A.D.* Walnut Creek, CA: Altamira.

Clark, R., Lab, S., and Stoddard, L. (1995). Environmental equity: A critique of the literature. *Social Pathology, 1*(4), 253-269.

Clark, R. D., Lab, S. P., and Stoddard, L. (1995). Environmental equity: A critique of the literature. *Social Pathology, 1*(3), 253-269.

Clear, T. (2001). Thinking strategically about the American Society of Criminology. *The Criminologist, 26,* 1, 3-7.

Clear, T. R., and Cadora, E. (2003). *Community justice.* Belmont, CA: Wadsworth.

Clifford, M. (Ed.). (1998). *Environmental crime: Enforcement, policy, and social responsibility.* Gaithersburg, MD: Aspen.

Clifford, M., and Edwards, T. D. (1998). Defining 'environmental crime'. In M. Clifford (Ed.), *Environmental crime: Enforcement, policy, and social responsibility.* Gaithersburg, MD: Aspen.

Clinard, M. B., and Yeager, P. C. (1980). *Corporate crime.* New York, NY: The Free Press.

Cockrell, R. (1992). *A green shrouded miracle: The administrative history of the Cuyahoga Valley National Recreational Area.* Omaha, NE: National Park Service.

Coglianese, C., and Nash, J. (2006). *Beyond compliance: Business decision making and the U.S. EPA's Performance Track Program.* Cambridge, MA: Mossavar-Rahmani Center for Business and Government, the John F. Kennedy School of Government, Harvard University.

Cohen, B. R. (1998, August 1). Polluted agency. *National Review, 50,* 38-39.

Cohen, M. A. (1992). Environmental crime and punishment: Legal/economic theory and empirical evidence on enforcement of environmental statutes. *The Journal of Criminal Law and Criminology, 82,* 1054-1108.

Cohen, M. A. (1998). Sentencing the environmental criminal. In M. Clifford (Ed.), *Environmental crime: Enforcement, policy, and social responsibility* (pp. 229-249). Gaithersburg, MD: Aspen.

Cohen, M. J. (2004). George W. Bush and the Environmental Protection Agency: A midterm appraisal. *Society and Natural Resources, 17,* 69-88.

Cohen, S. A. (1986). EPA: A qualified success. In S. Kamieniecki, R. Obrien and M. Clarke (Eds.), *Controversies in environmental policy* (pp. 174-198). New York, NY: State University of New York Press

Colborn, T., Dumanoski, D., and Meyers, J. P. (1998). *Our stolen future: Are we threatening our fertility, intelligence and survival? A scientific detective story.* New York, NY: Penguin.

Cole, D., Todd, L., and Wing, S. (2001). Concentrated swine feeding operations and public health: A review of the occupational and community health effects. *Environmental Health Perspectives, 108,* 685-699.

Collin, R. W. (2006). *The Environmental Protection Agency: Cleaning up America's act.* Westport, CT: Greenwood.

Conca, K. (2000). American environmentalism confronts the global economy. *Dissent, 47,* 72-78.

Corson, W. H. (1995). Priorities for a sustainable future: The role of education, the media, and tax reform. *Journal of Social Issues, 51*(4), 37-61.

Couch, S. R., and Kroll-Smith, S. (1997). Environmental movements and expert knowledge: Evidence for a new populism. *International Journal of Contemporary Sociology, 34*(2), 185-210.

Crump, K. S., Canady, R., and Kogevinas, M. (2003). Meta-analysis of dioxin cancer dose response for three occupational cohorts *Environmental Health Perspectives, 111,* 681-687.

Cutter, S. (1994). The burdens of toxic risks: Are they fair? *Business and Economic Review, 41,* 3-7.

Cutter, S., and Solecki, W. (1996). Setting environmental justice in space and place: Acute and chronic airborne toxic releases in southeastern United States. *Urban Geography, 17*, 380-399.

Daley, B. (2006, March 27). Whodunit?; A Coast Guard chemist identifies the unique fingerprints of oil spills to help determine who is responsible. *Boston Globe*, C1.

Daly, H. (1991). *Steady state economics*. Washington, DC: Island Press.

Daly, H. (1993). *Valuing earth: Economics, ecology, ethics*. Cambridge, MA: MIT Press.

Daly, H. (1996). *Beyond growth: The economics of sustainable development*. Boston, MA: Beacon Press.

Daniels, B., and Friedman, S. (1999). Spatial inequality and distribution of industrial toxic releases: Evidence from the 1990 TRI. *Social Science Quarterly, 80*, 244-262.

Daugherty, J. (1997). *Assessment of chemical exposure: Calculation methods for environmental professionals*. Boca Raton, FL: CRC Publishers.

Davies, J. C. (1970). *The politics of pollution*. New York, NY: Bobbs-Merrill.

Davis, D. (2002). *When smoke ran like water: Tales of environmental deception and the battle against pollution* New York, NY: Basic Books.

Daynes, B. W. (1999). Bill Clinton: Environmental president. In D. L. Soden (Ed.), *The environmental presidency* (pp. 259-312). New York, NY: State University of New York Press.

d'Eaubonne, F. (1974). *Le feminisme ou la mort*. Paris, France: Pierre Horay Editeur.

Deffeyes, K. S. (2001). *Hubbert's peak: The impending world oil shortage*. Princeton, New Jersey: Princeton University Press.

Del Olmo, R. (1998). The ecological impact of illicit drug cultivation and crop eradication programs in Latin America. *Theoretical Criminology, 2*(2), 269-278.

Denno, D. (1990). *Biology and violence: From birth to adulthood*. Cambridge: Cambridge University Press.

Derezinski, D., Lacy, M., and Stretesky, P. B. (2003). Chemical accidents in the United States, 1990 - 1996. *Social Science Quarterly, 84*(1), 122-143.

DeRoos, A. J., Hartge, P., Lubin, J. H., Colt, J. S., Davis, S., Cerhan, J. R., et al. (2005). Persistent organochlorine chemicals in plasma and risk of non-Hodgkin's lymphoma. *Cancer Research, 65*(23), 11214-11226.

Devall, B., and Sessions, G. (2001). *Deep ecology: Living as if nature mattered*. Layton, UT: Gibbs Smith.

Dickason, C. (1975). Efficiency and equity in natural-resource and environmental-policy - Comment. *American Journal of Agricultural Economics, 57*(1), 127-127.

DiMento, J. F. (1990, April). Polluters beware. *The Economist, 315*, 58.

DiMento, J. F. (1993). Criminal enforcement of environmental law. *The Annals, 525*, 134-146.

Domhoff, G. W. (2005). *Who rules America: Power, politics and social change, 5th Ed.* NY: McGraw-Hill.

Doughty, R. W. (1975). *Feathers, fashion and bird preservation: A study in nature preservation*. Berkley, CA: University of California Press.

Dowie, M. (1995). The fourth wave. *Mother Jones, 20,* 34-36.

Dowler, K., Fleming, T., and Muzzati, S. L. (2006). Constructing crime: Media, crime and popular culture. *Canadian Journal of Criminology and Criminal Justice, 48*(6), 837-850.

Downey, L. (1998). Environmental injustice: Is race or income a better predictor? *Social Science Quarterly, 79*(4), 766-778.

Downey, L. (2005). Assessing environmental inequality: How the conclusions we draw vary according to the definitions we employ. *Sociological Spectrum, 25*(3), 349-369.

Drielak, S. C. (1998). *Environmental crime: Evidence gathering and investigative techniques.* Springfield, IL: C.C. Thomas.

Drielak, S. C. (2004). *Hot zone forensics: Chemical, biological and radiological evidence collection.* Springfield, IL: C.C. Thomas.

Drielak, S. C. (2006). The collection of chemical, biological, and radiological evidence in a global justice environment. *The Police Chief, 73*(3), 48-53.

Dunlap, R. E., and Mertig, A. G. (Eds.). (1992). *American environmentalism: The U.S. environmental movement, 1970-1990.* Washington, DC: Taylor and Francis.

Earickson, R. J., and Billick, I. H. (1988). The areal association of urban air pollutants and residential characteristics: Louisville and Detroit. *Applied Geography, 8*(1), 5-23.

Edwards, B., and Ladd, A. (2000). Environmental justice, swine production and farm loss in North Carolina. *Sociological Spectrum, 20,* 263-290.

Edwards, S. M. (1996). Environmental criminal enforcement: Efforts by the states. In S. M. Edwards, T. D. Edwards and C. B. Fields. (Eds.), *Environmental crime and criminality: Theoretical and practical issues* (pp. 205-244). New York, NY: Garland.

Edwards, S. M. (1998). A history of the U.S. environmental movement. In M. Clifford (Ed.), *Environmental crime: Enforcement, policy and social responsibility* (pp. 31-56). Gaithersburg, MD: Aspen.

Edwards, S. M., Edwards, T. D., and Fields., C. B. (Eds.). (1996). *Environmental crime and criminality: Theoretical and practical issues.* New York, NY: Garland.

Ehrlich, P. R. (1969). *The population bomb.* New York, NY: Ballantine Books.

Ehrlich, P. R., and Ehrlich, A. H. (1995). *Extinction: The causes and consequences of species extinction.* N.Y., New York: Random House.

Ehrlich, P. R., and Ehrlich, A. H. (1996). *Betrayal of science and reason: how anti-environmental rhetoric threatens our future.* Washington, D.C.: Island Press.

Eichenberg, T. (2002). Testimony before the U.S. Commission on Ocean Policy. Washington, D.C.

Eichenberg, T. (2006). Testimony before the Senate Committee on Commerce, Science, and Transportation. Washington D.C.: National Ocean Policy Study.

Eldredge, N. (1998). *Live in the balance: Humanity and the biodiversity crisis.* Princeton, NJ: Princeton University Press.

Elkington, J. (1998). *Cannibals with forks: The triple bottom line of 21st century business.* Stony Creek, CT: New Society Publishers.

Elliott, M. R., Wang, Y., Lowe, R. A., and Kleindorfer, P. R. (2004). Environmental justice: Frequency and severity of U.S. chemical industry accidents and the socioeconomic status of surrounding communities. *Journal of Epidemiology and Community Health, 58*(1), 24-30.

Engineer Professional Advisory Committee, U.S. Public Health Service. Engineer's career planning handbook (January 2003). Available at http://www.usphsengineers.org/handbook.

Environmental Council of the States. (2001). *State environmental agency contributions to enforcement and compliance*. Washington, D.C.: The Environmental Council of the States.

Epstein, J. (1998). State and local environmental enforcement. In M. Clifford (Ed.), *Environmental crime: Enforcement, policy, and social responsibility* (pp. 145-169). Gaithersburg, MD: Aspen.

Epstein, J. J., Hammett, T. M., and Collins, L. (1995). *Law enforcement response to environmental crime*. Washington, D.C: U.S. Dept. of Justice, Office of Justice Programs, National Institute of Justice.

Erickson, M. D. (2001). PCB Properties, Uses, Occurrence, and Regulatory History. In L. W. Robertson and L. G. Hansen. (Eds.), *PCBs - Recent advances in environmental toxicology and health effects* (Vol. xi-xxx). Lexington, KY: The University Press of Kentucky.

Eschholz, S., Mallard, M., and Flynn, S. (2004). Images of prime time justice: A content analysis of NYPD Blue and Law and Order. *Journal of Criminal Justice and Popular Culture, 10*(3), 161-180.

Fagin, D., and Lavelle, M. (1999). *Toxic deception: How the chemical industry manipulates science, bends the law, and endangers your health* (2nd ed.). Monroe, Me.: Common Courage Press.

Farber, D. R., and Krieg, E. J. (2002). Unequal exposure to ecological hazards: environmental injustices in the Commonwealth of Massachusetts. *Environmental Health Perspectives, 110*(S2), 277-288.

Feagin, J. (1977). Indirect institutionalized discrimination: A typological and policy analysis. *American Politics Quarterly, 5*, 177-200.

Ferkiss, V. (1995). Strong winds from D.C. *Commonweal, 122*, 4-5.

Ferrey, S. (1997). *Environmental law: Examples and explanations*. New York, NY: Aspen.

Findley, R. W., and Farber, D. A. (2000). *Environmental law: In a nutshell*. St. Paul, MN: West Group.

Fishbein, D. (1990). Biological perspectives in criminology. *Criminology, 28*, 27-72.

Flippen, J. B. (1995). The Nixon administration, timber, and the call of the wild. *Environmental History Review, 19*(2), 37-54.

Flippen, J. B. (1996). Containing the urban sprawl: The Nixon administration's land use policy. *Presidential Studies Quarterly, 26*(1), 197-207.

Flippen, J. B. (2000). *Nixon and the environment*. Albuquerque, NM: University of new Mexico Press.

Frank, N., and Lynch, M. J. (1992). *Corporate crime, corporate violence: A primer*. New York, NY: Harrow and Heston.

Freeman, M. (1973). The distribution of environmental quality. In A. Kneese and B. Bower (Eds.), *Environmental quality analysis* (pp. 243-278). Washington, DC: Resources for the Future.

Friedrichs, D. O. (1992). *Trusted criminals: White collar crime in contemporary society.* Belmont, CA: Wadsworth.

Frysinger, G. S., Gaines, R. B., and Reddy, C. M. (2002). GC x GC - A new analytic tool for environmental forensics. *Environmental Forensics, 3*(1), 27-34.

Gelobter, M. (1987). *The distribution of outdoor air pollution by income and race: 1970-1984.* Unpublished Master's Thesis, University of California at Berkeley, Berkeley, CA.

Genovese, M. A. (1990). *The Nixon presidency: Power and politics in turbulent times.* Westport, CT: Greenwood.

Gerber, S. M. (1997). Forensic science in detective fiction. In S. M. Gerber and R. Saferstein (Eds.), *More chemistry and crime.* Washington D.C.: American Chemical Society.

Gibbs, L. (1995). *Dying from dioxin: A citizens guide to rebuilding our heath and reclaiming democracy.* Boston, MA: South End Press.

Goldman, B. A. (1991). *The truth about where you live.* New York, NY: Random House.

Goldstein, A. (2002, August 26). Too green for their own good. *Time, 160,* A58-A60.

Goodstein, D. (2004). *Out of gas: The end of the age of oil.* New York, NY: W.W. Norton.

Gorman, C. (2006, September 21). A compromise on clean air. *Time.* Accessed December 13 at: http://www.time.com/time/nation/article/0,8599,1537817,00.html.

Gottlieb, R. (1993). *Forcing the spring: The transformation of the American environmental movement.* Washington D.C.: Island Press.

Gould, J. (1986). *Quality of life in American neighborhoods.* Boulder, CO: Westview Press.

Greene, D. L. (2003, May 22). EPA chief Whitman resigns from post GOP moderate perceived by some as lacking will, influence on environment. *The Baltimore Sun,* p. 1A.

Gwartney, J. (1985). Private property, freedom, and the West. *The Intercollegiate Review, Spring,* 39-49.

Habicht, H. F. (1984). Justice cracks down on environmental crimes. *EPA Journal, 10*(2), 16-17.

Hamilton, J. (1993). Politics and social costs: Estimating the impact of collective action on hazardous waste facilities. *Rand Journal of Economics, 24,* 101-125.

Hamilton, J. (1995). Testing for environmental racism: Prejudice, profits, political power? *Journal of Policy Analysis and Management, 14*(1), 107-132.

Hays, S. P. (1959). *Conservation and the Gospel of Efficiency: The Progressive Conservation Movement, 1890-1920.* Cambridge, MA: Harvard University Press.

Hebert, H. J. (2006, September 19, 2006). EPA inspector criticizes agency on fairness of reviews. *Associated Press Financial Wire.*

Hedman, S. (1991). Expressive functions of criminal sanctions in environmental law. *The George Washington Law Review, 59,* 889-899.

Heinberg, R. (2003). *The party's over: Oil, war and the fate of industrial societies.* Gabriola Island, BC: New World Publishers.

Helvarg, D. (2001). Bush unites the enviros. *The Nation, 272,* 5-6.

Henry, J. (1963). *Culture against man.* New York, NY: Vintage.

Hertsgaard, M. (2006). Green goes grassroots: The environmental movement today. *The Nation*(July 31 / August 7), pp. 11-15, 17-18.

Hird, J. (1993). Environmental policy and equity: The case of Superfund. *Journal of Policy Analysis and Management, 12*(2), 323-343.

Hird, J. (1994). *Superfund: The political economy of environmental risk.* Baltimore, MA: Johns Hopkins University Press.

Hird, J., and Reese, M. (1998). The distribution of environmental quality: An empirical analysis. *Social Science Quarterly, 79*(4), 693-716.

Hoff, J. (1994). *Nixon reconsidered.* New York, NY: HarperCollins.

Holbrook, A. R., and Hill, T. (2005). Agenda setting in priming prime time television: Crime drama as political cues. *Political Communication, 22*(3), 277-295.

Hughes, B., and Suggs, J. A. (2003). Accreditation of an environmental forensic center. *Environmental Protection, 14*(2), 66-74.

Humphreys, S. L. (1990). An enemy of the people: Prosecuting the corporate polluter as a common law criminal. *American University Law Review, 39*(311-354).

Hunter, S., and Waterman, R. W. (1996). *Enforcing the law: The case of clean water acts.* Armonk, NY: M.E. Sharpe.

Hurly, A. (1997). Fiasco at Wagner Electric: Environmental justice and urban geography in St. Louis. *Environmental History, 2,* 460-481.

Hyatt, B. (1988). The federal environmental regulatory structure. In M. Clifford (Ed.), *Environmental crime: Enforcement, policy, and social responsibility* (pp. 115-141). Gaithersburg, MD: Aspen.

Innis, P. (2004). *Hazardous waste site sampling basics: Technical note 414.* Accessed December 10, 2007 at: http://www.blm.gov/nstc/library/pdf/HazWaste414.pdf.

Ireland, D. (2001). A toxic choice. *The Nation, 272*(4), 18.

Javaux, M., Kasteel, R., Vanderborght, J., and Vanclooster, M. (2006). Interpretation of dye transport in a macroscopically heterogeneous, unsaturated subsoil with a one-dimensional model *Vadose Zone Journal, 5,* 529-538.

Javaux, M., Vanderborght, J., Kasteel, R., and Vanclooster, M. (2006). Three dimensional modeling of the scale- and flow-rate dependency of dispersion in a heterogeneous unsaturated sandy monolith. *Vadose Zone Journal, 5,* 515-528.

Jeffords, J., and Gorte, J. F. (2006). A dark cloud over disclosure. *New York Times,* p. A21.

Johnson, G. W., and Ehrlich, R. (2002). State of the art report on multivariate chemometric methods in environmental forensics. *Environmental Forensics, 3*(1), 59-79.

Johnson, H. (1991). *Sleepwalking through history: America in the Reagan years.* New York, NY: W.W. Norton.

Karliner, J. (1997). *The corporate planet: Ecology and politics in the age of globalization*. San Francisco, CA: Sierra Books.

Kennedy, L. W., and Sacco, V. F. (1998). *Crime victims in context*. Los Angeles, CA: Roxbury Publishing.

Kline, B. (1997). *First along the river: A brief history of the U.S. environmental movement*. San Francisco, CA: Acada Books.

Korc, M. (1996). A socioeconomic assessment of human exposure to ozone in the South coast air basin of California. *Journal of the Air and Waste Management Association, 46*, 547-557.

Kormondy, E. J. (1970). Lake Erie is aging, but effort can save it from death. *Smithsonian, 1*, 26-35.

Kraft, M. E. (1996). *Environmental policy and politics*. New York, NY: Harper Collins.

Kraft, M. E. (2001). *Environmental policy and politics* (second edition ed.). New York, NY: Longman.

Kraft, M. E., and Scheberle, D. (1995). Environmental justice and the allocation of risk: The case of lead and public health. *Policy Studies Journal, 23*(1), 113-122.

Kreig, E. (1995). A socio-historical interpretation of toxic waste sites. *The American Journal of Economics and Sociology, 54*, 1-14.

Kruvant, W. (1975). People, energy, and pollution. In D. Newman and D. Day (Eds.), *The American energy consumer* (pp. 125-167). Cambridge, MA: Ballinger.

Kulldorff, M., Feuer, E. J., Miller, B. A., and Freedman, L. S. (1997). Breast cancer clusters in the Northeast United States: Geographic analysis. *American Journal of Epidemiology, 146*(2), 161-170.

Landrigan, P. J., Claudio, L., Markowitz, S. B., Berkowitz, G. S., Brenner, B. L., Romero, H., et al. (1999). Pesticides and inner-city children: Exposures, risks, and prevention. *Environmental Health Perspectives Supplements 107*(S3), 431-437.

Landy, M. K., Roberts, M. J., and Thomas, S. R. (1990). *The Environmental Protection Agency: Asking the wrong questions*. Oxford: Oxford University Press.

Lappe, M. (1991). *Chemical deception, the toxic threat to health and the environment: Exposing ten myths that endanger us all*. San Francisco, CA: Sierra Club Books.

Lash, J., Gillman, K., and Sheridan, D. (1984). *A season of spoils: The Reagan Administration's attack on the environment*. New York, NY: Pantheon Books.

Lasser, M. d. S.-O.-L. E. (2002). Comparative readings of Roscoe Pound's jurisprudence. *American Journal of Comparative Law, 50*, 719-751.

Lavelle, M., and Coyle, M. (1992). Unequal protection: The racial divide in environmental law. *National Law Journal, 21*(September), S1-S11.

Lazarus, Richard J. (2006). *The making of environmental law*. Chicago: University of Chicago Press.

Lester, J. P. (1989). *Environmental politics and policy: Theories and evidence*. Durham, NC: Duke University.

Lev, L. (1996). Dealing with consumer and environmental issues. Tucson, Arizona: Department of Agricultural and Resource Economics at the University of Arizona. Accessible at: http://cals.arizona.edu/arec/wemc/papers/DealingConsumer.html

Liu, F. (2000). *Environmental justice analysis: Theories, methods, and practice*. Boca Raton, Florida: Lewis.

Logan, W. P. (1953). Mortality in the London fog incident, 1952. *Lancet, 14*(February), 336-338.

Loomis, D., Castillejos, M., Gold, D., McDonnell, W., and Borja-Aburto, V. H. (1999). Air pollution and infant mortality in Mexico City. *Epidemiology, 10*, 118-123.

Lovelock, J. (2006). *The revenge of Gaia: Earth's climate crisis and the fate of humanity*. New York, NY: Basic Books.

Luneberg, W. V. (1995). The legal context of environmental protection in the United States. In E. O. Talbott and G. F. Craun (Eds.), *An introduction to environmental epidemiology*. Boca Raton, FL: CRC Press.

Lynch, M. J. (1990). The greening of criminology: A perspective for the 1990s. *The Critical Criminologist, 2*(3), 3-4, 11-12.

Lynch, M. J., McGurrin, D., and Fenwick, M. (2004). Disappearing act: The representation of corporate crime research in criminological literature. *Journal of Criminal Justice, 32*(5), 389-398.

Lynch, M. J., and Michalowski, R. J. (2006). *A primer in radical criminology*. Monsey, NY: Criminal Justice Press.

Lynch, M. J., and Patterson, E. B. (1991). *Race and criminal justice*. New York, NY: Harrow and Heston.

Lynch, M. J., and Stretesky, P. B. (2001). Toxic crimes: examining corporate victimization of the general public employing medical and epidemiological evidence. *Critical Criminology, 10*(2), 153-172.

Lynch, M. J., and Stretesky, P. B. (2003). The meaning of green: Towards a clarification of the term green and its meaning for the development of a green criminology. *Theoretical Criminology, 7*(2), 217-238.

Lynch, M. J., and Stretesky, P. B. (2007). Critical criminology and the investigation of environmental crime in the Americas. In P. Beirne and N. South (Eds.), *Issues in green criminology*. Devon, UK: Willan.

Lynch, M. J., Stretesky, P. B., and Burns, R. G. (2004). Determinants of environmental law violation fines against petroleum refineries: Race, ethnicity, income, and aggregation effects. *Society and Natural Resources, 17*(4), 333-347.

Lynch, M. J., Stretesky, P. B., and Burns, R. G. (2004). Slippery business: Race, class and legal determinants of penalties against petroleum refineries. *Journal of Black Studies, 34*(3), 421-440.

Lynch, M. J., Stretesky, P. B., and Hammond, P. (2000). Media coverage of chemical crime, Hillsborough County, Florida, 1987-97. *British Journal of Criminology, 40*, 112-126.

Lynch, M. J., Stretesky, P. B., and McGurrin, D. (2002). Toxic crimes and environmental justice: Examining the dangers of hazardous waste. In G. Potter (Ed.), *Controversies in white-collar crime* (pp. 109-136). Cincinnati, OH: Anderson.

Mackie, D., Junfeng, L., Yeong-Shang, L., and Thomas, V. (2003). No evidence of dioxin cancer threshold. *Environmental Health Perspectives* (111), 1145-1147.

Manaster, K. A. (2002). *Environmental protection and justice: Readings and commentary on environmental law and practice.* Cincinnati: Anderson.

Mann, C. R. (1993). *Unequal justice: A question of color.* Bloomington, IN: Indiana University Press.

Marcus, A. A. (1980). *Promise and performance: Choosing and implementing an environmental policy.* Westport, CT: Greenwood Press.

Markham, A. (1994). *A brief history of pollution.* New York, NY: St. Martin's

Markowitz, G., and Rosner, D. (2002). *Deceit and denial: The deadly politics of industrial pollution* Berkeley, CA: University of California Press / Milbank Memorial Fund.

Marland, G., Boden, T., and Andres, R. J. (2006). National CO_2 emissions from fossil-fuel burning, cement manufacture, and gas flaring: 1751-2003. In C. D. I. A. Center (Ed.). Oak Ridge, TN: Oak Ridge National Laboratory.

Maurray, R. C., and Tedrow, J. C. (1998). *Forensic geology.* Upper Saddle River, NJ: Prentice-Hall.

McCarthy, T., Thompson, D., and Thornburgh, N. (2000). How green was Bill. *Time, 156*(25), 64-65.

McCormick, J. (1989). *Reclaiming paradise: The global environmental movement.* Bloomington, IN: Indiana University Press.

McGowan, E. (2006, January 30). Ex-EPA chiefs want action on greenhouse gases. *Waste News.*

McGurty, E. (2000). Warren County, NC, and the emergence of the environmental justice movement: Unlikely coalitions and shared meanings in local collective action. *Society and Natural Resources, 13*(4), 373-387.

McMahon, R. (2006). *The Environmental Protection Agency: Structuring motivation in a green bureaucracy.* Portland, OR: Sussex Academic Press.

Mcmurry, R. I., and Ramsey, S. D. (1986). Environmental crime: The use of criminal sanctions in enforcing environmental laws. *Loyola of Los Angeles Law Review, 19,* 1133-1170.

Merchant, C. (1992). *Radical ecology: The search for a livable world.* New York, NY: Routledge.

Merchant, C. (1995). *Earthcare: Women and the environment.* Oxford, UK: Routledge.

Mertig, A. G., Dunlap, R. E., and Morrison, D. R. (2002). The environmental movement in the United States. In R. E. Dunlap and W. Michelson (Eds.), *Handbook of Environmental Sociology* (pp. 448-481). Westport, CT: Greenwood Press.

Metzger, R., Delgado, J. L., and Herrell, R. (1995). Environmental health and Hispanic children. *Environmental Health Perspectives, 103*(S6), 25-32.

Meyer, J. M. (2005, Spring). Does environmentalism have a future? *Dissent,* 69-75.

Michalowski, R. J., and Kramer, R. C. (Eds.). (2006). *State corporate-crime: Wrongdoing at the intersection of business and government.* Piscataway, NJ: Rutgers University Press.

Milbank, D., and Nakashima, E. (2001, March 25). Bush team has 'right' credentials: Conservative picks seen eclipsing even Reagan's. *Washington Post,* p. 1.

Miller, J. G. (1996). *Search and destroy: African-American males and the criminal justice system.* Cambridge; New York, NY: Cambridge University Press.

Mintz, J. A. (1995). *Enforcement at the EPA: High stakes and hard choices.* Austin, TX: University of Texas Press.

Mitchell, J., Thomas, D., and Cutter, S. (1999). Dumping in Dixie revisited: The evolution of environmental injustices in South Carolina. *Social Science Quarterly, 80,* 229-243.

Mohai, P., and Bryant, B. (1992). Environmental racism: Reviewing the evidence. In B. B. a. P. Mohai (Ed.), *Race and the incidence of environmental hazards* (pp. 163-176). Boulder, CO: Westview.

Morello-Frocsh, R., Pastor, M., and Sadd, J. (2001). Environmental justice and southern California's riskscape: The distribution of air toxics exposures and health risks among diverse communities. *Urban Affairs Review, 36,* 551-578.

Motavalli, J. (2005, May/June). Trashing the greens: Reports of environmentalism's death may be exaggerated. *E Magazine, 16,* 26-33.

Mott, L. (1995). The disproportionate impact of environmental health on children of color. *Environmental Health Perspectives, 103*(S6), 33-35.

Murphy, B., and Morrison, R. (2002). *Introduction to environmental forensics.* New York, NY: Academic Press.

Nader, R., Brownstein, R., and Richard, J. (Eds.). (1981). *Who's poisoning America: Corporate polluters and their victims in the chemical age.* San Francisco, CA: Sierra Club Books.

Nash, J. L. (2000). Browner outlines environmental protection future. *Occupational Hazards, 62*(11), 19.

Nash, J. L. (2001). Whitman brings new direction to EPA. *Occupational Hazards, 63*(2), 29.

Nash, R. (1967). *Wilderness and the American mind.* New Haven, CT: Yale University.

Nash, R. (1976). *The American environment: Readings in the history of conservation.* Reading, MA: Addison-Wesley.

Nash, R. (1990). *American environmentalism* (Third ed.). New York, NY: McGraw-Hill.

Needleman, H. (1990). The future challenge of lead toxicity. *Environmental Health Perspectives, 89,* 85-89.

Needleman, H., Riess, J. A., Tobin, M. J., Biesecker, G. E., and Greenhouse, J. B. (1996). Bone lead levels and delinquent behavior. *JAMA-Journal of the American Medical Association, 275*(5), 363-369.

Neimark, P., and Mott, P. R. (Eds.). (1999). *The environmental debate: A documentary history.* Westport, CT: Greenwood Press.

Nevin, R. (2000). How lead exposure relates to temporal changes in IQ, violent crime, and unwed pregnancy. *Environmental Research, 83*(1), 1-22.

Northrop, D. (2002). Forensic applications of high performance liquid chromatography and capillary electrophoresis. In R. Saferstein (Ed.), *Forensic Science Handbook, Volume 1* (pp. 41-116). Upper Saddle River, NJ: Prentice Hall.

Oakes, J., Anderton, D., and Anderson, A. (1996). A longitudinal analysis of environmental equity in communities with hazardous waste facilities. *Social Science Research, 23*, 125-148.

O'Connor, J. (1973). *The fiscal crisis of the state.* New York, NY: St. Martin's Press.

O'Connor, J. (1985). *Accumulation crisis.* New York, NY Basil Blackwell.

O'Connor, J. (1997). *Natural causes: Essays in ecological Marxism.* New York, NY: Guildford Press.

O'Grady, Michael J. (2002). *Environmental statutes outline: A guide to federal environmental laws.* Washington, D.C.: Environmental Law Institute.

O'Hear, M. (2004). Sentencing the green collar offender: punishment, culpability and environmental crime. *The Journal of Criminal Law and Criminology, 95*(1), 133-276.

O'Riordan, T., Clark, W. C., and Kates, R. W. (1995). The legacy of Earth Day: Reflections at a turning point. *Environment, 37*, 6-10.

O'Rourke, D., and Macey, G. (2003). Community environmental policing: Assessing new strategies of public participation in environmental regulation. *Journal of Policy Analysis and Management, 22*(3), 383-414.

Paehlke, R. (2003). Environmental sustainability and urban life in America. In M. E. Kraft and N. J. Vig (Eds.), *Environmental policy: New directions for the twenty-first century* (Fifth ed., pp. 57-77). Washington, DC: CQ Press.

Page, J. A., and Sellers, G. B. (1970). Occupational safety and health: Environmental justice for the forgotten America. *Kentucky Law Journal, 59*(1), 114-144.

Pastor, M., Sadd, J., and Hipp, J. (2001). Which came first? Toxic facilities, minority move-in, and environmental justice. *Journal of Urban Affairs, 23*, 1-21.

Pastor, M., Sadd, J. L., and Morello-Frosch, R. (2002). Who's minding the kids? Pollution, public schools, and environmental justice in Los Angeles. *Social Science Quarterly, 83*(1), 263–280.

Pearce, F., and Tombs, S. (1998). *Toxic capitalism: Corporate crime and the chemical industry.* Aldershot, UK: Ashgate.

Pellow, D. (2000). Environmental inequality formation: Toward a theory of environmental injustice. *American Behavioral Scientist, 43*(4), 581-601.

Pellow, D. (2002). *Garbage wars: The struggle for environmental justice in Chicago.* Cambridge, MA: MIT Press.

Perlin, S., Seltzer, W., Creason, J., and Sexton, K. (1995). Distribution of industrial air emissions by income and race in the United States: An approach using the toxic release inventory. *Environmental Science and Technology, 29*(1), 69-80.

Perlin, S., Sexton, K., and Wong, D. (1999). An examination of race and poverty for populations living near industrial sources of air pollution. *Journal of Exposure Analysis and Environmental Epidemiology, 9*(1), 29-48.

Perman, R., Ma, Y., and McGilvray. (1996). *Natural resources and environmental economics.* Boston, MA: Addison Wesley Longman.

Phil, R. O., and Ervin, F. (1990). Lead and cadmium levels in violent criminals. *Psychological Reports, 66*, 839-844.

Pollock, P., and Vittas, E. (1995). Who bears the burdens of environmental pollution? Race, ethnicity, and environmental equity in Florida. *Social Science Quarterly, 76*(2), 294-310.

Pope, A. C., Burnett, R. T., Thun, M. J., Calla, E. E., Krewski, D., Ito, K., et al. (2002). Lung cancer, cardiopulmonary mortality, and long term exposure to fine particulate air pollution. *Journal of the American Medical Association, 287*(9), 1132-1141.

Postrel, V. (1990). Forget left and right, the politics of the future will be growth versus green. *UTNE Reader, 40*, 57-58.

Poulsen, T. G., Moldrup, P., Jonge, L. W. d., and Komatsu, T. (2006). Colloid and bromide transport in undisturbed soil columns: Application of two-region model *Vadose Zone Journal, 5*, 649-656.

Pound, R. (1921). *The spirit of the common law*. Francestown, NH: Marshall Jones.

Pound, R. (1967). *Interpretations of legal theory*. Gloucester, MA: P. Smith.

Pound, R. (1969). *Law and morals*. South Hackensack, NJ: Rothman Reprints.

Pound, R. (1982). *An introduction to the philosophy of law*. New Haven, CT: Yale University Press.

Quinney, R. (1970). *The social reality of crime*. Boston, MA: Little, Brown.

Rampton, S., and Stauber, J. (2001). *Trust us, we're experts: How industry manipulates science and gambles with your future*. New York, NY: Tarcher/Putnam.

Reaves, B. A. (2006). *Federal law enforcement officers, 2004*. Retrieved July 14, 2007. from http://www.ojp.gov/bjs/pub/pdf/fleo04.pdf.

Rebovich, D. J. (1998). Environmental crime research. In M. Clifford (Ed.), *Environmental crime: Enforcement, policy, and social responsibility* (pp. 341-354). Gaithersburg, MD: Aspen.

Rebovich, D. J. (2002). Prosecuting environmental crime in the twenty-first century. In R. Muraskin and A. R. Roberts (Eds.), *Visions for change: Crime and justice in the twenty-first century* (pp. 331-350). Upper Saddle River, NJ: Prentice Hass.

Reiman, J. (2005). *The rich get richer and the poor get prison: Ideology, class, and criminal justice* (6th ed.). Boston, MA: Allyn and Bacon.

Rhodes, E. (2003). *Environmental justice in America: A new paradigm*. Bloomington, IN: Indiana University Press.

Ringquist, E. J. (1998). A question of justice: Equity in environmental litigation, 1974-1991. *Journal of Politics, 60*(4), 1148-1165.

Ritz, B., Yu, F., Fruin, S., Chapa, G., Shaw, G. M., and Harris, J. A. (2002). Ambient air pollution and risk of birth defects in Southern California. *American Journal of Epidemiology, 155*(1), 17-25.

Rosenbaum, W. A. (2003). Still reforming after all these years: George W. Bush's 'new era' at the EPA. In N. J. Vig and M. E. Kraft (Eds.), *Environmental policy: New directions for the twenty-first century* (Fifth ed.). Washington, DC: CQ Press.

Ross, D. (1996). A review of EPA criminal, civil and administrative enforcement data: Are the efforts measurable deterrents to environmental criminals? In S. M. Edwards, T. D. Edwards and C. B. Fields. (Eds.), *Environmental crime and criminality: Theoretical and practical issues* (pp. 55-78). New York, NY: Garland.

Runyan, C., and Norderhaug, M. (2002). The path to Johannesburg summit. *World Watch, 15*(3), 30-35.

Saad, L. (2007, March 21, 2007). Did Hollywood's glare heat up public concern about global warming? Retrieved May 16, 2007, from http://www.galluppoll.com/content/?ci=26932

Saferstein, R. (2002a). Forensic applications of mass spectrometry. In R. Saferstein (Ed.), *Forensic science handbook, Volume 1* (pp. 117-159). Upper Saddle River, NJ: Prentice Hall.

Saferstein, R. (Ed.). (2002b). *Forensic science handbook, Volume I.* Upper Saddle River, NJ: Prentice Hall.

Saha, R., and Mohai, P. (2005). Historical context of hazardous waste facility siting: Understanding temporal patterns in Michigan. *Social Problems, 52*(4), 618-648.

Samet, J. M., Dominici, F., Curriero, F. C., Coursac, I., and Zeger, S. T. (2000). Fine particle air pollution and mortality in 20 U.S. cities, 1987-1994. *New England Journal of Medicine, 343*(24), 1742-1749.

Sanderson, S. (2002). The future of conservation. *Foreign Affairs, 81*(5), 162-173.

Sanger, D. E., and Kahn, J. (2001, May 18). Bush, pushing energy plan, offers scores of proposals to find new power sources. *New York Times,* p. 1.

Schaeffer, E. (2002). Clearing the air. *The Washington Monthly, 34,* 20-25.

Schaeffer, E. J. (2003). Clearing the air: Why I quit Bush's EPA [Electronic Version]. *Washington Monthly.* Retrieved 8/25/2007 from http://www.washingtonmonthly.com/features/2001/0207.schaeffer.html.

Schindler, G. (1995). It didn't begin with Earth Day. *E: The Environment Magazine, 6,* 32-35.

Schmidt, C. W. (2004). Environmental crimes: Profiting at the earth's expense. *Environmental Health Perspectives, 112*(2), A96-A103.

Seis, M. (1999). A community-based criminology of the environment. *Criminal Justice Policy Review, 10*(2), 291-317.

Sexton, K., Marcus, A. A., Easter, K. W., and Burkhardt, T. D. (Eds.). (1999). *Better environmental decisions: Strategies for governments, businesses, and communities* Washington D.C.: Island Press.

Shackelford, C. D. (1989). Diffusion of contaminants through waste containment barriers. *Transportation Research Journal, 1219,* 169-182.

Simon, D. (2000). Corporate environmental crimes and social inequality. *American Behavioral Scientist, 43*(4), 633-645.

Simpson, S. (2002). *Corporate crime, law, and social control.* Cambridge, UK: Cambridge University Press.

Situ, Y., and Emmons, D. (2000). *Environmental crime: The criminal justice system's response in protecting the environment.* Thousand Oaks, CA: Sage.

Smith, A. (1776). *The wealth of nations.* Middlesex, England: Penguin.

Soden, D. L. (1999). Presidential roles and environmental policy. In R. P. Watson and B. Hilliard (Eds.), *The environmental presidency* (pp. 1-13). Albany, NY: State University of New York.

South, N., and Beirne, P. (Eds.). (1998). *Special Issue: Green Criminology* (Vol. 2).

South, N., and Beirne, P. (Eds.). (2006). *Green criminology*. Aldershot, UK: Ashgate.

Spangler, J. D., and Dougherty, J. M. (2003). The heat's on Leavitt. *Deseret News*, p. A1.

Spitzer, S. (1975). Toward a Marxian theory of deviance. *Social Problems, 22*(5), 638-651.

Stafford, S. (2003). Does self-policing help the environment? *Vermont Journal of Environmental Law, 6*(2), 1-22

Staniloae, D., Petrescu, B., and Patroescu, C. (2001). Pattern recognition based software for oil spills identification by gas-chromatography and IR spectrophotometry. *Environmental Forensics, 2*(4), 363-366.

Starr, J. W. (1991). Turbulent times at justice and EPA: The origins of environmental criminal prosecutions and the work that remains. *The George Washington Law Review, 59*, 900-915.

Stauber, J., and Rampton, S. (1995). *Toxic sludge is good for you: Lies, damn lies and the public relations industry*. Monroe, ME: Common Courage Press.

Steenland, K., Hein, M. J., Cassinelli, R. T., Prince, M. M., Nilsen, N. B., Whelan, E. A., et al. (2006). Polychlorinated biphenyls and neurodegenerative disease mortality in an occupational cohort. *Epidemiology, 17*(1), 8-13.

Steingraber, S. (1998). *Living downstream: A scientist's personal investigation of cancer and the environment*. New York, NY: Vintage.

Stine, J. K. (1998). Environmental policy during the Carter presidency. In G. M. Fink and H. D. Graham (Eds.), *The Carter presidency: Policy choices in the post-new deal era* (pp. 179-201). Lawrence, KS: University Press of Kansas.

Stretesky, P. B. (2003). The distribution of air lead levels across U.S. counties: Implications for the production of racial inequality. *Sociological Spectrum, 23*(1), 91-118.

Stretesky, P. B. (2006). Corporate self-policing and the environment. *Criminology, 44*, 671-708.

Stretesky, P. B., and Hogan, M. J. (1998). Environmental justice: An analysis of Superfund sites in Florida. *Social Problems, 42*(2), 268-287.

Stretesky, P. B., Johnston, J. E., and Arney, J. (2003). Environmental inequity: An analysis of large-scale hog operations in 17 states, 1982-1997. *Rural Sociology, 68*(2), 231-252.

Stretesky, P. B., and Lynch, M. J. (1999). Corporate environmental violence and racism. *Crime, Law and Social Change, 30*, 163-184.

Stretesky, P. B., and Lynch, M. J. (1999). Environmental justice and the prediction of distance to accidental chemical releases in Hillsborough County, Florida. *Social Science Quarterly, 80*(4), 830-846.

Stretesky, P. B., and Lynch, M. J. (2001). The relationship between lead exposure and homicide. *Archives of Pediatrics and Adolescent Medicine, 155*, 579-582.

Stretesky, P. B., and Lynch, M. J. (2002). Environmental hazards and school segregation in Hillsborough County Florida, 1987-1999. *Sociological Quarterly, 43*(4), 553-573.

Stretesky, P. B., and Lynch, M. J. (2004). The relationship between lead and crime. *Journal of Health and Social Behavior, 45*, 214-229.

Strock, J. M. (1991). Environmental enforcement priorities for the 1990s. *The George Washington Law Review, 59*, 916-937.

Sturgeon, N. (1997). *Ecofeminist natures: Race, gender, feminist theory, and political action*. London: Routledge.

Suggs, J. A., Beam, E. W., Biggs, D. E., Collins, W., Dusenbury, M. R., MacLeish, P. P., et al. (2002). Guidelines and resources for conducting an environmental crime investigation. *Environmental Forensics, 3*, 91-113.

Suggs, J. A., and Yarborough, K. R. (2001). Environmental crime investigations, *14th Interpol Forensic Science Symposium*. Lyon, France.

Switzer, J. V., and Bryner, G. (1998). *Environmental politics: Domestic and global dimensions* (2nd ed.). New York, NY: St. Martin's Press.

Szasz, A. (1986). Organizations, organized crime and the disposal of hazardous waste: An examination of the making of a criminogenic regulatory structure. *Criminology, 24*(1), 1-27.

Szasz, A. (1994). *Ecopopulism: Toxic waste and the movement for environmental justice.* Minneapolis, MN: University of Minnesota.

Taylor, B. (2003). Threat assessment and radical environmentalism. *Terrorism and Political Violence, 15*(4), 173-184.

Taylor, D. E. (2000). The rise of the environmental justice paradigm: Injustice framing and the social construction of environmental discourses. *American Behavioral Scientist, 43*(3), 508-580.

Taylor, J. (2002, September 16). Greeniacs in Jo-burg. *National Review, 54*, 29-30.

The Environment: Green Bush. (2001, May 14). *National Review, 53*, 14-16.

Theodoropoulou, M., Karoutsos, V., and Tsakiroglou, C. (2001). Investigation of the contamination of fractured formations by non-Newtonian oil pollutants. *Environmental Forensics, 2*(4), 321-334.

Thornburgh, D. (1991). Criminal enforcement of environmental laws--A national priority. *George Washington Law Review, 59*, 775-780.

Tiefenbacher, J., and Hagelman, R. (1999). Environmental equity in urban Texas: Race, income, and patterns of acute and chronic Toxic Air Releases in metropolitan counties. *Urban Geography, 19*, 516-533.

Tonry, M. H. (1995). *Malign neglect: Race, crime, and punishment in America*. New York, NY: Oxford University Press.

Train, R. E. (1996). The environmental record of the Nixon administration. *Presidential Studies Quarterly, 26*, 185-196.

Tucker, W. (1982). *Progress and privilege: America in the age of environmentalism*. New York: Anchor Press/Doubleday.

UCC. (1987). *Toxic wastes and race in the United States: A national report on the racial and socio-economic characteristics with hazardous waste sites*. New York: United Church of Christ, Commission for Racial Justice.

U.S. EPA. (1992). *Reducing risk: setting priorities and strategies for environmental protection: The report of the Science Advisory Board, Relative Risk Reduction Strategies Committee to William K. Reilly*. Washington, DC (401 M St., S.W., Washington 20460): The Board.

U.S. EPA. (1996). Environmental justice implementation plan: USEPA Office of Environmental Justice.

U.S. EPA. (1998). *Final guidelines for incorporating environmental justice concerns in EPA's NEPA compliance analysis.* Washington, DC: Office of Federal Activities.

U.S. EPA. (1999). *Enforcement and compliance assurance: FY 98 accomplishments report.* Washington DC: U.S.EPA.

U.S. EPA. (2000a). 2000 National water quality inventory: USEPA.

U.S. EPA. (2000b). Incentives for Self-Policing: Discovery, Disclosure, Correction and Prevention of Violations. *Federal Register,* 65 (70): 19617-19627.

U.S. EPA. (2001). Environmental investigation: Standard operating procedures and quality assurance manual. Athens, Georgia: EPA Region 4.

U.S. EPA. (2006). National Environmental Performance Track: Basic Information. Washington, DC: U.S. Government Printing Office. www.epa.gov/performancetrack/about.htm.

U.S. EPA. (2006). Polychlorinated biphenyls (PCBs). Retrieved October 5, 2006, 2006, from http://www.epa.gov/pcb/

U.S. EPA. (2007). *FY 2006 OECA accomplishment report.* Retrieved. from.

U.S. EPA. (2007). 2005 TRI public data release eReport: USEPA. Accessed December 18, 2007 at: http://www.epa.gov/tri/tridata/tri05/pdfs/eReport.pdf.

U.S. GAO. (1983). *The siting of hazardous waste landfills and their correlation with racial and economic status of surrounding communities* (No. RCED-83-168). Washington DC: General Accounting Office.

Uwe Totsche, K., Jann, S., and Kögel-Knabner, I. (2006). Release of polycyclic aromatic hydrocarbons, dissolved organic carbon, and suspended matter from distributed NAPL contaminated gravelly soil material. *Vadose Zone Journal, 5,* 469-479.

Van Putten, M. (2005). Rebuilding a mainstream consensus for environmentalism. *BioScience, 55*(6), 468-469.

Vermette, S. (2007). Environmental Neighborhood Policing: Officer Safety, Environmental Crime, and Working with Community. Boston Police District E-18. Boston. Retrieved December 15, 2007 from http://www.p2pays.org/ref/38/37465.pdf.

Vig, N. J. (2003). Presidential leadership and the environment. In N. J. Vig and M. E. Kraft (Eds.), *Environmental policy: New directions for the twenty-first century* (pp. 103-125). Washington, DC: CQ Press.

Vig, N. J., and Kraft, M. E. (Eds.). (1984). *Environmental policy in the 1980s: Reagan's new agenda.* Washington DC: CQ Press.

Vig, N. J., and Kraft, M. E. (2003). Toward sustainable development? In N. J. Vig and M. E. Kraft (Eds.), *Environmental policy: New directions for the twenty-first century* (Fifth ed., pp. 391-407). Washington DC: CQ Press.

Vlachou, A. (2002). Nature and value theory. *Science and Society, 66*(2), 169-201.

Vlachou, A. (2004). Capitalism and ecological sustainability: The shaping of environmental policy. *Review of International Political Economy, 11*(5), 926-952.

Vlachou, A. (2005). Environmental regulation: A value theoretic and class based analysis. *Cambridge Journal of Economics, 29*(4), 577-599.

Vogel, D. (2003). International trade and environmental regulation. In N. J. Vig and M. E. Kraft (Eds.), *Environmental policy: New directions for the twenty-first century* (pp. 371-389). Washington DC: CQ Press.

Walljasper, J. (1990). Who are the greens and what do they believe? *UTNE Reader, 40*, 58-60.

Wang, X., Ding, H., Ryan, L., and Xu, X. (1997). Association between air pollution and low birth weight: a community-based study. *Environmental Health Perspectives, 105*(5), 514-520.

Wargo, J. (1998). *Our children's toxic legacy: How science and law fail to protect us from pesticides.* New Haven, CT: Yale University Press.

Warren, C. (2001). *Brush with death: A social history of lead poisoning.* Baltimore, MD: Johns Hopkins University Press.

Waterman, R. W. (1989). *Presidential influence and the administrative state.* Knoxville, TN: University of Tennessee Press.

Weida, W. (2001). *A review of the proposal to construct a 3700 sow farrow to finish hog operation in Gray County, Texas.* Unpublished manuscript, Colorado Springs, CO.

Weidenbaum, M. L. (1986). *Business, government, and the public* (3rd ed.). Englewood Cliffs, NJ: Prentice Hall.

Wernette, D. R. a. L. A. N. (1992). Breathing polluted air: Minorities are disproportionately exposed. *EPA Journal, 18*(1), 16-17.

Whitaker, J. C. (1976). *Striking a balance: Environmental and natural resources policy in the Nixon-Ford years.* Washington, DC: American Enterprise Institute.

Wilson, E. O. (1992). *The diversity of life.* Cambridge, MA: Belknap Press.

Wing, S., and Wolf, S. (2000). Intensive livestock operations, health, and quality of life among eastern North Carolina Residents. *Environmental Health Perspectives, 108*, 233-238.

Wolff, E. N. (2002). *Top heavy: A study of increasing inequality of wealth in America.* New York, NY: The New Press.

Wright, E. O. (1985). *Classes.* London: Verso.

Yauck, J. S., Malloy, M. E., Blair, K., Simpson, P. M., and McCarver, D. G. (2004). Proximity of residence to trichloroethylene-emitting sites and increased risk of offspring congenital heart defects among older women. *Clinical and Molecular Teratology, 70*(10), 808-814.

Zeitz, P., Berkowitz, Z., Orr, M. F., Haugh, G. S., and Kaye, W. E. (2000). Frequency and type of injuries in responders of hazardous substances emergency events, 1996 to 1998. *Journal of Occupational and Environmental Medicine, 42*(11), 1115-1120.

Zilney, L. A., McGurrin, D., and Zahran, S. (2006). Environmental justice and the role of criminology. *Criminal Justice Review, 31*(1), 47-62.

Zimmerman, R. (1993). Social equity and environmental risk. *Risk Analysis*(13), 549-666.

Index